Reservation Politics

Reservation Politics

Historical Trauma, Economic Development, and Intratribal Conflict

RAYMOND I. ORR

UNIVERSITY OF OKLAHOMA PRESS : NORMAN

This book is published with the generous assistance of
The McCasland Foundation, Duncan, Oklahoma

Library of Congress Cataloging-in-Publication Data

Name: Orr, Raymond I., 1980– author.
Title: Reservation politics : historical trauma, economic development, and
  intratribal conflict / Raymond I. Orr.
Description: Norman, OK : University of Oklahoma Press, [2017] | Includes
  bibliographical references and index.
Identifiers: LCCN 2016022318 | ISBN 978-0-8061-5391-9 (hardcover) ISBN
978-0-8061-9489-9 (paper) Subjects: LCSH: Indians of North America—Politics
and government. | Indians

  of North America—Economic conditions. | Indians—Ethnic identity. |
  Memory—Social aspects—United States—History. | Lakota Indians—Politics
  and government. | Melancholy—Social aspects—United States—History. |
  Indians of North America—History. | United States—Ethnic relations. |
  Political culture—United States.
Classification: LCC E98.T77 O77 2016 | DDC 970.004/97—dc23
LC record available at https://lccn.loc.gov/2016022318

The paper in this book meets the guidelines for permanence and durability of the
Committee on Production Guidelines for Book Longevity of the Council on Library
Resources, Inc. ∞

To my brother, Yancey,
for his help, and to the Olmstead, Anderson,
Dowgialo, Gartenberg, Hurley, Otter, Lickliter,
Hassid, Tsai, Harvey, Watson, and Upchurch
families, for their kindness

Contents

Illustrations

Figures

Tables

Acknowledgments

The subject matter of this book—the politics on reservations and among tribal members—and my interest in it reach back before my graduate training. My interest first developed while I was a resident at Akwe:kon, an American Indian–themed dorm in the style of an Iroquois longhouse, as an undergraduate at Cornell University. The variety and richness of tribal political life was made apparent to me through the stories of my fellow residents and peers. Whether involving religious functions, economic development projects, witch hunts, or corruption trials, the everyday lives of American Indians as tribal members were undeniably vivid.

My time spent working at First Nations Development Institute allowed me to extend my interest in American Indian economic development from theory to practice. The opportunity and mentorship offered by Rebecca Adamson, Terry Douglas, and Sarah Dewees broadened my understanding and experience in Indian country. Jerry Reynolds's breadth of knowledge, intellectual generosity, and friendship added much to this project.

It is perhaps misguided to try to thank institutions, but the support of the University of California, Berkeley, was instrumental in the research and writing of this book. I would like to thank members of my dissertation committee for their support and guidance. Taeku Lee, my dissertation adviser at Berkeley, provided patience and insight and supported me through the difficulties of writing a dissertation and book with the calm demeanor characteristic of the best advisers. *I gweyen nikan.* Tom Biolsi's knowledge and sense of overall perspective about what could be a meaningful contribution to the study of American Indians were essential in both creating the motivation to do this work and the background to put it in context. Todd LaPorte's enthusiasm, creativity, and ability to comprehend the jumbled ideas of a graduate student and to rearticulate them into something clear did much for the trickiest parts of this book. This book benefited from conversations at Berkeley with George Tsai, Dann Naseemullah, Bart Watson, Carmon Foghorn, Jon Hassid, Jakuba Wrzesniewski, Andrew Janos, Gloria Chun, Carolyn Arnold, Chris Ansell, Cindy Andallo, Kiren Chaudhry, John Hanley, Sam Hanlin, and Sandy Muir. Both my time at Berkeley and this project were enhanced as well by Dean Harvey, David Anderson, Liz Griegg, Amanda Hassid, Barbara Anderson, Ally and Matt Dodson, and Fernando Torres.

My time as a postdoctoral fellow with Yale University's Race, Ethnicity, and Migration Program aided me in the formation of this manuscript from a dissertation. The advice of Ned Blackhawk, Alicia Schmidt Camacho, and Steve Pitti was extraordinarily helpful. The camaraderie of Lourdes Gutiérrez Nájera, Ted Van Alst, Ashley Makar, and Rani Neutill brought much-needed joy and ideas to the task of writing.

Princeton University's Department of Politics generously offered me a fellowship. While at Princeton, I appreciated the comments given during a workshop on the manuscript from a group that included Alan Patten, John Borrows, Anna Stilz, Andrea Benjamin, Larry Rosen, James Tully, and Sandra Field. Thank you to Melissa Lane, Helen Milner, and Jennifer Widener.

Yancey Orr, Bart Watson, Jon Hassid, Emily Dowgialo, Gary Gartenburg, Dann Naseemullah, and, most of all, Caley Otter, provided needed editorial suggestions.

"Thank you" to this book's editor, Thomas Krause, who supported and advised this project to publication, and to the anonymous reviewers for the fair, critical, and important perspectives.

This work was made possible by the time and knowledge shared by those who participated in the research. Individuals across the United States were willing to spend a considerable amount of time—some even spent days—talking with me about what was important to their lives as American Indians, tribal members, and human beings. Only with their contributions was I able to write this book. It is to these participants who shared their perspectives and life experiences that I am most indebted. I refer to participants generically as *informants* in this book. *Informant* might seem insensitive given the sometimes personal and sensitive information they talked about with me, but I use the term to protect the anonymity of these sources. Even referring to these participants by general identifiers such as demographic characteristics, occupations, where I met them, or where they reside could potentially compromise their anonymity.

This book is in debt to those who participated in telling stories, their own and their peoples'. *Migwetch jak she gego ga gishtoyen.*

Reservation Politics

CHAPTER 1

American Indian Politics as Behavior and Variation

1.1 INTRODUCTION: BLACK HILLS AND TO TAKE THE MONEY OR NOT?

Lakota communities in South Dakota are some of the poorest in the United States. On the Pine Ridge Reservation, 80 percent of tribal members are unemployed. In 2012, the median per capita income on the reservation hovered near $8,000 compared to the national median of $42,000 (U.S. Census Bureau 2012). Compared to the average American life expectancy of seventy-seven years, Lakota men and women on the reservation live an average of forty-eight and fifty-two years, respectively (Mitchell 2011; Schwartz 2006), which makes tribal members' lives the shortest in the Western Hemisphere, with the exception of those of Haitians. Though in poverty and despair—youth suicide is more than three times the national average (Nieves 2007)—along with several other Lakota tribes, the Pine Ridge Reservation refuses to accept $1,200,000,000 in reparations. This money comes from a 1980 Supreme Court decision that upheld a decision by the federal Indian Claims Commission in 1974 that offered compensation for nineteenth-century land seizures from several of the region's tribes. To accept the settlement would require that the tribes relinquish all possible claims to their ancestral lands. Known as the Black Hills, these lands span the Dakotas, Wyoming, and Nebraska and will almost certainly never be returned to the Lakotas under the conditions they demand because the lands are now privately owned by tens of thousands of individuals and have become national or state parks.

The Lakotas have two choices: (*a*) take the money or (*b*) do not take the money. It appears that choice *a* is clearly preferable and the *dominant strategy* in the nomenclature of behavioral economics. By selecting to reject the money, choice *b*, the Lakotas are not engaging in a negotiation ploy, as no better propositions are created by rejecting the offer (Giago 2010). Thus, the Lakotas receive no material benefit from this refusal, but claim that it honors their ancestors' efforts to protect the Black Hills. To the Lakotas, the choice over the Black Hills is framed differently than that of a material perspective and might resemble something like this: choice *a* dishonors their ancestors and the land and choice *b* honors their ancestors and the land.

It is likely that the Lakotas would be forced to accept a lesser deal than the one that exists. Under these conditions, the decision makes no rational sense if rationality is construed economically. Naturally, the question arises: why is it that such a destitute people refuse such a large amount of money? This book is broadly about such questions as they pertain to American Indian politics and how people—not just American Indians—respond to and frame such political decisions differently. Though most American Indian tribes and indigenous populations as polities—to speak globally—do not face as dramatic a choice as the Lakotas do about the Black Hills, they make collective decisions that evoke competing moral or ideological commitments.

How should we understand the Black Hills impasse? Is it strategic and are these American Indians holding out for better compensation? The Lakotas' strong opposition to any deal and the absence of an additional settlement for the last thirty years is clear evidence that the community is not looking for or expecting greater compensation short of the return of the Black Hills to its ownership (Giago 2010). Alternatively, we could examine the institutions involved in the settlement. Are there courts, congressional committees, state agencies, or tribal constitutions whose rules make the return currently impossible? For instance, why did efforts by U.S. senator Bill Bradley in the 1980s fail to resolve the dispute? Certainly the outcome is shaped by legal rules and institutional constraints. Perhaps even a powerful court or a committee might grant the Lakotas control of the Black Hills, and this would solve the dispute, but it would only get to the surface political question. Both strategic and institutional ways of approaching this issue would leave untouched perhaps the most fascinating feature of the Lakota example, which is behavioral; it is the striking desire of the Lakotas to control the Black Hills. Strategic and institutional analyses do not provide a legitimate explanation or capture why the Lakotas prefer something other than material resources.

What people want and what they give up in order to achieve those wants are both questions with as much relevance to political outcomes as strategy and institutional constraint. If we are to look at the Lakotas' prevailing view of the Black Hills settlement, it is clear that in this instance, material maximization is not their highest political preference nor is it the tribe's defining motivation. When confronting a political puzzle such as the Lakotas' rejection, George Homans suggests, "It is seldom enough to ask whether or not [people are] rational. The relevant question is what determined their behavior" (1974, 81). The basic premise of this book is that the calculus behind how we decide, and the provenance of many key political behaviors, depends upon a great many things, but that our worldview is central to these decisions. A *worldview* is a broad term, but for this book's purposes, it is the interpretation about the world and our role in it—what Jürgen Habermas refers to as the "life world" (1984). More specifically, it is constituted from the intersection of our motivations and how we frame or perceive our surroundings, including our individual and collective experiences. As important components of worldview, these two terms, *motivation* and *frame*, are abstract so allow me to specify how these terms will be used.

A *motivation* refers to our wants or desires. Often associated with motivations is the term *preference*, which is a selection among a limited choice of actions that seeks to satisfy certain motivations. These desires can be conscious or unconscious, material or emotive, helpful or harmful. In the case of the Lakotas' refusal, the motivation would be, at least at the surface level, to possess the Black Hills.

A *frame* refers to our perception or ordering of the world. Such perception could be our place in what is around us, our views of others such as their motivations or character, our history (or their history), and even our moral outlook or sense of right and wrong (see Goffman 1974; Snow et al. 1986 for more detailed discussion of frame analysis). *Worldview* is a grander term often used to capture this system of perception. *Framing*, the act of using or creating a frame, is a type of cognitive organization that facilitates better sense of the world's complications and guides our decisions and actions. In the case of the Lakotas' refusal, how they frame the situation is unclear from the limited information provided, but rejecting the money is likely a function of how enough tribal members perceive the world.

I have outlined frames and motivations somewhat separately, but perception and motivation are interrelated, mutually reinforcing and structuring our decisions along with helping us to establish goals and set permissible and desirable behavior.

Why we might perceive choices *a* and *b* differently depends upon our worldview. Similar questions to what I have described in the Lakota Black Hills example, about the intersection of worldview and decision, have been approached in urban poverty research (see Small, Harding, and Lamont 2010 for descriptions of the "culture of poverty" debate). Compared to the long history of research around worldview (often referred to as "ideology") and material condition of urban and black communities (see Banfield 1970 and Young 2004 for examples of poverty and culture research; see Cohen 1999 and Dawson 2001 for studies of black political ideology and identity), the origin of American Indian belief receives less attention, particularly as it pertains to material "irrationality." Despite important works by Duane Champagne (1983, 1985), among others, the study of whether contemporary American Indian belief systems come from historical experiences has a limitation in how critical it might be. Perhaps there does not need to be an American Indian version of Thomas Sowell's *Black Rednecks and White Liberals* (2005), which argues that much of urban black culture is residue of white rural culture (i.e., "redneck"). However, that decisions such as that of the Black Hills are taken at face value deserves consideration itself. In fact, the hermetical or interpretative suspicion seems rather shallow in the refusal of the Black Hills settlement. I believe this is less the case in scholarship on other racial and ethnic groups. A common and provocative theme in urban poverty research, and one shared with this work, is why marginalized communities seem to further their plight (hence, select choice *b*). An answer depends upon their motivations and perceptions, which in turn, this book claims, depend upon their experiences and the meaning found in these experiences—what will be called *lived experiences.*

Such a dynamic, whereby we find meaning in our experiences, was identified by anthropologist Clifford Geertz (1973) over forty years ago. It is a sentiment echoed by anthropologist Audra Simpson, when she states, "The culture and issues of native peoples can best be examined in terms of the lived experience of nationhood" and "To appreciate that experience, one must take account of the shared set of meanings that are negotiated through narrations—through the voices" (2000, 127). This book follows an approach to American Indian political decisions recognized by Geertz and Simpson but does so through considering the historical processes of exploitation and traumatic events—abundant in American Indian history and the lives of contemporary American Indian peoples—and their role in providing experiences upon which meaning is derived, decisions are made, and intratribal politics is organized. We know lived experience is important, and this book seeks to add to that knowledge by considering these experiences comparatively in order to know, maybe only in rough estimation, what experiences do to meaning. On the surface, my question about American Indians' decision-making, as encapsulated in the Black Hills example, follows a similar path to how poverty is studied from a cultural analysis perspective, whereby decisions, and the worldviews they are grounded in, provide insight into larger social processes hewn from historical experience. This book also argues through its case studies of contemporary conflict in American Indian tribal politics that the provenance of worldviews should take place in an intellectual arena with deeper ties to political theory, political economy, historical exploitation, and social change. This book, therefore, seeks to extend the importance of intratribal conflict as an established theme in writing on American Indian history (see Blackhawk 2006; Dowd 1992; Foster 1991; Green and Perdue 2008; Hamalainen 2008; Lewis 1991; Wilson 1985 for a few of many historical accounts of this conflict) to the American Indian politics of the contemporary period where we find substantially less scholarly work—a body of literature which will be discussed in the next chapter.

As distinct polities, American Indians are in a unique position to situate such analyses, as they add two features to the urban poverty research and cultural analysis that allow for a deeper intellectual discussion to take place. Unlike black Americans, whose choices and culture were the focus of urban poverty research, American Indians have tribes, which are formal polities that engage in communal decision-making and allow for examination at the collective level. Second, as polities, American Indian tribes can be traced historically with greater distinction and allow for linkages between experiences and perceptions in a way that is less apparent among other minority groups (Champagne 1983, 1985, 2007; Cornell and Gil-Swedberg 1995; Cornell and Kalt 2010). Examining American Indian tribal politics opens the potential for powerful comparative studies that link collective experience to contemporary beliefs.

That American Indians have defined polities allows us to answer another question about worldviews: why are they dispersed the way they are? (My assumption is that American Indians might be sympathetic to choice b more than whites; if that is true, then why?) Certain motivations are more desirable and certain frames more accurate to some than to others. For instance, the Lakotas often say that whites are more likely to select choice a and take the money. This book examines how American Indians frame political choices differently from one another, not only compared to whites. At its core, this book rejects the notion that shared ethnicity, even at the tribal level, connotes a shared or agreed-upon worldview. Rather, it argues that a shared experience around distinct historical processes, which is often, but not always, located in ethnicity creates a commonality of worldview. This book's argument, not a provocative or novel one, is that worldviews are historically created or conditioned, and that such variations in worldviews—between those who would take the money and those who reject it or between those who perceive the choice materially and those who see it morally or ethically, for instance—are not random, but are the result of interplay between two types of experiences that exert a strong influence over such divergence in motivations and frames. In essence, worldviews arise from experiences and these experiences differ from one experiential group to another.

That historical experience shapes current action is neither a new perspective nor provocative. Yet what this book offers that is new and potentially theoretically provocative is the selection of experiences that matter. The first historical experience to profoundly shape worldviews was incorporation into market economies and new forms of wealth. We might refer to this experience as a process of *economic development*, a softer and less abrasive term for *wealth*. Economic development promotes what I call the *rise of self-interest* or the *rise of the self-interested worldview* as materially construed. Economic development or wealth creation is the experience, and the rise of self-interest is the associated behavioral change in motivation, perception, or frame (i.e., worldview). The second of these historical experiences, and the admittedly controversial thesis of this book, is that of historical trauma. Historical trauma promotes what I call the *rise of melancholia* or the *rise of the melancholic worldview*, which is a drive to reject self-interest in favor of furthering individual and collective mourning. The more specific claim made about historical trauma throughout this book is that the behaviors associated with traumatized individuals emerge and persist at the collective polity level decades and even centuries after the initial traumatizing events. Traumatic events are recognized in American Indian communities as creating terrible ruptures and needing healing (Brave Heart 2003, 2007; Duran and Duran 1995), but trauma has been less understood as shaping collective political behavior.

Let us return to differences in preferences, motivations, values, attitudes, moral outlooks, worldviews, and ideologies—just a few of the many concepts scholars employ to discuss why people act and decide the way they do. Our motivations and perceptions might arise randomly or be entirely irrelevant or trivial to the study of politics. Why some people prefer apples to cranberries, red to blue, burgundy to periwinkle, and so on and so on might be random or not, but these preferences are certainly beyond what is worth predicting for our interest in politics. However, there are certain types of preferences that may be less random and more worth our inquiry. Why one community might accept an offer of redress or reconciliation, another reject an offer, and another be completely un-inclined to barter over an issue are differences worth thinking about. Needless to say, these elemental inclinations would be more important for political life than selection of color or taste in fruits.

Few claim that the past does not matter. That the past shapes motivation and perception is accepted from Freud to Geertz. At the individual level, motivations typically involve the future and what we want in that future, but frames are often historically formed and our available preferences politically limited. If our history, and the experiencing of it, creates patterns in our worldviews, then are there experiences that are strong enough to make claims about—in a broad sense—vis-à-vis such an experience's impact on motivation and, ultimately, preference? Yes, with the caveat that my claim is not that experience with market incorporation and historical trauma explains every motivation or perception but rather that much of the behavior we see in American Indian communities would not make sense without understanding their histories and especially the role of wealth and trauma. I advocate an approach where the experiences of historical trauma (especially relocation and genocide) and economic incorporation were significant enough to create a pattern in the alteration of worldviews. This is referred to as the *pain and profit approach*, and its evidence is borne out in the discussions and disagreements that American Indians have between each other within their own tribes. Such disagreements might be about what a tribe is for, whether to accept or reject a specific policy, or what tribal history and identity means. These are worth sustained inquiry because these show fissures in worldviews and also the behavioral terrain that tribes draw upon to make decisions.

Returning to the Lakotas and their potential billion dollars, let us evaluate how trauma, self-interest, motivation, and perception might help an observer understand their decision. Both by collective and individual standards, the Lakotas have a painful past. The Lakota tribes actively fought nineteenth-century white encroachment to little avail: most of their territory was taken, including the Black Hills, as war concessions resulting from repeated military defeats. The horrors associated with military loss paled in comparison to the multiple massacres of women and children during the late nineteenth century. Such troubling events are not relegated to the past or forgotten, but continue on in the form of painful and brutal experiences in contemporary reservation life. The Lakotas have developed a process of commemoration and of framing the world that includes introducing themselves at meetings in relation to which of their ancestors were murdered during nineteenth-century massacres. For the traumatized, the past is not the past and the future is rarely new. And whatever overtly colonial danger left in the nineteenth century has now given way to widespread social violence that is prevalent on reservations in the northern plains. Traumatic events on reservations in this region are significantly higher than in other regions (see Manson 1996). Over 60 percent of children on reservations in the northern plains are exposed to a traumatic event (Jones et al. 1997), such as parental violence, and the adult post-traumatic stress disorder (PTSD) prevalence is twice the national average (see Manson 1996). The brutal affinity between the past and present, the individual and the collective, intensifies the relationship the Lakotas have with their own suffering and how they frame this suffering. In interviews, politics and life history become intertwined and framed in such a way that the two features of painful ethnohistory and interpersonal violence combine into a polity that perpetually seeks to re-create and re-experience the trauma that formed it. To sacrifice and to suffer as the Lakotas do not only honors ancestors and the loss of the Black Hills but has the potential to place them in a communion with this trauma.

The claim that historical and individual traumas serve as central features in many American Indian communities is not original to this work. Research over previous decades has sought to understand the degree and characteristics of these traumas. Such trauma research focusing on American Indians is typically in the areas of public health (Beals et al. 2013; Deschenie 2006; Manson 1996; Whitbeck et al. 2009) or psychology, or on traumatic origins and healing (Brave Heart 2000, 2003, 2007; Duran and Duran 1995; Million 2013). This book offers trauma as an explanation for collective political behavior, which is witnessed in some of the decisions tribes make, the perspectives of tribal members, and the conflicts within tribes. Trauma not only shapes feelings; it also shapes perceptions and actions with political consequence. As a political force motivating behavior and informing perspectives, trauma should be elevated to the same status as concepts such as self-interest and fellow feeling.

Let us examine the suggestion further that a painful, traumatic past is motivating the Lakotas' refusal. Many Lakotas suggest that the Black Hills refusal endows their community with a cultural but not a tangible good. It is not trauma but honor that is cited as being what informs the decision from the Lakota perspective. For them, relinquishing their rights to the Black Hills is tantamount to signing away their commitment to the past. But what about the past is so seductive and why does it create an absolute devotion to it such that a people in desperate circumstances would refuse possible help, condemning themselves, their children, and their communities to further poverty? One answer is that by ending this grievance and focusing away from the loss itself, the Lakotas may sever the ties to injustice but also to the comfort found in its pain at the individual, familial, social, and political levels. To interpret this refusal as gamesmanship—holding out for a better offer—or a result of institutional alignment would be neat and clean, when in fact the motivation might be the drive toward further trauma and dissatisfaction. Despite the reported desire by many Lakotas to want to live safer, more stable, and prosperous lives as evidenced in the interviews that this book comprises, a paradoxical feature of historical trauma is that it drives the traumatized to pursue the opposite. Trauma's perplexing pattern, that it re-creates itself, pertains not only to the individual but also to the collective when that collective has undergone sustained trauma across enough of the polity's population. The mechanisms of this are described in chapter 3, which addresses causal dynamics. The perpetuation of these traumas to the present day includes the social, political, economic, and life ruptures associated with genocide and forced relocation, which facilitate higher levels of interpersonal violence and re-create the instability and danger in the next generation—thus informing the framing of its world by melancholia and the motivation of future pain.

Though trauma is in the past, the profound and puzzling legacy of those who experience trauma is that these initial traumas bind our future selves and future generations to lives of trauma with greater frequency than among those who did not experience said trauma. To relinquish the Black Hills is to relinquish the pain of loss itself—the one feature of the past the Lakota people would seemingly want to avoid if we are to believe that people go toward pleasure and away from pain. To many readers and scholars, this statement constitutes an insult to humanity's self-esteem. Trauma and its legacy might indeed be that. Understanding behavior through trauma is possibly the least normatively acceptable premise in which to understand human motivations—particularly regarding marginalized populations. It harkens back to the social sciences' dark ages in the 1960s and *culture of poverty* theories that blamed the victim (see Stack 1974). Such a perspective of trauma that includes perverse preferences and distorted perception lends itself to being an indictment of the abused by pathologizing the choices of the abused and reducing our belief in their agency. Yet this understanding of trauma and choice is the very source of psychology's inception since Charcot and Janet (Brown et al. 1996; Perez-Rincon 2011). The terms by which traumatic events operate unavoidably implicate their victims through the ungracious view that their later hardships are self-induced. But worse than accepting this harsh and unflattering aspect of the human psyche verboten (which knows not race, class, ethnicity, or gender) is to reject it solely because it is against our normative commitments. To abscond from the searing and peculiar effects of trauma with the safest version of human motivation intact serves neither the interests of social science research nor the communities we are intent on protecting.

Pain is a second currency in our world. As early as Hobbes's *Leviathan* in 1651, there was a recognition that polities control via application or suppression of fear and violence—two attributes of trauma. Yet the psychological and political potential that historical trauma can have on contemporary politics is mostly left unexamined (see Garbarino 2010; Myers, Hewstone, and Cairns 2009 as recent exceptions). Not only might traumas have political sources, such as colonization, but also trauma affects political actors. Traumatic experiences produce worldviews whose motivations are likely to, at least in the Lakota Black Hills example, promote frames and motivations that reject other options in order to continue the trauma or recount its loss. At the very least such a profound loss contributes to what legal and political scholar David Wilkins calls the "bitter frustration and profound disillusionment" (2013, 1) in contemporary American Indian politics. Though historical or social trauma does not easily conform to measurement, as in the case of biological or physical trauma, these less measurable experiences leave identifiable and peculiar legacies. At the individual level, evidence of trauma's legacy is clear in emotional dispositions and even in the biology of the traumatized. Trauma alters perceptions and twists motivations, and the evidence of a traumatic past is found in the physical architecture of the brain, which becomes a biological record of abuse (see Carrion and Wong 2012; McEwen 2001; Sapolsky 1996; Sapolsky 2000).

Trauma is studied retrospectively. The events that sear our minds usually take place in the past but are also cast or projected into the future. It is logical therefore that this book, because it is located in reservation politics at the local level, considers ethnohistory (the experiences of a tribe) at the communal level in its analysis, in line with the work of Audra Simpson (2000). Equally, this book examines how the personal experiences of those participating in its research draw meaning from tribal history into their worldviews. Because tribes, like all other polities, do not have biological nervous systems in the same sense that people do, the inclusion of individuals is required to show how perspectives might be formed out of a socioeconomic context set by ethnohistory and the interpretation of ethnicity.

If we believe the Lakotas make pain and not profit and seek to self-wound over self-heal, then why would they select a more painful existence and focus on what harms them? Why would people be, in essence, pain seekers instead of pleasure seekers or profit seekers? On the surface, this does not make sense, or at least not in the orthodox meaning of *sense* within a standard view of practical rationality. Yet, within what is known about psychological trauma, such paradoxical behavior fits the pattern that trauma reproduces itself.

The money from the settlement would seem to increase Lakota stability and prosperity and distance the people from the conditions that historical trauma helped induce. Children could go to more generously funded clinics, elders would have more to eat, adults would have greater access to employment and social services, young adults would have further funding for education, and cultural centers could rely on greater resources for community programs. But this logic excludes the charisma that pain and trauma might have over a polity and its constituency. As rational as taking the compensation might seem, it overlooks the possibility that the very loss and trauma that the tribe suffered from colonization, exemplified in the Black Hills, along with the decades of living in dire poverty and interpersonal violence that followed, produced a set of motivations and frames hostile to material utility and self-interest but comfortable with an array of forms of suffering. The identified reality that trauma seeks to reproduce itself, so apparent to scholars who work on trauma, is likely to be overlooked if we solely consider institutions or strategies. So treacherous are the horrors of the past that they must be relived—what Freud termed the *repetition compulsion* ([1920] 1961). Such a reality should either complicate assumptions made about political actors or at least provide a different perspective to understand certain forms of perception, political behavior, and decision-making.

1.2 AMERICAN INDIAN VARIATION OVER CHOICE *A* AND CHOICE *B*: THE PAIN AND PROFIT APPROACH

From a decade of researching, living with, or working for American Indians, it is clear to me that most American Indians believe that they are different from whites. For instance, the Lakotas in the Great Plains say that whites are less likely to understand the reasons why they refuse such a substantial amount of money. If you ask the Lakotas, they will tell you that they are a more principled or honorable people. To act white in Indian country is to resemble something near to Max Weber's entrepreneurial miser. Of course, not all Lakotas agree with this decision. But disagreement came at a cost for one Lakota man I spoke with, who declared, "I don't live in South Dakota because I can't stand that all people talk about are the Black Hills" (Informant 2007). And even if whites were to understand the Lakota remonstrance to material rationality and appreciate the principled sources of their rejection, whites would likely still accept the money themselves. The question of why this difference between Lakotas and whites emerges.

We have taken the self-interest and materialistic perspective as the starting point, where those who identify with the Lakotas are cast as abnormal. We should ask the question in reverse, where choice *a*, the self-interested materialist motivation, is the abnormal position. This was in fact believed to be the case for most of western and world history (see Hirschman 1997; Polanyi 2001 for an account of the transition to material self-interest). To answer questions similar to the Lakotas' decline of compensation for the Black Hills—i.e., the world is framed in a way that poverty rejects prosperity—should prompt us to examine our own preferences (assuming that most of us would be inclined to accept the money over the honor). In accepting material compensation, we might tell ourselves that our children would not have to go hungry, that health services might improve, that our future would be better than the past, and that maybe we could even put the Black Hills behind us. In fact, about half of the American Indians I spoke with disagree with the Lakotas' decision to bequeath poverty to the next generation or said that their tribe would have accepted the compensation and moved forward. Why might certain Indians prefer the money and others not? Where, then, might this *material rationality, instrumental,* or *self-interested motivation*—all terms scholars use to capture our preference for the money and amoral maximizers—originate? This book is about us, assuming we are materially self-interested profit seekers, and those who would advocate taking the money as well, but more importantly, it is about how we have come to have variance in these important worldviews and why we sympathize with one perspective over another.

I offer a historical explanation for how the variations in worldviews are constructed, how this past ultimately helps frame political commitments and political decisions. A conceptual model of this is in figure 1.1. I argue

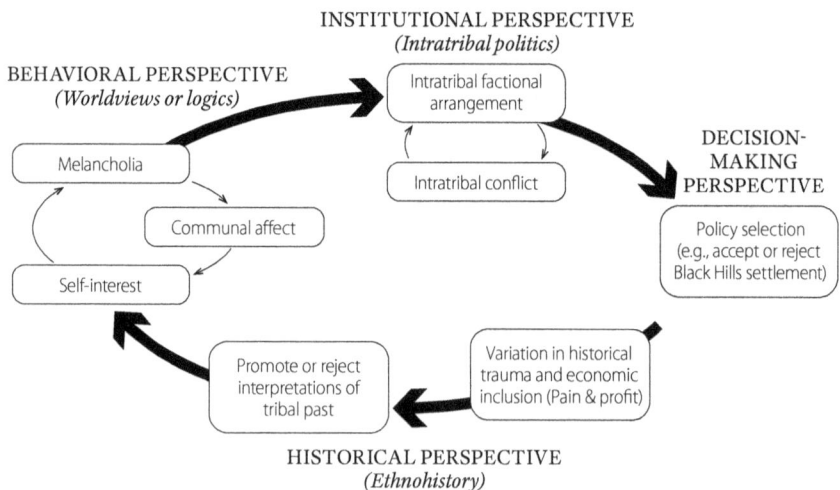

FIGURE 1.1 Visualization of pain and profit model: from historical experience, to preferences, to factional arrangement, to tribal decision-making

that variation in ethnohistory around trauma and economic incorporation has promoted different physical or material conditions.

These conditions, wealth or poverty, are the intermediaries between historical events and behavioral or psychological perspectives. This argument observes that certain tribes, though relatively few, experienced periods of substantial economic growth during the oil and mineral booms of the last 150 years. This is the historical stage of the model. These tribes are more inclined to be motivated by, and frame their world through, material self-interest. This is the behavioral or psychological stage of the model. Other tribes were repeatedly abused, murdered, dispossessed of land, and starved on reservations for decades. These tribes are more likely to be motivated by, and frame their world through, melancholia and display behavior that resembles anti–self-interest. Certain tribes were not conditioned by either context, and their previous motivations around communalism are reflected in the term *communal affect* (a concept I will explain shortly). A contemporary example is offered by the Pueblos in the Southwest, who were not geographically removed or massacred and whose politics are the subject of chapter 5. Certain tribes received both pain and profit and, as we will see in chapter 4 on the Citizen Potawatomis, have an acrimonious political climate where both frames and motivations inspire conflicting tribal factions. The psychological perspective utilized includes three categories of motivational sets and frames that function as organizing worldviews (self-interest, melancholia, and communal affect). These worldviews compete for primacy of preferences and ultimately inform tribal decisions. As American Indians differ according to what they want and how they see their moral universe, these worldviews inspire and reinforce different internal tribal factions. This is the institutional level of the model. The relative power of these factions determines the directions tribes take, such as rejection or acceptance of the money. I propose that the relative power of these three motivations in relation to each other can be witnessed by both the decisions tribes make at the end of the model and in how they structure internal conflict and factional politics within tribes. The claim here is that when a tribe has experienced significant forms of pain and profit, there is a greater heterogeneity of preference (many tribal members are sympathetic toward choice *a* or self-interest and many sympathetic toward choice *b* and melancholia) or worldview; this leads to greater factional organization, but also to conflict between factions within a tribe over its direction and meaning.

1.3 EXTENDING THE STUDY OF TRAUMA TO POLITICS

There is currently an impressive set of studies and approaches relating to the conceptualization of trauma in American Indians. Epidemiological studies have examined the high prevalence of post-traumatic stress disorder on reservations (Bassett, Buchwald, and Manson 2014), trauma has been linked to contemporary forms of human rights violations (Million 2013), and historical loss and its transition in American Indian communities has been understood in comparison to that of other ethnicities (Brave Heart 2000, 2003, 2007; Brave Heart and DeBruyn 1998). These themes are important and further work should be undertaken. What has yet to be examined in previous studies of trauma, however, and a lacuna that this work seeks to address, is the expression of trauma as a political form that explains the political decisions and ideological orientations of tribes. This work differs from these previous approaches to trauma in American Indian communities by showing that trauma and loss shape worldviews, organize political factions, and have significant consequence for the directions tribes take on major issues such as economic development. Trauma is not only a public health crisis, emotional state, historical grievance, or something in need of healing, therapy, or working through, but a force endowed with political agency and associated costs whereby decisions and the reasons given, such as refusal to settle the Black Hills claim because of principled commitment, may be cover stories for traumatic forms of attachment.

1.4 METHOD

Theoretical models and frameworks, as intriguing as they may be, need support in the empirical reality they purport to explain. Only a few tribes are involved in the Black Hills impasse, so we have to cast a broader net elsewhere to evaluate whether this book's perspective adds to our understanding of American Indian politics and the origins of worldviews. A rich but overlooked location in which to situate a story about differing worldviews is the conflict between tribal members.

By probing the continuity between tribal ethnohistory and preferences that may include traumatic events, this book illustrates the dynamics behind two outcomes not specific to American Indian peoples: (*a*) how people come to hold specific grouped perspectives, frames, worldviews, preferences, values, meanings, or motivations over others; and (*b*) what factors inform the political decisions of marginalized—and typically abused—communities. Not only might trauma potentially help us to understand the Lakota refusal (and this decision is returned to in chapter 6), but the presence or absence of collective or individual trauma aids in our understanding of broad features in American Indian politics at multiple levels as described in figure 1.1. This book claims that the presence or absence of trauma shapes widespread features in American Indian politics: (*a*) it creates intertribal differences in preferences and behaviors; (*b*) it inspires intratribal differences within the same tribe through factionalism; and (*c*) it shapes the types, and intensity, of social and political conflicts within tribes.

This work is based in an ethnographic account of the ways in which individuals see themselves as part of their tribe and the degree to which they differ in worldview. American Indians involved in tribal politics and non-Indians who were aware of tribal politics served as the informants for semi-structured interviews. As this book is interested in meaning and perception, it therefore utilizes interviews as a method to generate material best suited for analysis. Most of these interviews took place near tribal reservations in person or via telephone. Working in Indian country before attending graduate school resulted in a wide set of contacts for me to draw upon for informants. Interviews with tribal members were taken from three communities and form the basis of this book. The study was to include a fourth community, the Mashantucket Pequot tribe. However, due to previous accusations that the tribe and its members are not a legitimate tribe or "authentic" American Indians and have committed a form of ethnic fraud, the tribe prohibits its members from talking with researchers. After describing my research topic and gaining verbal consent required by ethics committees at my university, a typical interview began with my asking participants about the history of the area and their tribe. This was in part for my knowledge, but it has been my experience that when talking about the past one quickly arrives at the present—and this is where most of my interest in American Indian politics lies. This is also true about starting with questions about important events in tribal ethnohistory, which would transition to an individual informant's beliefs, attitudes, and worldviews. In total, the interviews collected in this research and presented in this book show a complexity of worldviews among American Indians on subjects ranging from what a tribe means, to what a tribe should aspire to be (and to avoid), to what are fault lines within the ethnicity, to who is an Indian, and to the degree to which outsiders might be trusted. These are a few of the many themes embedded in intratribal politics.

1.4.1 COMPARATIVE CASE STUDY

This work relies upon a comparative case study approach. In exploring the two units of analysis—tribal political conflict and the worldviews of tribal members—this book points to historical variation in tribal experiences. A comparative approach to tribal historical experiences selects representative tribes for a particular historical experience and examines variations in the outcomes (tribal political conflict and the worldviews of tribal members). The cases selected for study in this book were arrived at by access to tribal politics in addition to how they fit into the theoretical concerns of the project. The comparative method, as it is used here, is at best semi-scientific as it relies upon a small set of cases that might not represent the larger categories of historical experiences of interest. This book examines 3 tribes out of 566 and cannot claim the degree of scientific validity that accompanies large-number studies. This book, therefore, does not claim to prove a particular theory but looks for inference using this comparative method. In other words, what might such a perspective glean about tribal politics on these reservations? This book argues not only that much is gained in terms of insights about tribal politics, the dispersal of factions on reservations, and how tribes might differ in how they approach conflict but also how historical experiences shape what we think is valuable.

Within the collected interviews, and in this book's analysis of worldviews and what interviewees find important, a subtext will emerge that weaves a paradox of time and freedom. If certain motivations, frames, preferences, and, ultimately, values are a function of our lived experience—or more so than they are not, as this book contends—then such lived and remembered experiences, whether individual or tribal, simultaneously give and rob us of life and meaning. Experience not only endows our identity and humanity with values but also constrains our agency with respect to our freedom to relinquish such values. On the surface, it seems that we are free to wish for a future based on the rejection or acceptance of our experiences, yet, even in the case of rejection, we cannot fully escape the past and those experiences. Perhaps, as Nietzsche suggested, the past is doomed to "become the gravedigger of the present" (2007, 62). With no available reconciliation, only an acknowledgment of this universal snare is possible. This work seeks to capture responses to the fact that time, in the form of lived experience and framed by ethnohistory, on the one hand provides contexts of agency and, on the other, imposes ever-looming structure.

1.5 BOOK CONTENTS AND WHAT COMES NEXT

This book suggests that examining the politics between American Indians on reservations is a method to understand the potential origin and effects of worldviews. Intratribal politics, what I will call the political relationships between American Indians, is worth studying in addition to the historical provenance of worldviews. Relatively few works engage with the harshest part of intratribal politics in the contemporary period from a political perspective, compared to the volume of attention given to those from historical periods or the relationship between Indians and outsiders. Chapter 2 deals in detail with how intratribal conflict is studied. Chapters 1 through 3 are theoretically focused, and chapters 4 through 6 are case studies based on three reservations. A curiosity about the politics on American Indian reservations and the lack of previous writing on the subject may motivate some readers to have this book on their desk, more so than a desire to involve themselves with the social science theory. Readers may also not have deep interests in the conversations that social scientists forward regarding the theories around trauma and self-interest. For such readers interested primarily in what reservation political life and intratribal conflict looks like, they are invited to move forward to chapter 4, where the book turns to intra-ethnic competition over values and political conflict on the author's own reservation in Oklahoma. I encourage them to do so if they wish.

American Indian intratribal politics are a virtually unknown political space in the field of political science. The next chapter expands upon why the omission of intra-ethnic or intratribal politics and conflict should end. Chapter 2 introduces the concept of the *common secret*. Whether overlooked by convention or through discomfort about reporting adversarial relationships, the disparity between the knowledge that is discussed, but not reported, in scholarship—such as the centrality of intratribal politics and historical trauma and political life—is an example of a common secret. The relatively small theme in the field that is American Indian intratribal politics, despite the informal awareness of these politics as a key feature of American Indian life, is what motivates the common secret perspective. Chapter 2 describes how common secrets form a tacit knowledge base that has served empirical political theories in the social sciences.

For those readers interested in perspectives on the historical origins of motivations and frames, chapter 3 covers how the combination of colonially induced trauma, periods of economic development, and the desire to maintain traditional values shapes a great deal of reservation politics. Chapter 3 exposes a common secret: like all peoples, American Indians are socially constructed through experience and are neither immune from deep transformation nor "hewn" from a primordial rock (see Biolsi 1989 for critique of the primordial perspective on American Indian worldview). In fact, this chapter argues that contemporary worldviews are misidentified as being principled or traditional and are actually informed by trauma (such as the refusal in the Black Hills case). This chapter identifies various causal mechanisms in the pain and profit approach to the creation of worldview. Similarly, studies in trauma, psychology, neuroscience, social psychology, and established works in political theory and economic anthropology that support this book's claim that ethnohistory and lived experience can shape worldviews are identified.

This book's core lies in the reservations themselves, which take the form of three tribally based chapters on North American indigenous communities: the Citizen Potawatomis; the Isleta Pueblos; and the Rose-bud Lakotas (also referred to as the "Sioux"). Chapters 4, 5, and 6 ground themselves inside of tribes and explore the themes of trauma, conflict, economic development, self-interest, and preference. Each tribally organized chapter addresses a different perspective on the aforementioned themes. This ethnographic research took place on these reservations in 2007 and 2008.

Chapter 4 considers the harsh discord found among Citizen Potawatomi tribal politics as a competition between factions, families, and worldviews that originated during a complex and extreme set of colonial experiences in their ethnohistory. Forced removal from the Great Lakes to Oklahoma during the nineteenth century is more than a memory for the Citizen Potawatomis; it has become a narrative to help intensify more recent family experiences during a period of twentieth-century oil extraction that divide the tribe between the disenfranchised Indian and the Indian oil baron who did the disenfranchising. In the minds of certain Citizen Potawatomis, oil and now the casino are threats to the meaning of being an Indian. Such economic enterprises run parallel to the exploitative and unfair practices of the past that now serve as the grounds for trauma, loss, and grievance-based worldviews, or what I will come to call *melancholic worldviews*. Experiences with such drastic processes, both geographic dispossession from removal and oil wealth, register high in contemporary Citizen Potawatomi communal life. Certain tribal members have preferences that emerged from the painful events and others from radically different experiences of economic incorporation. The attempt at cohabitation by two factions within the same tribe, one inspired by pain and the other profit, has created a politics of mutual vilification.

Chapter 5 examines the crypto-politics of an American Indian village in New Mexico. In contrast to the Citizen Potawatomis of the previous chapter, the Isleta Pueblos did not lose significant ancestral lands, experience massacre, or endure removal efforts over the last three hundred years. The absence of such experiences has meant the Isletas escaped those radicalizing processes that have led to situating politics on either extreme of self-interest or melancholia. The result is greater homogeneity of experience, economic class, and life course among tribal members and less acceptance of conflict than what was apparent among the Potawatomis. If trauma and violence emerge as prominent themes in the American Indian historical landscape, then alcoholism, substance abuse, suicide, and family violence refresh similar sensations in the contemporary period.

Chapter 6 returns to the Black Hills dilemma. The chapter traces historical and individual trauma to ethnic identity, political culture, perception, preferences, as well as to how the tribe frames outsider economic offers. This chapter contends that the history of massacre, relocation, and land loss, along with extensive poverty (Pickering 2004), high levels of child abuse, and post-traumatic stress, has set the condition for an unusual type of political motivation to emerge: a melancholic worldview. In addition to living in extensive poverty, depression, and ill health, and rejecting development funds totaling over $1 billion, the tribe also delays in bringing in needed businesses, such as a grocery store, and does so through relying on a sense of continual threat. Using Nietzschean and Freudian frameworks, intergenerational trauma theory, and recent discoveries in neuroscience, I explore these political decisions made by the Lakotas through the lens of trauma and melancholia. This chapter refutes some of the core assumptions in American Indian and ethnic studies (see Perry 2008; Smith 2005 for examples of intra-ethnic conflict avoidance) by engaging with the possibility of intra-ethnic violence and exploitation.

The concluding chapter of this book revisits the themes of lived experience and worldview and places them within the normative project of American Indian and indigenous intellectual activism. If one desires American Indian and indigenous freedom, self-determination, and liberation—so much the normative focus of contemporary scholarship on American Indians—it becomes essential to ask upon what grounds motivations might unify them. And through the difficulty of establishing interest and common history, this book questions the terms *indigenous* and *colonized peoples* as adequate categories in which to organize these political communities and ethnic identities. Imagining a collective interest between American Indians is an inadequate substitute for a collectivity. Only an honest appraisal of political preference, motivation, identity, worldview, and other forms of behavioral politics in their contradictory forms will allow for a more robust collaboration within and between peoples.

CHAPTER 2

The Reservation of Common Secrets
The Suppression of Intra-Ethnic Conflict

2.1 INTRODUCTION

American Indian communities display staggering diversity in socioeconomic conditions, political behaviors, preferences, and values. Of the 566 federally recognized tribes in the United States as of 2014, several communities operate billion-dollar casino monopolies, whereas many others endure economic destitution. Reservations, therefore, have a place at both extremes of America's economic spectrum, making Indians simultaneously the poorest and the richest communities in the United States.

According to the U.S. Census Bureau and Department of the Interior, the median income of American Indian households in 2013 was approximately $36,000 (2014), but the variation can be stark: while the Shakopee Mdewakanton Sioux in Minnesota pay each adult tribal member $920,000 per year as their share of casino revenues (McNaney and Nahm 2010), the household income on the Pine Ridge Lakota Reservation is about $8,000. Contemporary economic disparity between tribes undoubtedly produces tensions, resentments, and animosities. In one of many typical examples from my conversations about conflict in politics, an informant from an economically modest tribe described the experience of attending the opening of the National Museum of the American Indian as witnessing ethnic fraud. Members of wealthy tribes near New York City, who donated large sums of money to the museum, were "sit[ing] on the stage looking down at us like they are the real Indians" (Informant 2007). To my informant, this "said they were [the] real Indians" but that it "didn't look that way," a remark that suggested this group looked black or white but not "red" (Informant 2007). In other words, to this informant, those on stage, holding center attention, committed ethnic fraud.

Intra-ethnic resentment and slander is as much a part of any polity as the formal and informal rules that govern it. In what could be described as everyday talk, American Indians remark upon economic disparity and discuss it as any community would (see Foster 1991; Garroutte 2003 for discussion of animosity in everyday talk among American Indians). Critical everyday talk betrays a brutality between people, in which the grievance and resentment is hard to ignore, especially if you are interested in politics between people in a polity charged with making difficult decisions over limited resources, which tribes are. It is hard to ignore as well when people become unwilling to contain their resentment, disagreements, and adversarial relationships and consider it an important part of the story of their *community*—a word itself that conveys a togetherness, rather than *polity*, which makes discord natural. But what was not initially apparent, at least for me, was where such harsh everyday talk, discord, disagreement, and resentment belong in scholarship on American Indians. It was also possible it did *not* belong at all, or that the perceived liabilities outweighed the benefits of studying intratribal conflict. Reporting conversations that point to intra-ethnic and intratribal conflict can conjure anxiety when placed into written scholarship; it did for me. Transforming spoken words to written words and then written words into published words was not an easy decision, and I would imagine that this is equally true for most scholars studying American Indian communities. The trepidation arrives from the possibility that your writing could be interpreted or construed as exposing community secrets, as easily as it could be seen to be bringing the most important, but difficult, political relationships to light.

The first part of this chapter outlines a few ways in which conflict has been studied in American Indian history and politics. Such an effort cannot be completely comprehensive in the sense of canvassing all published work on American Indian conflict, but it does make some points about the character and distribution of how and when conflict is studied. Scholars in the field will have to judge for themselves if my characterizations are accurate. Two major points are conveyed: the first is that writing about conflict between American Indians and settlers is more established than writing about conflict between American Indians; and the second is that writing about intra-ethnic and intratribal conflict that took place in the past involves less liability than does writing about that in the contemporary period. The result is that works on contemporary politics that examine intratribal conflict constitute a relatively small theme in the field. Within this smaller theme, I position this work as addressing the origin of intratribal conflict as a function of different lived experiences. It does not seek to understand or explain all origins, but it uses a comparative approach to conflict across tribes to develop and reflect on large theories on social change. This method is borrowed from other comparative social scientists interested in tribal conflict and extends upon these works (Champagne 2007; see also Cornell and Gil-Swedberg 1995).

The second section of this chapter examines variation in tribal political behavior. By this, I mean the ways in which tribes might differ in terms of the intensity of conflict and the decisions they make. Here I outline the vibrancy of tribal politics and consider why it might not have gathered as much attention as it could have. I claim the presence of *common secrets* in this section, which is to mean that we know a great deal about tribal politics, but we do not write about it. This section positions this book as an extension of a relatively small theme in the study of American Indian politics.

The third and final section is an argument as to why research on intratribal politics and conflict is necessary, and of growing importance, along with the consequences of not exploring the rich fissures within tribal communities. It argues that not directing more research toward intratribal politics places the study of American Indian politics at a disadvantage and ignores the contemporary lived experience of American Indians. Not only is this variation missed in keeping the study of intratribal conflict a small theme in the field, but such limited research results in a diminished meaning of the intense historical experience of American Indian peoples and tribes.

2.2 STUDIES IN AMERICAN INDIAN CONFLICT: A BRIEF OVERVIEW

Conflict that is intercivilizational, and therefore is between outsiders and American Indians, is at the center of scholarly research on American Indians. Many of the studies on intercivilizational conflict take a historical approach, and this is in line with the fact that the study of American Indian history is a highly developed field. That historical approaches to American Indians, and to conflict in earlier periods, constitute a prevalent theme is understandable, as the dynamics and shifts in American Indian lives and powers are a result of these conflicts. Similarly, conflict that is intracivilizational, meaning between tribes (intertribal) or within a tribe (intratribal), is also a developed theme in historical approaches. Earlier periods are not only saturated with intense and open conflict, but this conflict was formative in creating the contemporary lives of American Indians and was a function of Indian-to-Indian relationships. Temporal distance found in historical research also provides a shelter to explore what might be intra-ethnic and intratribal riffs, not just intercivilizational or ethnic conflict. At least one of the many reasons for this is easily apparent: when the informants or the agents pushing these events are themselves a part of the historical record, perhaps long dead, they cannot claim wound or affront to our characterization and analysis. Indeed, when scholars explore conflicts around key decisions that were made decades or centuries in the past, enough distance is afforded for those writing about conflict to either maintain greater neutrality or freely commit to advocating one position without having to take responsibility for the outcome—the decision has long passed. This, of course, does not mean that writing history is not without its own politics, sensitivities, moral conventions, and anxieties, but that as a general rule we are typically not contemporaries of the participants of historical research. Imagine writing about an instance of elite conflict in the nineteenth century. One might face scrutiny for much of the usual scholarly fare—that the work is mistaken about the facts, lacks conceptual rigor or fails to chart fresh terrain, or even that your interpretation has negative connotations for contemporary American Indians (see Clifford 1990 as an example)—but these accusations, though uncomfortable, do not tread as much on the sensitivities of the now. Imagine the position of writing on American Indian elite conflict that is ongoing today when the participants are still alive. The sensitivities about what should be said, and the liabilities, increase. Alternatively, it might be more difficult to remain neutral as you are in the period and potentially invested in or subject to the outcome. Perhaps it is better to stay quiet on contemporary intratribal and intra-ethnic politics, and I believe many scholars do. The living can protest on their own behalf, whereas the dead cannot or at least need proxies. Temporal distance might provide greater liberty to pursue difficult questions, hence the vibrant and wide debates in American Indian history on conflict.

The field of American Indian history—including social scientists using a historical perspective—has flourished and writing on conflict has made it lively, vivid, and powerful. Facilitating this, in part, is the rich work on intratribal and intra-ethnic conflict. Take, for instance, Paul Rosier's exploration of the fault lines about creating a tribal constitution in *Rebirth of the Blackfeet Nation, 1912–1954* (2001) and the need to draw members in despite the divisions that constitutional production creates. Rosier's work in part follows from a series of important works by Loretta Fowler on tribal conflict (Fowler 1982, 1984, 1989), which collectively show an effort by tribes to maintain cohesion—with varying success—in the face of significant ruptures. Of course, historical experience unites and creates people through making weaker ties stronger. An example of this is Frederick Hoxie's *Parading through History* (1997), which charts how responding to dispossession and abuse helped the Crow Nation. The integrative effect of mass social change is certainly undeniable, but divisions or divergence within a group also occur when a change happens, especially when change is uneven in a population (see Cattelino 2008; Dombrowski 2001; Harmon 2010; Wilson 1985 for discussion of change and division).

Elite conflict has been addressed in historical studies of tribes. Theda Perdue and Michael Green's *The Cherokee Nation and the Trail of Tears* (2007) displays the internal strife among the Cherokees around the time of removal from the Southeast. These conflicts led to the assassination of Major Ridge, the Cherokee factional leader who signed the Treaty of New Echota (1835), which relinquished tribal lands to settlers. In an article that examines Ute politics in the mid-nineteenth to early-twentieth century, David Lewis's *Reservation Leadership and the Progressive-Traditional Dichotomy* (1991) provides a thick analysis of elite conflict. Lewis argues that reservation conflict involved ideological middlemen and that the study of conflict has relied upon simplistic "grouping" traits or characteristics, rather than studying the individual leaders who demonstrate complexity (1991, 125–26). Work such as Lewis's follows a general trend toward complicating simplistic ideology, exemplified in the work of Robert Berkhofer (1971), which provides further depth to the study of factionalism and worldviews through biographical studies.

In *Organizing the Lakota* (1992), Thomas Biolsi describes reservation resistance in the 1930s to the Indian Reorganization Act and the conflicts over the nature that such resistance should take. Morris Foster's *Being Comanche* (1991) tracks the social history and internal conflicts of the Comanches through a nearly three-hundred-year period (1700–1990). Foster's evidence suggests that the tribe was able to maintain cohesion through ceremony despite ruptures brought on by colonization. Though Foster's work carries right into the period in which he is writing and is impressive in its scope, other historical research also draws upon themes and moves between tribe and time liberally, such as the subject of wealth and the resulting fissures in Alexandra Harmon's *Rich Indians* (2010), which documents the role that wealth has in reordering power within tribes. Competition for power across tribes and the violence endemic to colonialism has produced many recent award-winning books. Ned Blackhawk's *Violence over the Land* (2006) and Pekka Hamalainen's *The Comanche Empire* (2008) are two that probe the violence in the central basin. Each year dozens of books are published by university presses using a historical approach examining conflict, and many of these books are based in the uneasy and hostile terrain between Indians themselves. This is less true, I believe, of these conflicts in the contemporary period.

In comparison to works on earlier historical periods, fewer works on contemporary conflict that is intra-ethnic or intratribal have been produced than scholarship that studies the interethnic or intercivilizational. That the volume of literature on intra-ethnic and intratribal conflict seems more historical is understandable. For one, more has happened during the five hundred years of North American colonization than in the last twenty years. But the barriers to researching conflict in contemporary periods are high. Instead of seeking permission to use an archive, researchers need cooperation from participants involved in conflict. In many cases, tribes reject such research in their institutional review boards, which are tasked with determining what research might be supported by the tribe. These boards can be substantial barriers to research, even if the project is not on internal conflicts. Those in power have an interest in suppressing dissent, thereby making explorations on community fissures far from a priority. Researchers have mostly acquiesced to the legitimacy of tribal request. Whether or not a tribe has the authority to silence its members from talking with researchers, as far as I am aware, has not been legally tested as violating tribal members' rights to free speech. But the result is clear: research on contemporary intratribal conflict faces significant barriers.

Much of the intratribal scholarship in the contemporary period focuses on tribal membership and belonging. Determining who constitutes the polity is clearly a contentious debate as interethnic marriage is high among American Indians (Snipp 1989; Sandefur and Liebler 1996) and tribes become locations for economic development. Eva Garroutte's *Real Indians* explores everyday talk on the nature of who is and is not an authentic Indian (2003). The increase in mineral resources and, in particular, gaming (a euphemism for casinos) revenue has drawn significant interest. As revenues increase, the material rewards resulting from tribal membership increase (such as those mentioned among the Mdewakanton Shakopee Sioux at the start of this chapter) and create an incentive to expel members from tribal rolls. Gonzales described the influence of gaming enterprises as a source of much-needed economic revenue but also as initiating a de-enrollment of tribal membership and an increase in "social conflict, factionalism and cultural antagonism" (2003, 123). Another work on intratribal conflict around membership debates is Jean Dennison's *Colonial Entanglement* (2012), which examines reforms to the tribal constitution and how this activated intratribal interests and factionalism. Central to Dennison's analysis are the alternating approaches to membership and belonging, along with the tensions between these views. Another major recent work on intratribal conflict around identity is Circe Strum's *Blood Politics*

(2002). Like Garroutte and Dennison, Strum examines conflict from the perspective of different understandings of membership criteria. As a social construction with biological, cultural, geographical, and economic issues, identity is a contentious issue among many tribes, and Strum's exploration points to the difficult nature of these discussions and what is at stake in drawing borders within polities. Kirk Dombrowski's (2001) *Against Culture* explores how communal conflict over religion in the Native Alaskan villages he researches, a conflict that at times has resulted in the burning down of traditional totem poles, has its provenance in larger economic and political shifts. My argument and method bears a family resemblance to Dombrowski's interest in expanding upon the meaning of communal conflict and its roots in social and historical change.

Another theme in contemporary conflict is the drafting of tribal constitutions. Often tribes operate with constitutions that were created by the federal government. As an important step toward self-determination and better governance, tribes are starting to design their own constitutions. Conflict over these constitutions have emerged, as was the case in the White Earth Ojibwe Nation discussed in *The White Earth Nation* by Vizenor, Doefler and Wilkins (2012). The interest of this book is how tribes maintain order and build cohesion during these critical junctures.

These studies should continue, but I wish to merge my work with the focus of these works and with the previous works on intratribal political conflict, while also making the strongest available case for the importance of exploring politics at the tribal level. To demonstrate that tribal politics and conflict is central, we need only consider this quote from Robert Porter, a prominent legal scholar and former president of the Seneca Nation, in his assessment of tribal politics, conflict and its consequence:

> Throughout Indian country today, it seems that acrimony is the rule rather than the exception. Leadership challenges, membership disputes, constitutional crises, and often violence have afflicted both the largest and smallest Indian nations. While we know that there has always been some degree of internal turmoil, modern infighting seems exceptional both for its intensity and its effect. Today, it is entirely possible for tribal members to lose their lives and for tribal

sovereignty to be sacrificed solely as the result of internal conflict.
(Porter 1997)

It is the position of this book that American Indian political scholarship has not followed Porter's observation that conflict is central to tribal
politics, at least not to the degree necessary to understand these essential
political spaces. If conflict is central to tribal politics, why does it bear virtually no family resemblance to the study of American politics over the last
twenty years? Whereas the study of American politics has looked at culture wars, polarization, discrimination, gridlock, ethnic conflict, political
apathy, or party identification, to name just a few of the many subjects that
emphasize conflict, the study of contemporary American Indian politics
has only a handful of examples.

It is difficult to avoid intratribal conflict when including professional-
ized studies, such as those of judicial politics, law, or public health. Therefore, I do not mean to discount these accounts, but in terms of political
science and the study of politics, when it comes to intratribal conflict, this
work argues that more could be done and more should be done. Does this
mean that all 566 federally recognized tribal nations require research on
their internal conflict? Such a pursuit would not be feasible and perhaps
would not be the first step in addressing the importance of conflict. Rather,
I suggest that greater attention should be given to building an approach to
internal conflict that is nomological or theory-building. One way to do that
is by taking a comparative approach whereby we generate insights using
cases studies.

Previous comparative research on case studies, which have been both
comparative and interested in internal divisions, has focused on the relationship between internal cohesion and institutions. These studies have
been theory-building and testing. In "Sociohistorical Factors in Institutional Efficacy" (1995), Stephen Cornell and Marta Gil-Swedberg see conflict as providing a source of institutional volatility, which in turn affects
the economic prospects of tribes. They examine the economic profiles of
three Apache communities and explain disparities in performance according to effective governing institutions. Cornell and Gil-Swedberg identify
mismatches in norms and governing structures as contributing to volatility

in tribal politics. Volatility is also created by heterogeneity from forced mergers of tribes whereby two different tribes with different norms must operate under governing structures that do not accommodate both. Conflict becomes a key independent variable for economic development, and a theory emerges as to how development might work in Indian country. Cornell and Gil-Swedberg's work is illustrative of the comparative dimension in scholarship, and *Reservation Politics* follows both the approach and conclusions of their work, whereby ideological heterogeneity has an effect on contemporary politics.

Duane Champagne has perhaps been one of the scholars most associated with the comparative approach to American Indian politics. His work, starting in the 1980s, utilizes tribes as the unit of analysis in testing sociological theory regarding change and uses American Indian tribes as case studies specifically (Champagne 1983, 1985). Champagne's "Social Structure, Revitalization Movements, and State Building" (1983) uses a historical institutional approach and tests sociological assumptions about structural differentiation (see Parsons 1966; Parsons and Smelser 1956) using four tribal cases studies. In *American Indian Societies*, Champagne (1985) also uses this comparative approach to explore the variation in responses to colonial threats. Preexisting political conventions and values helped determine which tribes were able to overcome collective action problems to unify against colonial encroachment. There are limits to the comparative approach, which may in fact generate theories rather than validate them. Nevertheless, this book follows in the footsteps of the comparative approach adopted in the seminal studies of Champagne (1983, 1985, 2007) and Cornell and Gil-Swedberg (1995).

2.3 COMMON SECRETS

Identified thus far is what I consider a disparity between the importance and centrality of intratribal and reservation politics in American Indian lives and the less-developed theme of intratribal politics. It is also my sense that knowledge about intratribal politics is common among scholars but that its place in scholarship is not clear or comfortable. This dynamic, where phenomena are known yet are not brought in great abundance into scholarship, is what I term a common secret. These common secrets include perspectives that hold significance in observable social and political reality, though often tacitly so, but that scholarship fails to duly examine with according significance. This is not to say that common secrets are only that which is never mentioned; rather, common secrets are known and talked about, yet, given their importance, they are not recognized or made explicit in scholarship. In short, I suggest that we know intratribal and ethnic politics are important and we know a great deal about the politics internal to communities, but that this has not translated into a volume of work proportional to that importance or knowledge.

The examination of four of these common secrets forms the final part of this chapter: the first and already-mentioned secret is that there are discernible differences in political behavior and class among tribes and within tribes; the second is that the internal political relationships between American Indians are necessary to understanding the political lives of American Indians; the third is that American Indians are political co-competitors and mutual exploiters, who are capable of abusing one another or perpetuating acts of intra-ethnic violence and that these conflicts tell us something about how worldviews are shaped; and the fourth and final common secret is that a reluctance exists in American Indian political scholarship about expanding its existing paradigms to accommodate this knowledge. My thesis is that these four common secrets are co-constitutive and thus create a situation in which many of the relevant political questions about American Indian tribal political and social life are distorted by the liabilities of exposure. When works do engage with these topics, the authors risk accusations of sharing information that is harmful, unflattering, and so on.

Scholarship is motivated to discover and make the unknown known. An alternate motivation of knowledge is revelation, which is the act of bringing what is known into a more explicit plane of understanding. In part of his critique of Freud, Jean-Paul Sartre makes a similar distinction of knowledge as that of reflective self-consciousness or "thetic" against non-reflective consciousness or "non-thetic" ([1957] 1991). According to Sartre, this division was more nuanced than was Freud's of psyche into consciousness and subconsciousness; consciousness knowledge might not necessarily be recognized as knowledge; therefore, a distinction is necessary between discovery and revelation as well as a division between recognized and unrecognized conscious knowledge. A common secret is not repressed in the classical Freudian sense to the subconscious, but it is proportionally undervalued in its context. Common secrets as they pertain to this book are knowledge that is revealed rather than discovered, and by doing so, central features of American Indian politics are made more legible, as is the effect of historical experience and ethnohistory.

Noting the bounty absence provides, political theorist Ian Shapiro observes, "What people overlook might be more important, ideologically, than what they discern" (2007, 7). Critical disparities between reality and how one studies it pepper the social and political sciences as much as the political study of contemporary American Indian conflict. Such omissions supply a methodological leitmotiv for this book and, as I term them, are common secrets. The term implies a paradox: such phenomena are secrets because they survive surreptitiously, mentioned in academic literatures sparingly and at risk, yet are also common or regular to human and social life in that they are spoken about (often) informally. Though similar to an open secret, a common secret differs in an important way. Open secrets are not typically understood to have intrinsic weight to human affairs; they are instead seen as trivial. In tribal political everyday talk, common secrets are sometimes exchanged as gossip and are dismissed perhaps by the communities themselves as inconsequential. Common secrets might also be found in the tangled connection we have with our own knowledge.

A common secrets approach focuses on tacit knowledge deemed insignificant or marginal. Although this work proposes to identify such phenomena as common secrets, the concept of common secrets encapsulates a dynamic by no means new to scholarship. Similar to Sartre's distinction between thetic and non-thetic is that of revelation versus discovery, which dates as far back as Plato's allegory of the cave. Yet it was Freud's work at the turn of the twentieth century that perhaps attended human secrets and hidden knowledge by turning Enlightenment hermeneutics toward the human mind. In part, the premise of Freud's psyche was division along hidden knowledge. The psyche was fractured with consciousness and subconsciousness, the ego and the id, with the primary division between that of awareness and recognition (Freud 1923). Yet the idea or revelation of hidden knowledge is not relegated to European or classical perspectives. The common secret and its revelation are elemental features of contemporary American Indian literature. Like the established theme of historical research in intratribal conflict, American Indian fiction has traded extensively on tribal secrets, and these secrets' path to exposure is a well-travelled motif. For instance, Sherman Alexie and David Treuer, two of Indian country's most recognized contemporary authors, have both turned the unveiling of community secrets into a career and have provided insight into American Indian communal life as a result.

Significant change to how social and political inquiry is carried out was in part the result of exposing common secrets. The tragedy of the commons is a prominent example of a common secret whose revelation has become a touchstone or sacred text to twentieth-century social sciences and is foundational for rational choice theory (Appell 1993). Recognizing the poor condition of shared land due to overgrazing existed before publication of Garrett Hardin's "The Tragedy of the Commons" (1968), which explained the poor condition as an elemental failing of interhuman cooperation (the more profound tragedy). The tragedy of the commons was more a realization of known phenomenon than discovery. Literally surrounding agricultural societies, common land existed for millennia as an exploited and potentially ugly terrain—an observation certainly discussed by peasant, lord, and yeomen alike in their own argot long before it was unveiled and adopted in scholarly discourse. The prisoner's dilemma offers another foundational rational choice observation that is, in essence, a common secret exposed. The informational asymmetries around the prisoner's dilemma was an interrogation tactic before Merrill Flood, Melvin Dresher, and Albert W. Tucker (the latter of whom coined the term "prisoner's dilemma") formalized the outcomes and sketched the celebrated two-by-two boxes (Poundstone 1993).

Unease also assists in creating common secrets. Timur Kuran's *Private Truths, Public Lies* (1997) describes a dynamic similar to common secrets in its description of political censure in Soviet Russia. To Kuran, certain political communities live in fractured political spaces defined by disconnects between public and private discourse. Take the rapid fall of the Soviet Union that Kuran examines, in which the disparity between what citizens knew or believed privately was significantly different from what they professed publicly. Soviet subjects saved most of their honesty for the kitchen table. In such a system of censure, citizens could only exist in private; in public, they were subjects.[1] Truth and honest opinion were a commodity for the black market, and in the 1980s, the Soviet system was rapidly undermined by the preestablished counter ideologies that had been exchanged at kitchen tables long before the political and public opportunity arose. Reservation Politics suggests that conversations about tribal politics, which have existed in a near black market, be more freely discussed.

The exposure or revaluation of hidden knowledge is not necessarily a moral or ethical positive. Intellectual repression of contentious knowledge has legitimate justifications. In our case of American Indians, it might be desired to suppress fractiousness, communal conflict, and difference. Political theorist Stephen Holmes might argue that intellectual "gag rules" (1988, 208) function to facilitate the perpetuation of what this book identifies as common secrets. One can identify such "positive uses of negative liberty" (Holmes 1988, 209) as suppressing issues that, if openly discussed, would generate undesirable acrimony. This "strategic self-censorship" (1988, 221), as Holmes puts it, diverts attention away from issues crucial to a polity. In "Gag Rules, or the Politics of Omission," Holmes observes how in the years leading to the American Civil War, society was divided not only about the issue of slavery but also even on the question of whether to discuss the issue of slavery. The logic supporting the decision to avoid difficult yet crucial topics is mixed. Such provocative issues might be terminal, as the American Civil War almost was, and in avoidance, polities might flee for their own survival. Essential and pressing issues can rankle polities and pollute the spaces between their members and may only sour one party against the next. In such a perspective—one that values harmony—certain knowledge may be best left confined and socially amputated. Such preference for harmony and unity in a polity might undermine a community's honesty, credibility, self-reflection, and self-appraisal, each necessary for progress. This book argues for less reticence over the study of American Indian politics, particularly when this reticence obscures basic political features that are standard to the understanding of every polity.

By revealing the degree, intensity, and shape of various forms of American Indian conflict, this book invests in the notion that examining the origins of conflict, and the divergent worldviews that create it, might reduce the least helpful dimensions of intratribal conflict. And by failing to fully pursue the origins of divergent worldviews, the standing assumption continues that rival tribal members frame the world in the terms they do as a result of defunct character, innate wickedness, foolishness, irrationality, or even demonic possession. Providing a context for why certain American Indian tribes and even intratribal factions perceive the moral world differently through their ethnohistories provides insight into why the conclusions they make in the form of worldviews are divergent. Such origins might encourage other scholarship on conflict around tribal membership to consider the origins of disagreement. By leaving the origins of factions and divergent values untouched, the worst interpretations of moral failure, cowardice, greed, ideological co-optation, ethnic assimilation, and even sorcery, remain unchallenged.

Intratribal politics and the conflict between American Indians have a historical centrality that should go without needing mention and is long recognized in historical approaches (see Blackhawk 2006; Champagne 1989, 2007; Hamalainen 2008; Lewis 1991; Perdue and Green 2007; Wilson 1985 as examples of historical perspectives of conflict and division). Take, for instance, a common question asked about American Indians: why didn't Indian tribes unify to repulse European invaders when they first arrived to avoid losing their lands? The first and most obvious answer is that the earliest Europeans appeared a motley, if not a sorry, crew to the people who were to shortly become American Indians. Unable to predict the future, American Indians did not view the Europeans as a threat (Harch 1979). The second and more telling answer is that the established relationships between Indians—in particular the conflicts and competitions—impressed American Indians substantially more than the newly arrived settlers (Dowd 1992). American Indians incorporated the Europeans they encountered into their existing paradigm—a paradigm that was primarily natively referential. American Indians viewed early contact with European settlers through a lens derivative of strategies concerning relations with other Indians—who, by then, had been aiding or slaughtering one another for centuries. This book suggests that the study of contemporary American Indian politics retrieves enough of the relationship between American Indians to understand their politics.

As the study of American Indian politics stands at present, American whites' perceptions of American Indians are more prevalent in the literature than the relationship between American Indians in the same polity. Acts of Congress, decisions of the Supreme Court, and public depictions of American Indians receive greater critical attention in political science than the polities themselves. The absence of intratribal politics is a result of the deep-rooted ambivalence to questioning ethnic unity. Politics between American Indians works against the interethnic narrative that has been the premise of political scholarship on Indians since sovereignty and Pan-American Indian identity movements of the 1960s and '70s (Cornell 1986, 1988; Nagel 1995, 1996). A tribally based understanding of politics opens the possibility of competition, conflict, discord, and exploitation within the tribe or ethnicity. Scholarship that reveals intratribal politics leaves a scholar vulnerable to anti-Indian criticisms that portray American Indian reservations as dysfunctional political units. What is missed by this view is that politics involves conflict and is inherent in all polities. The sentiment motivating the general ambivalence on intratribal conflict obscures the essential location that everyday political lives and local politics have in American Indian life. It is believed, and mistakenly so, that tribes and American Indians are so fragile that to explore the disagreements within tribes would damage political units and communities that have survived cultural, social, biological, and spiritual catastrophes during five hundred years of colonization.

2.4 THE CONSEQUENCES OF RETICENCE ABOUT INTRATRIBAL POLITICS

My speculation is that social science literature avoids intratribal or intra-ethnic or Indian-to-Indian political relationships due to a reluctance to expose adversarial relationships between American Indians. Malicious groups do indeed co-occupy single non-western ethno-political communities; whether scholarship engages in the discussion does not change this fact. Research is, of course, produced on intratribal conflict, but I cannot say it is a strong theme in the study of contemporary American Indian politics. The study of American Indian politics suffers from this, as political relationships are as much about conflict as cooperation, and as much about mutual vilification as mutual affinity. Without a willingness to engage in unflattering aspects of community, a full discussion of politics is not possible.

Before moving to how conflict has been distorted in studies of sexual violence, let me provide an example of how scholars have been generally unwilling to conduct research on tribal activities that are endangering tribal members. A case can be made that tobacco poses the most significant health hazard to American Indians, even more than diabetes or alcohol. American Indians smoke at twice the rate of the general public and the most of any U.S. ethnic group (Bachman et al. 1991; Centers for Disease Control and Prevention 2011). Smoking is associated with 40 percent of American Indian deaths (Choi et al. 2011), twice that of non-Hispanic whites (Centers for Disease Control and Prevention 2000), and theirs is the only ethnic group whose smoking prevalence is staying the same, if not increasing (Hodge 2006). Whereas U.S. states seek to raise the taxes on cigarettes in part to dissuade use—particularly in relation to youth initiation, which is most sensitive to price and longer smoking (99 percent of long-term smokers start by age 25 [Chaloupka, Straif, and Leon 2011; Zhang et al. 2006])—many tribes have created economic development strategies based on the selling of inexpensive tobacco (Orr et al. 2015). Though it is a complicated legal arrangement, as tribes have agreements at the federal level, tribal status can avoid many of the sales taxes on reservations as state governments create most tobacco sales taxes. The result is that reservations are awash with cheap tobacco and advertising, and American Indians are dying at greater rates of tobacco-related illness than any other ethnicity (Bachman et al. 1991; Centers for Disease Control and Prevention 2011). Yet there is not a robust set of research projects and scholars who point fingers at tribes for their contribution to these outcomes. Undoubtedly, there are many factors that shape smoking behavior, but the fact that we do not directly research the implication of cheap tobacco-based economic development suggests the presence of spaces and dynamics that we will not openly research or would do so with trepidation. Few scholars want their work to accuse tribes of promoting policies that accelerate the demise of their own people. Could we imagine a similar trepidation by scholars if outsiders were pushing cheap and ultimately deadly tobacco on reservations?

By keeping the study of intra-ethnic conflict a relatively small theme, or what I consider a small theme compared to how conflict is studied in regions and populations other than Indian country by political science, American Indian intra-ethnic political conflict is at odds with the central feature of the contemporary political era of self-determination and sovereignty. If self-determination and sovereignty play essential roles in both American Indian politics—which is a normative commitment for most scholars in the field, including this author—and the political period in which American Indians now live, taken to its logical conclusion, wouldn't scholars want to know more about tribal-level politics and where power is exercised? Yet political scholars seem less inclined to conduct intratribal analysis in the United States, and counterintuitively, the period of American Indian self-determination (post-1960s) has witnessed a decline, not an increase, in scholarship on internal tribal politics in the United States, the very polities that have increased in relative importance.[2] It is also at odds with the study of contemporary American politics, which has focused intensely on the polarization often known as the "culture wars" (see D'Antonio, Tuch, and Baker 2013; Fiorina, Abrams, and Pope 2010; Jensen 1995; Lindaman and Haider-Markel 2002 for the hundreds of papers and books on polarization in contemporary American politics and society).

Without a sustained and explicit focus on intra-ethnic competition and conflict, we run the risk of suggesting that American Indians have no politics distinctly of their own, nor any valuable political spaces between them. Neglecting the potential aggression and tension within vulnerable communities owing to the assumption that it would be in poor taste to concentrate on these aspects actually fails to treat community vulnerability fairly. A telling example of the preference for neglecting conflict is how victimization is studied in American Indian communities. Criminal victimization differs from political competition and conflict, but both can be comparably distorted through racialization of conflict from intra-ethnic to interethnic.

Studies over the last thirty years have consistently shown that American Indians are violently victimized at the highest rates of all major ethnic groups in the United States. Between 1992 and 1996, the rate of victimization (number of individuals victimized per one thousand persons) for all violent offenses nationally was fifty (Greenfeld and Smith 1999). The white victimization rate occurred at forty-nine per one thousand and for blacks it was sixty-one (Greenfeld and Smith 1999). American Indian violent victimization was 124, twice the number of any other ethnicity (Greenfeld and Smith 1999). When economic status is taken into account, the rate of American Indian victimization remains twice that of their economic peers in other ethnicities and suggests that victimization is not a function of poverty (Greenfeld and Smith 1999).

The sources of American Indian victimization became an often written about topic in government agencies and scholarship. The Bureau of Justice Statistics published a study on American Indian victimization in the late 1990s. The report, authored by Lawrence Greenfeld and Steven Smith, found that in 70 percent of crimes committed against American Indians, the assailant was non-Indian (1999). Scholarship that used this bureau report reached improbable conclusions, with claims that non-Indians committed 99 percent of the acts of sexual violence against American Indian women (Smith 2005).

The interethnic interpretation of American Indian violent crime, where the victim and assailant were of differing ethnicity or race, became a common and accepted theme in scholarship. From the period of 2000 to 2008, American Indian studies and scholars did not openly question the interethnic source of violence. Conclusions about interethnic violence would be unobjectionable if the evidence did not ultimately support the very opposite, that violence was intra-ethnic and between American Indians. The serious issue of victimization makes the misrepresentation of crimes against American Indians disturbing. That the studies, which found crime against American Indian victims as interethnic, were not scrutinized earlier is surprising, as literature in criminology has consistently found that violence, especially intimate violence, is intra-ethnic (see O'Brien 1987;

Wilbanks 1985 for research on the intra-ethnic nature of violence and intimate violence).

Research initiated by the Office of the Attorney General of South Dakota and by political scholars whose primary research focus was outside of American Indians concluded that the results of earlier studies were based on mistakes from biased data collection (Long et al. 2008). This review of American Indian victimization found that earlier research that pointed to interethnic violence based its findings on state but not federal crime data. Major crimes on reservations fall under federal jurisdiction, and the result is that earlier studies excluded reservations—where half of American Indians live—entirely (Long et al. 2008), thus distorting the results.

The attorney general's study, which was published in a research journal on American Indians, limited its scope to an analysis of crimes where the perpetrator was identified and convicted. This minimized the speculative aspect based on previous survey data of the early studies, in which neither the presence of a crime nor the ethnicity of the perpetrator were established. Using reservation and non-reservation data, the study concluded that American Indian violent crime was as intra-ethnic as in other ethnic groups (Long et al. 2008). The findings of this study concluded that American Indian victims of intentional homicide were killed by American Indians 82 percent of the time. The attorney general's study found that 83 percent of American Indian women who were raped were assaulted by another American Indian. This is equivalent to the white intra-ethnic sexual assault rate of 85 percent (Long et al. 2008).

Within the subject of victimization, the study of violence in American Indian communities has become a central topic. Andrea Smith, a highly cited author in American Indian studies over the last few decades and most associated with the study of interethnic preponderance of sexual violence, went as far as to suggest that rape may not have even existed as a form of political violence in North America before European arrival (2003). In addition to being factually inaccurate, the misrepresentation of the nature of violence has implications for policy. The earlier studies that pointed to interethnic violence resulted in attention being focused on non-Indians who used various legal loopholes to reduce the likelihood of prosecution for committing crimes against American Indians (see Duthu 2008; Perry

2008 for advocacy for legal change). I could find no retractions issued by scholars who had used the original and flawed study. As of 2012, no further research has followed that of Long et al. (2008) to further understand the intra-ethnic sources of American Indian victimization, nor has their article been cited in American Indian studies journals. In fact, despite being found to be faulty and perhaps even dangerous in policy implications, the conclusions from the interethnic violence research are still accepted in the field with an event taking place at Harvard's Radcliffe Institute for Advanced Study in 2015, titled Sliver of a Full Moon, commemorating the faulty study and its conclusion that sexual violence against American Indian women is interethnic.

Not enough scholarly attention is devoted to those political decisions that American Indians make that negatively affect their lives. To put this slightly differently: our impulse is to consider outsiders as those who start conflicts and exploit our people rather than ourselves. Though this might have been true historically, or even true today, it should not blind us from looking inward. Extending upon the recognition of the lacuna of research around tribal tobacco policies, such an impulse is easy to see in how violent victimization has been studied over the last few decades in American Indian studies. The bulk of American Indian studies positions conflict historically or on American Indian reservations as between Indians and outsiders; works by Dennison (2012) and Strum (2002) among others seem the exception rather than the rule, which rarely highlights the harshness of political disagreement inside tribes and the ethnicity. The study of American Indian victimization is not the study of politics, but there are parallels where conflict is posited. Yet this view is also understandable, as colonization is typically thought of as interethnic in its exploitative quality and is a vivid feature of American Indian history. By removing the possibility of exploitation by kinfolk, clansmen and clanswomen, family members, and even loved ones, scholarship on American Indians or other minority communities is not made better nor are the communities enhanced.

Sacrificing the critical importance found in unattractive political struggles within American ethnic groups in order to preserve the image of ethno-harmony has done little to protect such marginalized communities. The rejection of Harvard sociologist and U.S. senator Patrick Moynihan's study on the collapse of the black American family in the 1960s and its effect on income and class mobility (1965) serves as a standing example of how forced ignorance causes unjustified and dangerous socio-intellectual amputation (see Tierney 2011 for greater detail on the politics behind the Moynihan report). It is not only true that life, to quote Hobbes, has the propensity to be "solitary, poor, nasty, brutish, and short" ([1651] 1909, 99), but also that those who are geographically, phenotypically, and genetically close can further— with disappointing efficiency—the hideousness he so succinctly outlined. Perhaps Sartre did not go far enough when he wrote "hell is others" (1944).[3]

Those who are committed to the perspective that American Indians are unable to exploit each other or compete politically leave American Indian studies in conversations with its imaginary notion of what American Indian Life should be. The disinclination surrounding intra-ethnic research de-incentivizes inquiry about political relationships between Indians, which, to be accurate and valuable, should include the possibility that Indians work at cross-purposes, undermine each other, or arrive at conflicting worldviews as do participants in every polity.

2.5 CONCLUSION

This chapter explored two related themes and provided a context for how American Indians are typically not presented in the social sciences. The chapter proposed that politics between American Indians on their reservations, and the variation in these politics, needs greater consideration if we are to understand the collective behaviors of these communities. Examining the internal features of Indian communities requires that intra-ethnic, intratribal, and Indian-to-Indian relationships receive similar consideration as Indian-to-outsider relationships have received in the literature. Although the reservations on which this book is based remain demographically small and typically geographically isolated, I aim to place the study of Indian politics back inside Indian communities, which is a significant departure from the current concerns of American Indian political scholarship. The chapter also stakes claim to a second story about how empirical reality might be obscured by anxieties, the primary example being how the internal conflict within tribes is widely known but is only a small theme in social science literature. Scholars must be aware of the political dynamics between Indians, but such knowledge is either (*a*) not reflected upon as worthy of sustained and focused analytical attention, or (*b*) obscured by a sense that the liabilities do not outweigh the benefits. To those familiar with American Indian tribal life, it should be apparent that American Indians are in political and social competition over resources, narratives of their ethnohistory, the meaning of tribal identity, and the setting of tribal priorities. Intra-ethnic competition often elicits behaviors that work against the images of ethnic fraternity that contemporary scholarship tends to emphasize, as witnessed by how the study of American Indian violence could only be allowed to be interethnic.

Common secrets seek to restore evenness between reality and its study. My point is not necessarily to reject or reaffirm the findings of preceding academic literatures. Rather, the fundamental criticisms expressed in the following pages originate mostly from one main source worth summarizing: the disparity between how people live and how scholars imagine they live. As the term *common secret* suggests, it serves only as an intervention in the sense that it asks for an expansion of ongoing inquiry into what must already be semi-recognized. Most criticisms of previous scholarship expressed in this work are not as concerned with the abilities of previous scholars or the value of their work to American Indian politics. Rather, my hope is to broaden the focus of inquiry to capture the segment of American Indian community life that might be uncomplimentary to the harmonious image that outsiders grant Indians, but that is necessary to understanding reservation politics (or any form of politics for that matter). For those interested in American Indians and those interested in new ways to conceptualize the historical sources of divergent forms of human rationality expressed in political values and preferences—the two postulated audiences of this project—this book works to unveil self-undermining human dynamics, collective and individual, that scholars of social phenomena must recognize but have not yet elevated to serious analytic consideration in politics.

Opening reservation politics and conflict does not stain the collective American Indian character. Community strife, by definition, is not cordial. Communal acrimony offers an insight into deeper processes that may cause discomfort, as we shall see in the next chapters. But to proceed otherwise, hagiographically, about the internal conflict within ethnic communities or how trauma distorts our assumption of behavior, might constitute an insult to those who live, often very painfully, in these uneasy spaces with complex legacies. This sentiment—to confront unflattering features of human life—continues into the following chapter's discussion on trauma. To look at the effects of trauma at the individual and then at the communal level is an insult to humanity's self-esteem and is to consider something that our better nature wishes were otherwise: that life might be, in certain instances, against itself.

What might be known and avoided applies to the theoretical premise of this book as well and is the focus of the next chapter. That trauma, violence, loss, and pain leave complex and unhelpful legacies has been established in the fields of psychology, psychoanalysis, public health, epidemiology, and neuroscience. In private lives, violence and abuse is discouraged by many societies, not solely because it is distasteful or causes immediate damage but because it scars the possibility of a different future—a shared common secret about violence. Whereas this chapter explored the important relationships that Indians have with each other and how that is overlooked, the following chapter goes into detail about trauma's peculiar charisma over the human psyche.

The next chapter offers accounts for experiences that produce differing worldviews, motivations, and frames that shape the intratribal and intra-ethnic conflict discussed in this chapter. It takes the differences causing political conflicts that are at the center of this chapter and thinks about how historical and lived experience prompts individuals and groups to arrive at different conclusions regarding worldview.

CHAPTER 3

Categories, Logics, and Causal Mechanisms in "Pain and Profit"

3.1 INTRODUCTION

I make two broad assumptions about human behavior in this book. These assumptions are called *causal mechanisms*, which, if true, make viable my approach to understanding how historical processes and lived experiences have shaped worldview and ultimately contemporary American Indian politics.[1] By *causal mechanisms*, I mean the drivers behind why something either alters or supports something else. For example, that material wealth changes something that it is not, in our case worldviews, is an assumption and evidence to the effect of why this causal relationship might have the possibility of being true. I do this to both be as explicit as possible about my assumptions and present supporting evidence from a range of fields that these assumptions are merited and legitimate perspectives on understanding some of the empirical phenomena described in my case studies.

The first assumption is that the creation of wealth and experience of economic markets shifts individual and collective perspectives toward a self-interested worldview. Self-interest inclines individual and community motivation toward greater material accumulation at the expense of other values such as social harmony, the sense of togetherness or equality, and long-held communal norms. I call this the rise of self-interest. The second is that certain forms of traumatic experience, violent loss, and exploitation can alter the individual and collective perspective of a community toward a melancholic worldview. Melancholia inclines individual and community motivation toward perpetuating grievances, grieving, and reliving trauma to the detriment of material self-interest and community harmony. I call this process the rise of melancholia. The absence of rises in melancholia or self-interest is likely to allow for the continuation of communal affect, which emphasizes collectivism and social cohesion over self-interest and melancholia. When this system survives without disturbance by rises in self-interest or melancholic worldviews, I call this the *persistence of communal affect*.

This chapter first identifies categories of grouped motivations, frames, and worldviews that organize American Indian political behavior and serve as signal posts for comparison and changes through time. I refer to the grouped and broad nature of these concepts and how these weave between ethnohistory, lived experience, and worldview by using the term *logic*. I outline these three logics and then place them into theories of social transformation. This chapter then explores two important causal mechanisms that shape American Indian political behavior. The first is the rise of self-interested behavior and logics organized around gain. Supporting this causal mechanism is classical work in political economy (see Hirschman 1997 on the rise of self-interest in the Italian city state) and recent research in social psychology (see Kraus, Piff, and Keltner 2009 for the assocation between status and selfishness; see also Kraus et al. 2012; Piff 2013; Piff et al. 2012). The second causal mechanism is the rise of melancholic behavior and logics organized around loss. To support this causal mechanism, I rely upon conclusions generated by trauma theory (see Herman 1997 for general discussion of traumatic legacy) and neuroscience (see McGowan et al. 2009; McGowan et al. 2011; Sapolsky 1996; Uno et al. 1989 for recent findings on stress and cognition). This chapter concludes with an example of pain and profit being applied to the historical experience and current political behavior of the Citizen Potawatomi Nation, which will be the subject of chapter four.

The objective of this chapter is not to conclusively prove that either of these causal mechanisms hold direct responsibility for creating or causing the behaviors described in the following chapters. This chapter establishes perspectives on why the claims within the pain and profit framework are a viable method to understand the origins of the divergent political behavior in American Indian tribes through variance in historical experience.

3.2 CATEGORIES: THREE LOGICS

At this book's start was the claim that we frame the same political event or question differently, as in what one would do if faced with a decision similar to that of the Lakotas regarding the Black Hills. The discussion of what we wanted or thought was correct not only involved frames, world-view, and our motivations, but also showed that how we see the world and our motivations are logically linked. These logics are broad continuities between frames, worldviews, motivations, and the all-encompassing terms that bind these behavioral components. The term *logic* is selected because it ascribes value to the coherence between worldview, preference, frame, motivation, and action.

Let me provide an example to illustrate what I mean by how multiple aspects of behavior are grouped by logic into a coherency whereby experience, perception, preference, and behavior are cognates. If an individual's or community's worldview perceives outsiders as dangerous for whatever reasons and therefore frames outsiders as dangerous, and the individual or community values safety and not danger, it would follow that the individual or community will be motivated or prefer to avoid outsiders. *Logic*, as a categorical term, typically links these different behavioral components—perception, worldview, preference, value, and ultimately action—into coherency. Yet coherency comes at a cost. Logic implies a simplicity, exclusivity, and inflexibility to how individuals and communities "think." Though this is a perspective with multiple flaws, the widespread acknowledgment about confirmation bias in psychology whereby we interpret information as to fit our established worldviews (see Nickerson 1998 for a review of confirmation bias), or the presence of political parties and ideologies, suggests that thought is organized more by patterns and consistency than by random association. The following chapters will demonstrate, through examining intratribal conflicts, that it is difficult to satisfy multiple logics simultaneously, as each logic involves commitments mostly hostile to each other. This book nominates the logics of self-interest, communal affect, and melancholia as broad categories that aid in grouping varying aspects of behavior.

3.2.1 LOGIC OF COMMUNAL AFFECT

The logic of communal affect values community harmony and social cohesion above individual preference. In traditional or tribal societies, this is a standard or commonplace logic, and this sentiment—to preserve the whole and the connections between individuals—is recognized by social and anthropological theory (see Polanyi 2001; Scott 1976) and social psychology (see Nisbett 2003). Yet such communal mindedness is not relegated to only tribal peoples. Philosopher David Hume wrote of "the common blaze" ([1777] 1966, 275) that bounds individuals to social and political organization. A contemporary of Hume, the philosopher and early economist Adam Smith wrote on "fellow-feeling" or the need for compatriation between individuals (2010). Early in the American political tradition communal affect was an important commitment and was found in the ideological strain of civic republicanism, located primarily in colonial New England, which emphasized the citizens' obligation to place community interests above their own (Mansbridge 1990).

The commitment to community interest is typically strained and eventually undermined by economic shifts. Or at least this is what much of classical political economy and economic anthropology suggests. When the economic system is subordinate to social relations, and where self-interest is constrained by the need to preserve social relations, economic anthropology calls such systems *moral* or *embedded economies* (see Booth 1994; Polanyi 2001; Scott 1976 for further discussion of moral and embedded economies). In such systems, brazen and bold self-interest is contrary to the expectation that individual self-interest should be subordinated. The key to these economies is the centrality of social relationships above individual maximization. Communities, such as those of tribes in North America before contact, typically practiced these principles with the expectation of pooling resources for more even distribution. In subsistence economies with uncertain future food patterns, such redistribution increases the likelihood of collective survival (Scott 1976). For instance, a failed hunting expedition for one family unit would mean its potential starvation without a communal ethos and sanguine relations with neighbors or clan members. In this system, overt greed and the maximization of potential gains might yield greater rewards, but if such behaviors broke communal norms around sharing, it would jeopardize one's social standing and place one outside the communal safety net. This public-minded system, whereby social relationships and held norms are respected above individual maximization and strife violates the security provided by harmony, is the logic of communal affect. With community or group cohesion, the sine qua non of this logic, the other two logics—self-interest and melancholia—are therefore subordinate to group unity.

3.2.2 LOGIC OF SELF-INTEREST

Self-interest elevates individual material preferences higher than that of community harmony. As a concept, self-interest has had a long and checkered career in the social sciences. Self-interest is typically understood materially and is associated with terms such as *maximization, rational,* and *utilitarian,* and with the ideology of commerce. Collective interest is outweighed by individual materialism in the full commitment to self-interest, and as Thomas Jefferson remarked, "Merchants have no country [and] [t]he mere spot they stand on does not constitute so strong an attachment as that from which they draw their gains" (1814). The self-interested—merchants comprising the paradigmatic case—are not loyal to community or what this book calls *communal affect,* but to their profits and interests materially defined.

Self-interest has had a troubled career in scholarship. The difficulty of defining what is not self-interest is a prominent criticism of the term. For instance, economist Gordon Tullock has argued that every communally orientated decision may be motivated by self-interest and what benefits the collective would benefit the individual within it (1971). That individuals and people pursue their survival collectively, though usually true, is not ubiquitous, as collective prosperity often requires individual sacrifice or the absence of shirking. What is meant by *self-interested* in this sense is when collective interests or norms are broken by the pursuit of individual interest. Drawing the boundaries of self-interest so broadly, as in the view Tullock represents, results in the concept of self-interest becoming non-falsifiable and unhelpful. Self-interest at its conceptual essence is contrasted with public-regarding behavior. That is, self-interest is materialistic and individualistic. It is therefore contrasted against principled motives (hence material) and group solidarity (hence individualistic) (see Clark and Wilson 1961 for further discussion of these distinctions).

The self-interested image of humanity is best represented in the caricature *homo economicus*. A term first coined by John Stuart Mill in the nineteenth century, *economic man* as the rational economic actor compelled toward materialism had been a staple of eighteenth-century political thought (1836). Most associated with self-interest's positive externalities in the eighteenth century was Adam Smith. Thomas Hobbes had argued, incorrectly in Smith's perspective, for a centralized authority or *Leviathan* to prevent self-interest from devolving society into a war of all against all (Hobbes [1651] 1988). Centralizing authority, to Smith, was less necessary, as pursuit of self-interest would lead—the "invisible hand" metaphor—to a certain harmony of colliding interests (1994, 2010).

Self-interest as a guiding doctrine or charter as poised against collective concerns is not relegated to European classical thought. It was seminal to the ideologies that competed at the start of the American political system. In an example central to American political and intellectual history, *The Federalist Papers*, Alexander Hamilton, James Madison, and John Jay debate the virtues of individuals pursuing their own interests against the collective interest (Hamilton, Madison, and Jay [1787–88] 2003). In the early years of the American republic, much thought and contention went into the role of self-interest in government and its potentially corrosive effect of factionalism generated by that interest. As Madison in *No. 10* explains, "The latent causes of faction are thus sown in the nature of man. . . . A zeal for different opinions concerning religion, concerning Government and many other points . . . have divided mankind into parties, inflamed them with mutual animosity, and rendered them much more disposed to vex and oppress each other, than to co-operate for their common good" ([1787] 2003 50, 58). The founders concluded that factionalism could not be leveled in a liberal system, as the French would try in their revolution, but could be appropriately checked by an institutional arrangement by which individual interest was embraced. In the American case, Smith's self-interest won the ideological war within the revolution.

3.2.3 MELANCHOLIC LOGIC

The third category is melancholic logic. This logic recognizes the irrational preferences that fit neither communal affect nor self-interest. Melancholic logic broadly recognizes the tangled relationship humans have with loss, past trauma, and irrational drives (ones that may serve neither communal affect nor self-interest). This logic places the reliving of traumatic events as a critical motivation where worldviews and frames are developed from a lens focusing on the past and its trauma. Liability is emphasized over opportunity, yet a paradox emerges in this logic: we are driven toward contemporary and future forms of the very liability and trauma that we experienced and profess to avoid or abhor. Melancholic logic includes resentment toward the outside world and a tendency of those traumatized to brutalize the world closest to them. We see much of these behaviors—depression, violence, suicide, and substance abuse—inside American Indian reservations and described in the growing literature on trauma and intergenerational trauma (see Bassett, Buchwald, and Manson 2014 for a review of literature on trauma in American Indian communities). Melancholic logic also incorporates into the polity the preference for healing and therapy in a way that material self-interest might not. Such preferences include the redress of past wrongs through apologies, ceremony, and public mourning and remembrance. This trend is apparent in American Indian politics whereby political efforts internal and external to the tribe seek such recognition and remembrance.[2] Contrary to the self-interested logic, melancholic logic directs the polity away from a mechanism for the promotion of economic development, or an affirmation of togetherness as in communal affect. The melancholic logic might claim to pursue the remedy of an injury and loss, but within that claim it may seek the re-creation of that injury and loss.

3.2.4 CARICATURES AND IDEAL TYPES

At first blush, nominating three logics to understand human motivation and its change seems highly reductionist or at least ignorant of the complexities surrounding human political behavior and experience. It is easy to caricaturize these categories and reject them as overly simplistic. It is true these logics are simplistic, yet these three logics are proposed as

Weberian "ideal-types" if not caricatures (Weber 1949). No one is purely self-interested for instance, but instead has varying degrees of that motivation. The essence of these distinctions and their presentation as ideal types is to capture that self-interest is not equally distributed (similarly, this applies to communal affect and melancholic logics) and that experience is involved in this distribution.

These caricatures or ideal types serve as the boundaries or categories upon which we can understand differing patterns of behavior, worldviews, preferences, and so on. Such categories are necessary in order to understand both difference and change through time. How peoples differ politically is undoubtedly more complex, but these categories of logic and worldview aid in explaining the associated patterns of belief and its variation in multiple tribes.

3.2.5 CATEGORIES: CAUSAL MECHANISMS

Why (and where) might some of these broad logics become more dominant than others? This assumes that each logic has a role in each individual, and therefore the polities that individuals create, but that each logic is not necessarily equally salient to all individuals or polities. How is it that these become distributed? There are two assumed causal mechanisms that are critical to the movement between logics. The first assumption is that American Indians—though such mechanisms might apply to any group— shift from a logic of communal affect to a self-interested logic when new forms of wealth are brought to or forced upon their communities. The assumption in the model forwarded is that exposure to market forces and materialism in the form of wealth creation has the potential to alter frames and motivations.

I suggest four basic propositions:

Proposition 1: If American Indians are undisturbed, then communal affect continues as the dominant logic.

Proposition 2: If American Indians are exposed to processes that create new types of wealth, then the logic of self-interest increases in prominence and creates tension with the logic of communal affect.

Proposition 3: If American Indians are exposed to processes that traumatize, then the melancholic logic increases in prominence and creates
tension with the logic of communal affect.

Proposition 4: If American Indians are exposed to both processes leading
to traumatization and wealth, then the logics of self-interest and melancholia competing with communal affect are highly compromised.

Reducing the potential outcomes and processes to four possibilities
negates the complexity of hundreds of ethnohistories spanning multiple
centuries. Yet, as parsimonious as this perspective on American Indian
history is, it follows established themes in the American Indian experience that involve uneven processes of violent loss and economic change.
The pain and profit framework synthesizes three distinct themes about
American Indian change post-contact. The first is that many American
Indians lived according to different logics than Euro-American settlers
upon arrival and that colonization disrupted many of these logics due
to either material or geographic dispossession. The second theme the
framework engages with is that American Indians were exposed to new
concepts of property and acquisition that created inequality within their
tribes (Harmon 2010; Wilson 1985). The third theme is that colonization
produced violence, loss, suffering, and exploitation that is seared into
individual and collective worldviews; and these traumas, not unlike
wealth, might cross generations and become intergenerational (see Brave
Heart 2000, 2003, and 2007 for research establishing historical and intergenerational trauma among North American Indigenous populations).
The overarching effect is that these processes were uneven across tribes.
These propositions might not explain all or many of the features of tribal
political life, but they provide a framework to tether historical experiences
that broadly affected American Indians historically to the contemporary
polity's conflict and factionalism. This book's objective is to place these
three themes into contact with each other and identify the link between
historical processes and intratribal politics.

How do these historical and lived experiences create these logics? Let me
start by describing the causal mechanisms behind the creation of the self-interested logic before turning to melancholic logic and how this would vary.

3.3 RISE OF SELF-INTEREST THROUGH MARKETS

For self-interest to become a dominant logic, two events must take place. The first is the erosion of the logic of communal affect and the second is that, once exposed to new forms of wealth and trade, greater interest in material acquisition over social norms results. Many American Indians interviewed during research for this book thought whites were more individualistic and greedy than American Indians. That observation about communalism and anti-individualism is not without wider support from American Indian communities. In tribal societies, where food and survival is a function of cooperation and subject to uncertainty, individuals who are overly individualistic and ignore social bonds risk survival. The field of economic anthropology, which explores the economic systems of tribal societies, refers to this type of corporation as moral economies or economies embedded within social systems as embedded economies (Booth 1994). The rationale for being less individualistic was thus: if a hunter were unlucky and failed to secure a kill, which can happen to any hunter, then he and his family can survive if others are willing to share. Other successful hunters are willing to share if they know that if they were unfortunate to return without meat, the unsuccessful hunter they helped would share with them. The same goes for farmers whose crops might become wiped out by flood or disease. In a contemporary economy, with social welfare provisions and comparatively greater material abundance, this social dependence is unnecessary, as one might be highly individualistic without much risk of starvation.

Economic-maximizing behavior violates the moral economy and is dangerous in traditional systems. There are limits to how much food might be stored or how many items might be carried. Without markets, extra grain would spoil. Economic actors are also risk-averse in this system. Unlike today, where risk might create a windfall of wealth and profits, hunters and farmers in pre-market economies would see risks but no rewards. Introducing a new farming technique might risk starvation, with the payoff for success only being food that could not be eaten.

A claim made in economic anthropology is that these moral economies change (Polanyi 2001). The shift from a society organized by the logic of communal affect to self-interest has been well documented in political theory and political economy in sixteenth- and seventeenth-century Europe. Perhaps most recognizable is Albert Hirschman's seminal work *The Passions and the Interests: Political Arguments for Capitalism before Its Triumph* (1997), which identified the advent of self-interest among the ruling class in Europe as a function of greater stability and therefore a more virtuous society. Showing that the original arguments for capitalism and self-interest, from Machiavelli to Hume, were made on moral grounds, Hirschman questioned the assumption that self-interested behavior was originally understood as being wealth-creating instead of virtue-supporting. Hirschman's argument differed from Madison and Smith's on the moral justification for the rise of self-interest. Self-interest made for prudence, compared to passion and honor. A state, or ruler, that wished to rule effectively, as was Machiavelli's commitment, needed to abide by its own self-interest rather than passion or honor—even if it kept order through fear.

3.3.1 RISE OF SELF-INTEREST THROUGH WEALTH

Willingness to break social norms and harmony in pursuit of individual self-interest is unevenly distributed within a society as well as across societies (see Nisbett 2003 for comprehensive study of cultural differences around individualism and social order). Studies in social psychology have identified that those who have a comparatively high status display greater individualistic behavior. This research supports the claim I forward that the creation of wealth and greater socioeconomic status in American Indians has led to more self-interested worldviews. High-status individuals demonstrate a willingness to break societal norms and standards for their own benefits. Sociopsychologist Paul Piff and fellow researchers conducted seven studies that examine the behavior of high-status and low-status individuals around norm-breaking behavior for gain (2013). In naturalistic studies, such as observing individuals while driving, and laboratory studies, such as questionnaires on acceptable behavior, upper-class individuals demonstrated greater willingness to break social norms when it was to their advantage. High-status and wealthier individuals were found to have greater senses of entitlement and were more likely to show signs indicating narcissism. Such studies point to an association between wealth and self-interested worldviews.

The identified reasons for this disparity are many. High-status and wealthy individuals have greater independence than those in the lower classes, and wealthier individuals are able to suffer fewer social sanctions and costs for self-interested behavior (Galperin, Bennett, and Aquino 2011; Kraus, Piff, and Keltner 2009; Kraus et al. 2012). Wealthy individuals frame their behavior in terms of entitlement and are less concerned with the perceptions of others (Galinsky et al. 2008; Snibbe and Markus 2005). The upper class is oriented toward goals more than the lower class (Guinote 2007). Greed is also viewed more positively among the wealthy than the poor (Wang, Malhotra, and Murnighan 2011) and by those who are exposed to self-interested models of thinking (Frank, Gilovich, and Regan 1993).

Increased wealth and status not only are associated with norm-breaking behavior but also are linked to greater individualism. Linguistic studies have shown a relationship between wealth and individualism. The shift is away from communal terms and toward individualistic and self-interested words. Research in linguistics has identified a change in the frequency of individualistic-orientated words published in the United States throughout the twentieth century (Greenfield 2013). Whereas words that suggest communal demands such as *give, belong*, or *obliged* have declined in frequency, words that indicate self-orientation, such as *individual, unique*, and *get*, have increased in use. "Such adaptation," according to psychologist Patricia Greenfield, "prioritizes choice, personal possessions, and . . . foster[s] the development of psychological mindedness and the unique self" (2013, 1722). Greenfield also tracked the prevalence of the use of words *give*—indicating a perspective of obligation to a larger system—and *get*—indicating self-interest–centered perspectives—in the millions of books published over the last two hundred years to which Google has access, and found that as wealth increased during this period, *get* increased and *give* decreased (2013, 1727). If language represents the preferences and concerns of populations, this indicates that communal-mindedness diminishes as wealth and commerce increases.

There are limitations to these social psychology experiments for our purpose. Such research is not focused on American Indians and takes place in the contemporary period. Our concern is particularly with the past and is about historical change. Those limitations considered, research does strongly suggest that wealth and self-interested behavior is related.

3.4 RISE OF MELANCHOLIA

An experience that animates motivations similar to what Hume called the "dark passions" ([1777] 1966),[3] or what this book terms *melancholic logic* and *worldview*, is the experience of trauma or loss.[4] A retrospective term, trauma in its abstract and tautological definition captures experiences that lead to the end point of traumatization. The *Diagnostic and Statistical Manual of Mental Disorders* (DSM-IV) diagnoses individual psychological trauma if "(1) the person experienced, witnessed, or was confronted with an event or events that involved actual or threatened death or serious injury, or a threat to the physical integrity of self or others (2) the person's response involved intense fear, helplessness, or horror" (American Psychiatric Association 1994). Depending upon intensity and repetition of these experiences and the resilience of the individual who experienced it, the outcome is an identifiable way of relating to the world that involves perception, worldview, and motivation.

This section explores what a traumatic event is and three approaches to understanding trauma that contribute to the adoption of a melancholic logic. The first of these three approaches is the ideational or classical understanding of trauma being an idea; the second is the biological or neuroscientific understanding of trauma being a physical alteration; the third is how historical trauma passes from one generation to another.

3.4.1 TRAUMATIC EVENT

Trauma is born from a state of high or intense fear. This is different from low fear, which does not carry with it the same existential threat that high fear creates. Biologically based disciplines, such as neuroscience, will often use the term *high stress* or *stressor* in referring to what more humanistic or psychological fields call *traumatic events*. These fears or stressors are not standard everyday anxieties such as worrying about receiving a parking ticket, but rather result from experiences of physical or psychological harm or the perception of such harms to oneself, close relations, or those in phys-ical proximity (American Psychiatric Association 1994; Herman 1997). A traumatic event can be physical or sexual assault, torture, severe neglect, starvation, captivity, exposure to natural disaster, or automotive accidents. Traumatic events produce multiple effects the moment the event occurs but also hold consequences for the future behavioral pattern of an individual. In the classical perspective trauma, such events, in the moment they occur, alienate individuals from their sense of control. Psychologist Judith Herman identifies "the moment of trauma" as when "the victim is rendered helpless by overwhelming force" (1997, 33). To Herman and scholarship that empha-sizes the ideational quality of trauma, it is "an affliction of the powerless" (1997, 33), and the traumatic event and moment is one that overwhelms ordi-nary senses. In the neuroscientific approach, events that cause high stress prompt the nervous system to alter the chemical composition of the brain. In moments of fear, glands release initially helpful chemicals to heighten alert to manage a threatening circumstance. In both the neuroscientific and clas-sical approach, this state of heightened alert is called the *arousal state*. This state is where the body, mind, and brain prepare for the threat, perceived or real. The arousal state is initially useful but is a rupture to the psychic or biological continuity and a basis for traumatization after the event.

Not all events that could be traumatizing do in fact create later trauma. The likelihood of trauma, and therefore the degree to which an event is traumatizing, is a function of the event's severity and duration and the resilience of the person experiencing the trauma. Not all potentially trau-matizing events traumatize, and not all people are equally traumatized by the same event. Experiencing military combat, where one's life is directly in danger, is more likely to traumatize than returning to a burgled home. The typical rate at which individuals who experience what could be traumatic events exhibit symptoms of traumatization is approximately 40 percent (Patcho et al. 2013). The graver the traumatic event, the greater the risk of traumatization. As a single event might not lead to traumatization, the repetition and duration of these events is critical to later traumatization. Repeated traumatic events are more likely to generate chronic traumati-zation. One-off events such as car crashes are less likely to traumatize than residing with an abusive parent, where the fear is routinized.

Exposure to traumatic events is not evenly distributed. For instance, the most common traumatic events experienced by men are military combat and witnessing injury (deRoon-Cassini et al. 2010). For women, sexual abuse and intimate partner violence are the experiences most likely to create trauma (Pietrzak et al. 2011). Men experience traumatic events more, although women are more likely to be traumatized by those events, even taking into account the type of exposure (Pietrzak et al. 2011). The prevalence of traumatization, described as post-traumatic stress disorder, is about 6 percent in the general population. Compared to all ethnic groups in the United States, American Indians experience the most traumatic events (U.S. Bureau of Justice Statistics 2002). American Indian youth are the most likely of all racial groups in the United States to experience trauma leading to death as a child (see table 3.1), the most likely to suffer violent victimization (Truman, Langton, and Planty 2013; see table 3.2 below), and twice as likely to be suffering from associated aspects of trauma (Breslau et al. 1999; Manson et al. 2005; Stephens et al. 2010). Though essential to understanding how trauma is created, the traumatic event is of

TABLE 3.1 Leading causes of death among young people in American Indian and white populations nationally *(rate per 100,000 persons)*

	RATE		HAZARD RATIO of American Indians and Alaska Natives compared to Whites
	American Indians and Alaska Natives*	Whites	
Causes of death, ages 1–4			
All causes	81.2	28.5	2.8
Unintentional injuries	31.4	10.6	3.0
Homicide	6.4	1.7	3.8
Causes of death, ages 14–25			
All causes	185.5	75.8	2.4
Unintentional injuries	98.6	40.1	2.5
Homicide	21.0	6.9	3.0
Suicide	34.3	10.3	3.3

*Rate adjusted for missing race on death certificate.

Source: Indian Health Service (2011), *Indian Health Focus: Injuries, 2002–2003 Edition.* Washington D.C.: U.S. Department of Health and Human Services, Indian Health Service, Office of Public Health Support, Office of Environmental Health and Engineering, https://www.ihs.gov/dps/includes/themes/newihstheme/display_objects/documents/IHS-FOCUS_Injuries2002-2003a.pdf.

Table 3.2 Rates of victimization across race, 2012 *(rate per 1,000 persons, ages 12 or older)*

	American Indian/ Alaska Native	White	Black/African American	Hispanic/Latino
Violent Crime*	46.9	25.2	34.2	24.5
Serious Violent Crime+	26.2	6.8	11.3	9.3

* Includes rape, aggravated assault, simple assault, sexual assault, and robbery.
+ Excludes simple assault definition of violent crime.

Source: Jennifer Truman, Lynn Langton, and Michael Planty (2013), *Criminal Victimization, 2012*, U.S. Department of Justice, Bureau of Justice Statistics (October): 1–17, http://www.bjs.gov/content/pub/pdf/cv12.pdf.

secondary consideration in this work compared to the behavioral pattern associated with residual traumatization. To provide an overview of how trauma might operate as a causal mechanism, three approaches to trauma are discussed. The first is classical or ideational, the second is biological or neuroscientific, and the third is intergenerational.

3.4.2 CLASSICAL AND IDEATIONAL APPROACHES TO TRAUMA

In the classical approach, trauma is thought to consist of concepts and ideas. Referring to it as *ideation* is meant to differentiate it from the neuroscience approach to trauma, which will be discussed in the next section. Classical or ideational approaches to trauma revolve around the memory of a traumatic event or its repression. Trauma as an idea or memory hearkens back to late-nineteenth-century work by Freud and his contemporaries that came to be known as psychoanalytic theory; hence the use of the term *classical*. In the psychoanalytic tradition, a body of literature most aligned to the classical and ideational approach, a complex set of assumptions about cognition and emotion were utilized to treat psychological distress. Freud, among others, felt that the psychological distress, which he called "hysteria" or "psychological neurosis," was found in past experiences that had been repressed (Freud [1896] 1972). Such experiences, to Freud, were typically not memories in the sense that they were known or overly remembered, but instead were found in the unhelpful responses to non-traumatizing stimuli. These repressed memories existed in the subconscious, or id, and resurfaced in the behavioral condition of hysteria (Freud 1923). "Hysterics," as they were called, exhibited various afflictions that became the source of social ostracism and institutionalization. Rarely one to ingratiate himself to modern-day feminists, Freud's and his contemporaries' hysterics were initially all females, and the speculated cause of trauma was early sexual abuse. This grounded notion of trauma changed after the First World War, when the symptoms experienced by combat veterans, what might have been called *battle fatigue* or *shellshock*, resembled the hysteria of his early observations of sexually abused women.

The rich history of psychoanalysis and its many limitations is best described in works directly on trauma (Freud [1896] 1972), but for our purposes the essential aspect of the ideational or classical approach of understanding trauma is that horrific events leave legacies in the form of ideas or memories that we are aware of or repress. These events *haunt*, for lack of a better word, and have the capacity to modify how individuals engage with them.

Melancholia and trauma can be thought of as undermining an ideal or preferred (rational) state through two broad processes. The first is a traumatic event resulting in the new presence of something undesirable. The second is a traumatic event resulting in the absence or loss of something previously desired. These are nearly always interrelated. To illustrate this point, imagine that while depositing a check in a bank, armed robbers storm the lobby. After a few minutes of intimidating bank staff and patrons, they leave. Though there is no physical harm, assuming none are injured in the robbery, those present now will hold a new and undesirable memory. Something is lost as well in this experience. Perhaps just as significant in the legacy of the robbery is that those who experienced it might also have lost their sense of safety in public areas. They would now potentially carry with them the sense of fright and preparedness for a recurrence of the traumatic event. The world as they knew it, one of safety and nonviolence, might be diminished or even gone. Returning to a bank or a cash register might create severe discomfort. For some predisposed to the effects of traumatic experiences, agoraphobia might develop.

Traumatizing experiences are potentially devastating even in the absence of physical injury. In the ideational or classical perspective of trauma, an individual's perception and emotions suffer from the omnipresent sense of danger and the overwhelming potential for real injury. In remembering or sensing themselves powerless to the degree that they perceive threats that are not actually present, the traumatized may possess attachment disorders, express difficulty in forming new relationships, suffer depression, and, in the worst cases, experience hallucinations of the original event. As terrible and wounding as it is, one can appreciate and be awed by trauma and the potential of ideas and experiences to shape realities.

3.4.3 BIOLOGICAL AND NEUROSCIENTIFIC TRAUMA

Recent studies in neuroscience and biopsychology have typically held that the "structure of the brain is a history of its use" (Bahrick and Hollich 2008, 175). This perspective is one that emphasizes what can be literally seen in the brain (in contrast to the ideational or classical understanding of trauma, which is based on ideas of what cannot be seen). A tenet to the neuroscientific premise of traumatization is that, to some degree, nervous systems are physically malleable; they are altered through experience and products of conditions in what is termed *neuroplasticity*. In particular, neuroscientific research identifies fear and stress as having an unusually formative role in conditioning the nervous system and altering the physical structure of the brain.

What is understood as *high stress*—the product of fearful, abusive, traumatic, and violent experiences—is believed to alter the brain's chemical composition in the short term and physical structure in the long term (McEwen 1999, 2001; Sapolsky 1996). Structural changes have permanent implications for cognition, behavior, and perception (McEwen 1999; Dannlowski et al. 2011). The neuroscientific perspective on trauma looks at the change in brain regions during stressful, traumatic, and fear-inducing events. Fear is an emotive but also a biological state, as fear alters the brain's composition by introducing new compounds that stimulate certain regions (Sapolsky 2000). The biological system that is most associated with stress is the limbic system, which will be the subject of the next section.[5]

3.4.3.1 *The Limbic System and Stress*

The limbic system is at the center of regulating stress-induced arousal and preparing to sense danger. Within the limbic system, the glands responsible for regular chemical intervention and response during stress are the hippocampus and the amygdala. These two glands are the regions of the brain that are most biochemically altered by experiences of danger. The amount that each gland changes as a result of danger or abuse depends upon (*a*) the individual and (*b*) the type of abuse. It has been noted that all people, even those with high resistance, have a threshold at which high stress impacts their nervous system (Davis 1997).

The physiochemical mechanisms that fear-induced high stress provokes for survival are epinephrine (adrenaline), norepinephrine, and hydrocortisone. Epinephrine and norepinephrine are released and hydrocortisone regulates these interactions with synapses[6] (Munck, Guyre, and Holbrook 1984; Sapolsky 1996). The secretion of these compounds in a short period of time, such as a day or two, does not typically have adverse physiological consequences (Sapolsky, Romero, and Munck 2000). The release of these chemicals is a preservation mechanism designed to enable heightened responses for survival in potentially dangerous situations in the short term (Sapolsky 1996). Yet, when these chemicals are sustained through long-term danger, the results are possibly deleterious to future brain functioning. If the exposure to epinephrine (adrenaline), norepinephrine, and hydrocortisone is sustained, the consequences can be adverse to essential regions that process emotions, memory, and perception in the brain (Sapolsky 1996; Sapolsky, Romero, and Munck 2000).

A gland within the limbic system that is at particular risk is the hippocampus. During stress and arousal, hydrocortisone is secreted to stimulate the hippocampus; this can lead to erosion of the hippocampus and limbic system if the exposure is prolonged (Bechara, Tranel, and Damasio 2000; Dannlowski et al. 2011; Frodl et al. 2010; Grabenhorst, Rolls, and Parris 2008; Mueller et al. 2010; Rubia et al. 2006; Volz, Schubotz, and von Cramon 2006). There is a strong correlation between exposure to danger and hippocampal size in human populations that confirms the effects of stressors on the limbic system. Those suffering from depression and PTSD secrete greater amounts of stress compounds than the general population (McEwen 1992). Vietnam combat veterans who exhibited PTSD were found to have significant atrophy (8 percent) in the right hippocampal region and close to that amount in the left (Sapolsky 1996). Follow-up studies found that the hippocampal reduction of veterans compared to their non-veteran peers is 22 percent for the right and 26 percent for the left hippocampus (Bremner et al. 1995). Children who experienced abuse were found to have a 12 percent hippocampus atrophy compared to those who did not (Gurvits et al. 1996). The aforementioned studies controlled for gender, age, educational level, and drug abuse (Bremner et al. 1995).

3.4.3.2 *Behavioral Effects of Atrophy and Reduction of the Limbic System*

Life proves more challenging with a diminished hippocampal region. Prolonged stress degrades regions of the brain responsible for regulating tasks essential to social and communal activities (Sapolsky 1996). The legacy of abuse is as pernicious in the neuroscientific perspective as it is in the ideational. Glandular atrophy is associated with multiple behavioral conditions, none of which is considered helpful. The regions of the brain damaged by stress-induced arousal are critical to other functions such as memory, attention, IQ, perception, inhibition control, and learning.

The hippocampus is the region of the brain essential to cognition. A reduction in the hippocampus will affect or diminish the capacity of how individuals understand their environment, learn, remember, identify social norms, and assess risk. The temporal lobe, where the hippocampus is located, is essential to integrating experience with perception—what ultimately gets termed as *learning*. This region translates short-term memory into long-term memory. Stress and trauma will reduce the region of the brain in mammals responsible for processing information, perceiving the environment, making decisions, and calculating strategies. Laboratory studies on hippocampal reduction due to stress are usually conducted on rodents and not people, but these have been replicated in higher-level primates as well (Brand et al. 2007; Lindauer et al. 2006; Mueller et al. 2010; Sapolsky 1996; Villarreal et al. 2002).

Damage and atrophy to the limbic system and prefrontal cortex alters the assessment of risk and reward. Bechara and colleagues (2000) found in a study of gambling tasks based on real-life decisions that participants with atrophy or damage to the prefrontal cortex responded differently than control groups on choices involving risk. They found that those with atrophy to this part of the brain were hypersensitive to rewards and less sensitive to punishments and future consequences. The study group was guided by the immediate prospect of rewards and much less that of negative consequences (Magarinos et al. 1996; Uno et al. 1989). Such research suggests a change in perception caused by continued stress, which is further supported by another study that found that damage to the prefrontal cortex and amygdala also reduces the ability to make decisions under ambiguity or risk (Bechara, Tranel, and Damasio 2000).

The brain's cortex—which includes the frontal lobe, where much of our thinking capacity lies—is in continual communication with our limbic system, which includes the hippocampus and amygdala. In order to learn from experience, events must be allowed to settle or be recorded in the frontal lobe (Brand et al. 2007). During assault or threat of assault, the limbic system is activated before the frontal cortex can be stimulated. Furthermore, it is believed that the prefrontal cortex, instrumental in learning and problem solving, can only be activated from a situation of non-arousal where there is no sense of pending threat (Blair 2012). In short, when danger is perceived, the ability to learn and update knowledge is interrupted.

Social recognition and memory is also impaired by brain atrophy. Research examining the relationship between brain volume and PTSD has also shown that atrophy in the hippocampus, amygdala, and other parts of the brain can reduce the effective recall of people and knowledge. Both verbal memory and facial recognition were delayed in PTSD sufferers, whose magnetic resonance scan (MRI) showed reduced brain volume from atrophy (Streeck-Fischer and van der Kolk 2000). Impulsivity is also associated with a smaller and overstimulated hippocampus, amygdala, and prefrontal cortex. Overuse of these regions of the brain earlier in life reduces the capacity for these regions to be properly stimulated later in adulthood. A study of Romanian adults who were adopted from an orphanage (and presumably had greater stressors early in life) found that their limbic systems and prefrontal cortexes had lower metabolic rates compared to those of adults who were not orphans (Chugani et al. 2001). The conclusion of this research was that dysfunction in these brain regions resulted from early stress or deprivation and was possibly responsible for the later cognitive and behavioral deficits evident among the orphan group.

Early childhood abuse skews the adult survivors' perception and memory. Prolonged stress might not only alter the shape and capacity of the regions of the brain that manage danger and threat, such as the hippocampus, but also impact the connections between regions responsible for forming memories, solving problems, and developing reflections on previous events. This approach to trauma corroborates my assumption in this book that trauma and stress alter perception and affect the ultimate worldview of the traumatized.

3.4.4 INTERGENERATIONAL TRAUMA

Up to this point, a traumatic event has been described as affecting an individual or limited group. Traumatic events, such as muggings, for instance, might be pervasive in a society, but each event has a limited impact on a discrete set of victims. Yet researchers have expanded the concept of psychological trauma from an individual with a traumatic event as the unit of analysis to a collective and how trauma exists and is transmitted between individuals within these collectives. Ideational and neuroscientific aspects both operate within this broader and collective perspective of trauma.

Collectively traumatizing events could be wars, starvation, genocide, and forced relocation. Many of these events are present in American Indian history. For instance, the Lakotas engaged in multiple wars with the U.S. government in the late nineteenth century and suffered the massacre of women and children in conditions that amounted to biological and classical notions of trauma. Associated with the potential that trauma might be collective is a belief that these traumas might be passed from one generation to the next. Historical trauma (sometimes referred to as the transgenerational transmission of trauma) has been studied for more than half a century (see Fassin and Rechtman 2009 for critical perspective on trauma and victimhood; Kellermann 2009 for a history of transgenerational trauma studies). The historical trauma perspective recognizes the potential for the damage done by events to be passed from one generation to the next. Historical or intergenerational trauma need not be collective. For instance, individualized trauma is often carried within one family and between parents and children, which could be independent of the community or society at large experiencing something similar. I will use the term historical trauma to signify trauma that is both collective and intergenerational and distinguish it from non-collective types of intergenerational trauma, such as the idiosyncrasy of an abusive family.[7]

The concept of historical trauma has its origin in Danish studies in the 1950s on the mental health of Jewish Holocaust survivors. Herman and Thygesen observed that symptoms associated with direct traumatization nearly a decade earlier were not disappearing (1954). Their study found depression, fatigue, nightmares, anxiety, and reduction in memory. These Danish studies were followed by larger studies on the long-term traumatization of former American prisoners of war (POWs) from Japanese and North Korean camps (Beebe 1975; Keehn 1980; Nefzger 1970) with similar findings. Much of this earlier work was limited to individuals who directly experienced the trauma, such as POWs and concentration camp survivors, but within a decade, researchers expanded the potential for traumatic effects to those who did not directly experience the event.

It should not be unexpected that years of prolonged and direct experience with traumatic events in concentration or POW camps that prompted stress, danger, fear, and death would incline individuals toward a melancholic worldview. It is unexpected that the psychic results of direct trauma are transitive and could affect a secondary population decades later in contexts with little danger and in locations geographically far removed. Early recognition that trauma might be transitive between individuals gained prominence from studies conducted on the children and spouses of Holocaust survivors. This early work originates from engagement by Canadian psychiatrists with members of immigrant Jewish communities in the 1960s who sought treatment for their children (Rakoff 1966). One of these psychiatrists, Vivian Rakoff, noted a pattern of high anxiety, depression, and paranoia among children in families led by Holocaust survivors. These conditions, Rakoff believed, resulted from parental expectations that children replace the lives of those lost during the Holocaust. "The love and ambition of whole family members were," Rakoff observed, "resurrected in memory and imposed as hopes on the children who were expected to supply the gratification normally coming from mothers, fathers, brothers, sisters, cousins, uncles and aunts, and to live in their own lifetimes those truncated lives" (1966, 21). The observation that saw children as replacements was only the initial point of entry into what would become a sustained and continual interest in family dynamics of traumatized cohorts.

Such a perspective emphasizes the ideational dimension of trauma, but such Holocaust stories of lost loved ones and kin also robbed children of the sympathetic parent as much as it incorporated them into distressing content by the parents' sharing Holocaust experiences. The trauma originated in the next generation not only in the sharing of memories but also in the parental-child relationship. Rakoff and colleagues believed that when parents relived these traumatic memories, "Few emotional resources [were] left over to meet any but the most routine psychological pressures. [Children's] needs and their requests for attention and care [were] either ignored or dealt with as unfair demands" (Rakoff, Sigal, and Epstein 1966, 24f). Children's futures were made pallbearers of the past. Rather than having attentive parents, children of holocaust survivors were often relegated to the role of medium to past tragedy.

Further research over decades suggests that children of traumatized people share or are incorporated into the direct burden. In addition to depression, emptiness, and dispiritedness, traumatized parents pass on perceptions or worldviews from periods of danger and intensity in their own lives. Such worldviews are dominated by suspicion, fear, and an impending sense of danger (Podietz et al. 1984).

Hundreds of studies have examined intergenerational and historical trauma since it was first identified in the 1960s. Much of this research was done psychoanalytically, such as in Bergmann and Jucovy's 1982 *Generations of the Holocaust*, which is a collection of New York City psychoanalysts working with Holocaust patients and their children. Historical and intergenerational trauma research was initially self-selecting and therefore limited in rigor. As much of it is based in interviews and writings by practitioners, the generalizability to the entire population is compromised. Neither is the homogeneity of trauma well understood by these original studies. Community-level studies that emphasized randomization supported the proposition that children of Holocaust survivors did suffer from a higher prevalence of disorders associated with traumatic events (Bremner et al. 1993; Bremner et al. 1995).

Another explanation for how trauma moves between generations relies upon biological mechanisms. The biological basis for which trauma might be transmitted relies upon the relationship between environmentally induced stress, biochemistry, and genetics. Referred to as epigenetics, this perspective examines the heritable changes in genes due to environmental stimuli that are outside the DNA sequence. In the transition of trauma through epigenetics, like in the biological perspective, stressful experiences produce alterations in body chemistry. Hundreds of studies have found that chemical changes from stress alter the genes of multiple organisms (Sigal and Weinfeld 1989). This mark that stress has on genes, called imprinting, could occur in childhood and have consequences for future generations. In one of the earliest studies on epigenetic change in humans, Bygren and colleagues found that high calorie intake and overeating in youth as a result of famine could create a chain of events that might mean earlier death for their grandchildren (2001). Research on the adult brains of abused children found an abnormal chemical layer surrounding the genes in their brains during autopsies. More recent studies have shown that pregnant women who were near the World Trade Center on September 11, 2001, delivered babies with relatively high stress hormones thought to enact genetic changes that would last for generations (Yehuda et al. 2005).

Epigenetic research identifies parents' interactions with children as particularly important for imprinting in future generations. Studies suggest that a mother's level of stress will leave a chemical imprint in utero that affects the child's susceptibility to PTSD (Yehuda et al. 2009). Parental separation, a common occurrence in the uncertainty associated with historical trauma found in American Indian removal, was identified by epigenetic research as altering chemical levels in infants. Children's stress levels, as measured by chemical increases, increase and decrease when separated and reunited with their mothers (Yehuda et al. 2005). The presence of these chemicals is associated with the plasticity of genes. In a study on parenting quality and epigenetic outcomes, psychologists found a relationship between the parenting quality an individual experienced and that individual's stress levels fourteen years later. Those who experienced a stressful childhood and poor parenting were found to have greater changes to genes (Kochanska, Philibert, and Barry 2009).

3.4.5 LIMITATIONS TO THE STUDY OF TRAUMA

Skepticism arose shortly after the development of the concept of historical trauma being transmitted transgenerationally. Literature contrary to the vulnerability outlined in historical trauma research developed, and those who survived trauma and their offspring were thought to have highly developed coping mechanisms (Belsky and Beaver 2011; Dimsdale 1980; Harel, Kahana, and Kahana 1988). Such studies focused on survivors' coping ability (Leon et al. 1981). Some researchers saw no difference between the children of Holocaust survivors and the general population (Harel, Kahana, and Kahana 1988). Other studies found significant diversity in the attitudes of secondary populations (Aleksandrowicz 1973). Despite these concerns and doubts, evidence on these legacies is established in literature on both non–American Indian and American Indian populations (Danieli 1981a, 1981b).

3.5 THE PAIN AND PROFIT APPROACH: POLANYIAN TRIAD

Thus far, I provided support for the claim that the causal mechanisms of wealth and trauma support different worldviews. Offered now is an explanation of how such causal mechanisms might be imagined together and applied to American Indian ethnohistory, lived experience, and then to contemporary politics. The Citizen Potawatomis' historical experiences with wealth and trauma are used in describing the pain and profit framework, their Nation, and the creation of intratribal factionalism. Over the last two hundred years, the Citizen Potawatomis have experienced instances of significant trauma and wealth creation and therefore are placed within the high pain/high profit category. This means that the tribe was removed (and decimated in the process) but also came to have wealthy business or merchant classes. The historical source of the melancholia for the Potawatomi tribe originated in the tribe's removal from its traditional lands in the Great Lakes by westward-moving settlers in the

Precontact tribal worldview

COMMUNAL AFFECT
Features: Moral or embedded economy, risk aversion, social control

Ethnohistory *(Post-contact)*

Low in pain & profit *(Persistence of communal affect)*

High in profitable experiences: Market economy & merchant classes *(Rise of self-interest)*

High in painful experiences: Geographical removal or genocide *(Rise of melancholia)*

Lived experience *(Conditioned by & reinforcing ethnohistory)*

Features: Low social & economic differentiation, high social censure

Features: Business elite, integration into Euro-American institutions

Features: Generational poverty from historical exploitation, social vices

Contemporary worldview / Logic *(Case study)*

COMMUNAL AFFECT *(Isleta Pueblos)*

MELANCHOLIC *(Rosebud Lakotas)*

SELF-INTEREST & MELANCHOLIC *(Citizen Potawatomis)*

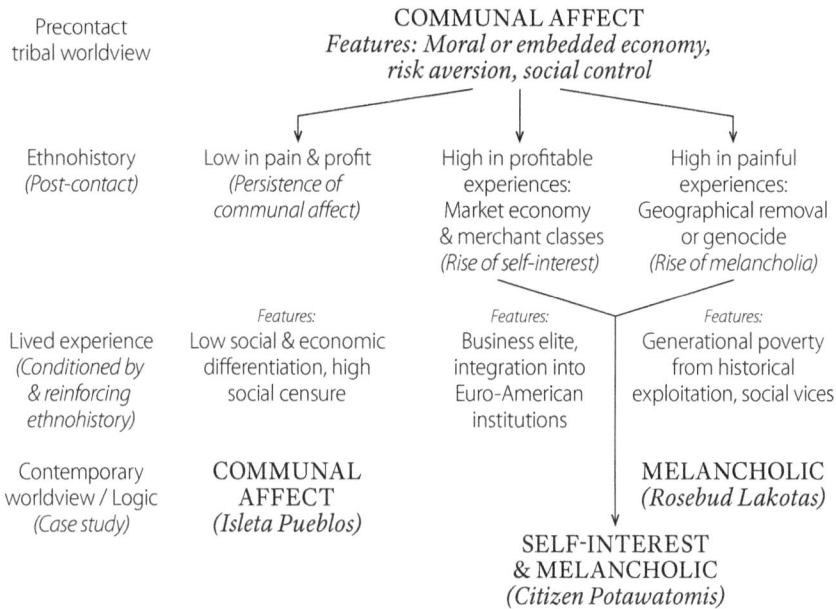

FIGURE 3.1   Visualization of pain and profit framework, starting with communal affect in traditional or moral economies

nineteenth century. This was a period of widespread death, upheaval, and disorganization for its members. Yet, within a few decades of arriving in Oklahoma, the location of their new reservation, oil was found, making many Potawatomis wealthy and giving rise to a self-interested logic for those who benefited. These contrary experiences sparked competing worldviews among the Potawatomis, which are expressed in an intense factionalism within tribal politics.

A split between one faction organized by the logic and worldview that is melancholic and another that is self-interested defines contemporary Citizen Potawatomi intratribal politics. To capture the transition to these self-interested and melancholic worldviews and logics, I draw upon the work of Karl Polanyi. In his work *The Great Transformation* (2001), Polanyi identified the transition from communal and reciprocal social organization to market-based organization. This transition, which he called the *great transformation*, saw economic profit increase but also the misery of those cast out of the system. Polanyi did not explicitly incorporate individual behavioral observations into his perspectives on market expansion; rather his perspective broke large-scale social change into three forms (original forms of communalisms, which were punctured by self-interest and then resulted in loss). It is these three categories that provide a model on which we might base the categories and causal mechanism in this work. Brought into a single visual representation at its most fundamental level is what I call the *Polanyian triad*. Individuals and communities can cycle through the logics of communal affect, melancholia, and self-interest depending upon experience. Painful experiences such as massacres and removal create classes of dispossessed with melancholic logics. Profitable experiences with development generally affirm logics of self-interest. A visual representation of this is as follows in figure 3.2.

The assumed standard is that communal affect logic is the default position, as described by economic anthropology. This assumes, to the extent accepted in studies of tribal and traditional societies, that American Indian tribes had a communal affect principle before contact and that their communities' dominant logic emphasized communalism.

The Polanyian triad "tilts" according to experience. Traumatic experiences including genocide and relocation undermine communal affect

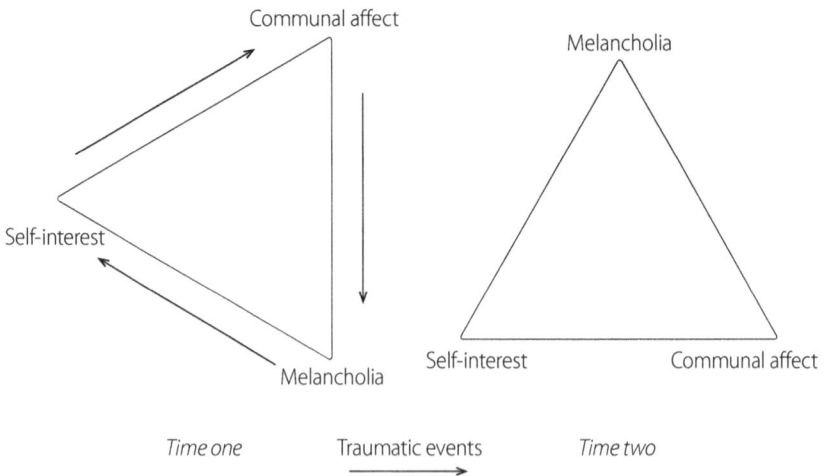

FIGURE 3.2 Impact of injury that diminishes communal affect and advances melancholic logics

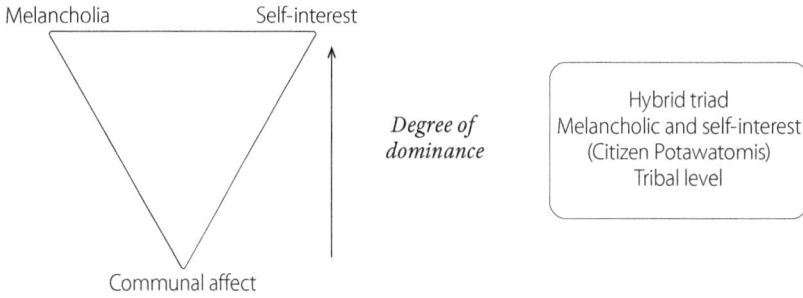

FIGURE 3.3 Rise of melancholia and self-interest, and competing logics within one tribe

logic. This is represented by a shift in the triad that replaces communal affect with melancholic logics (see figure 3.2).

In the case of the Citizen Potawatomis, where two factions are competing for dominance, the tribe is represented by a triad on its point, as in figure 3.3.

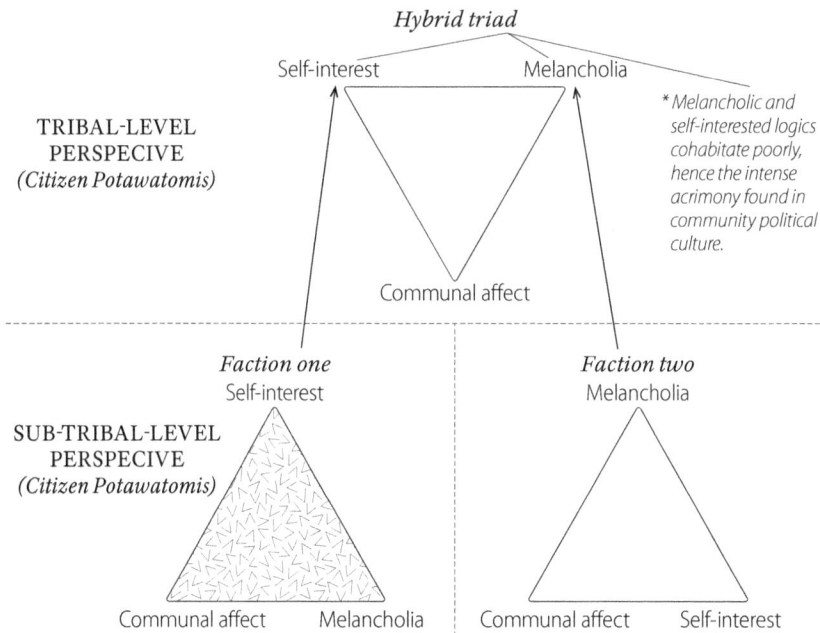

FIGURE 3.4 A representation of a hybrid form of political community, in which logics of self-interest and melancholia are dominant at a sub-tribal level, but are in competition at the tribal level

Citizen Potawatomi intratribal politics, as mentioned earlier, are filled with acrimony and conflict. The next chapter will show how melancholic and self-interested logics are in competition using the Citizen Potawatomis as a case study. Indeed, these two logics and worldviews make for an unusually severe culture of strife and acrimony.

At a sub-tribal and factional level, the Citizen Potawatomis' composition of these logics, as expressed by triads, is different and more precise. The Citizen Potawatomi members who comprise the self-interested faction are guided by self-interested logics and a utilitarian calculus. Let us call this group *faction one*. The Citizen Potawatomis who place melancholic preferences and worldviews over material self-interest have a triad that has a dominant melancholic logic. Let us call this group *faction two*. These tribal factions are discussed in the next chapter.

3.6 CONCLUSION

If we expand the theoretical approach in the pain and profit model to the empirical case studies, we see that each empirical chapter fits into a mix of experiences. Figure 3.4 outlines how the case studies in this work mix Polanyi's perspective on social change. With changes came challenges to communal affect and the rise of other logics depending upon the ethnohistory of the tribe. More recent experiences, represented at the lived experience level, broker the relationship that individuals have with their own sense of ethnicity and worldview in the contemporary period.

This chapter provides support to the premise that individuals and communities change their behavioral features as a result of experience. The next chapter returns to focus on the Citizen Potawatomis and illustrates the rise of self-interest and melancholia at the expense of communal affect. The next chapter examines how historical trauma and wealth creation have created two competing tribal factions that understand Potawatomi identity and tribal purpose in two distinct ways.

CHAPTER 4

The Politics of Nostalgia
Potawatomi Acrimony and Oklahoma Oil

"Indian country doesn't need another Don Quixote."
—John "Rocky" Barrett,
Citizen Potawatomi chairman

"The best way to get a room's attention is to throw a
rattlesnake in its middle."
—Sacred Heart Citizen Potawatomi

4.1 INTRODUCTION

If America had ruins, they would be in Oklahoma. Heading into the rolling hills, in the humid, heavy air of eastern Oklahoma, one crosses the Canadian River, among other small streams, with banks hollowed by wetter years. Wooden shacks, now abandoned, perch on hills and leave the valleys to the rusted skeletons of once-hammering oil pumps. Oil was a vital part of this region, employing many and making untenable land profitable. One moves between Citizen Potawatomi[1] and Oklahoma territory often, as the reservation borders are jagged, legacies of allotment and checkerboarding—a term used to describe land incongruence from trust and freehold status. Within this landscape and in many ways because of it, there are two American Indian histories in Oklahoma. Those once-hammering oil pumps drilled profit for some and pain for others.

What is not immediately felt in this movement through Oklahoma is that one is entering a contested region in Indian country. These

79

confrontations constitute a significant, if not a dominant, degree of the contemporary individual American Indian political experience in this region. The Citizen Potawatomi conflict is relatively passionate and open by contemporary American Indian standards. Accusations of corruption and slander are constant, and the strife is sporadically violent though continually organized. Unlike the Indians in New Mexico or South Dakota, the Citizen Potawatomis, for instance, have semiformal political parties.

This chapter contends that conflicts within the Citizen Potawatomi Nation mark a noteworthy feature of American Indian intratribal politics. The conflict makes clear the powerful rifts between worldviews that are possible within a single tribe. Such conflicts are also significant as they are attempts by intratribal factions to frame the purpose of a tribe based upon competing worldviews. The Citizen Potawatomi tribe itself is divided into two competing factions: one faction associated with the current tribal chairman, John Barrett, that has emphasized economic development grounded in what was described in the previous chapter as a self-interested worldview; the other faction, called the Sacred Heart Citizen Potawatomis, who reject Barrett's economic emphasis as violating the spiritual and social nature of the tribe, is grounded closer to what was described in the previous chapter as a melancholic worldview.

For some Citizen Potawatomis, this factional conflict proves meaningful; for others, it is a distraction. The conflict allows for narratives of colonial exploitation and resistance, foundational narratives for American Indian populations, to emerge within the contemporary setting and intratribally. For those with melancholic tendencies in their worldview, this conflict, whereby they struggle for the "soul of the tribe" as one informant told me, allows them to reach unusual communion with their imagined ancestral agony. In the attempt to possess what was lost or taken, a driving motivation of melancholic worldviews, these Citizen Potawatomis express nostalgic longings for a political and social past and complain of the disenfranchisement they experience within their own tribe. This factional group initiate grievance-based politics to reopen these historical losses but are not necessarily interested in leveraging these losses for material gain. For instance, many Sacred Heart Citizen Potawatomis refuse to accept settlements for mismanaged oil royalties even after initiating the lawsuits, claiming that doing so would violate their ancestors' sacrifice (not dissimilar to the Lakota view of the Black Hills in chapter 1). To reinjure is the object of melancholic motivations.

Opposing this melancholic group is a Citizen Potawatomi faction whose worldview resembles self-interest. This faction currently controls tribal government, and these Citizen Potawatomis also utilize the conflict with the Sacred Heart Citizen Potawatomis to reaffirm their conception of the tribe as a provider of social good through economic development. And, as will be discussed at the end of this chapter, this faction uses the mourning nature of the Sacred Heart Citizen Potawatomis to frame their tribal identity as one that is uniquely adept at prospering and "getting past" the colonial experience that still keeps other tribes poor.

This chapter is divided into four sections. The first is a short description of Citizen Potawatomi conflict and the intratribal groups involved. The second brings the concept of *nostalgia* to bear on our discussion of pain and profit. As both a sentiment and emotion, nostalgia mediates how individual worldviews make sense of lived experience, ethnohistory, and loss. Nostalgia is not always a unifying force, as this section describes an instance where nostalgia may further intensify communal acrimony when factions attempt to frame tribal direction and historical meaning from different worldviews. The third section navigates the issues on which factions disagree. Specifically, it attends to two political issues that produce the most acrimony: the direction the tribe should take and the interpretation of tribal or ethnohistory. A fourth section explores the origins of this conflict and sources of these divergent worldviews. This section places the contemporary Citizen Potawatomi conflict as stemming from the twentieth-century lived experiences of families and individuals as recounted by the Citizen Potawatomi interviewees. These sections may at times overlap, as these themes are interrelated.

4.2 BACKGROUND: CITIZEN POTAWATOMI CONFLICT

At first glance, central Oklahoma would be an unlikely location for ethnic conflict. A common image of American ethnic conflict is of nineteenth- and twentieth-century Irish and Italians clashing in various examples of

Hell's Kitchens. And in comparison with the 1960s and 1970s takeovers of the Pine Ridge Reservation, Alcatraz Island, and the Bureau of Indian Affairs in Washington, D.C., and the interethnic conflict in those events, Oklahoma's ongoing intratribal conflict seems unsensational. We, the observers, may be likely to not ascribe profound or grand narrative to these intratribal conflicts or be inclined to use these for nomological theory building. When Indians compete politically against each other, the dramatic and inspirational image of political awakening among dis-possessed groups, once passive but now asserting their political agency in active resistance to oppressive institutions and outsiders, is lost. That is not what the conflicts discussed here are or represent. Rather, these intratribal conflicts indicate the complexity of politics and also represent the false assumption of ethno-based confraternity.

When Indians in Oklahoma display animosity among themselves, the backdrops are neither dramatic nor inspirational. The settings are restau-rants such as Chili's, Checkers, and Sonic (a chain founded on Citizen Potawatomi tribal land by non-Indians), gravel and concrete yards, and narrow country highways. Understandably, with such uninspiring a back-drop, political scientists are apt to miss this conflict. It fails to provide the image of political awakening or fit within the established research focus of exploring the relationships between tribes and outside governments. This intratribal conflict is also unflattering to communities that might wish to hide such divisions.

Within the towns of Shawnee and Tecumseh, Oklahoma, where the primary residential and commercial centers of the Citizen Potawatomi Nation are located, intratribal politics is spiteful. Bulldozers have been used to protect tribal headquarters from building takeovers (essentially coup attempts). Less spectacular, though more common, is the practice of using websites to spread salacious accusation. For some, these websites are a nuisance and distraction from tribal operations. For others, these web-sites provide an objective and free press that is currently lacking in the local newspapers (De Koning 2009). According to one Shawnee resident, the defamation lawsuit (often arising from these websites) is the best-practiced, modern-day Citizen Potawatomi ritual. "They seem to sue each other an awful lot," another local resident told me (Informant 2008).

The intensity of Citizen Potawatomi conflict has part of its source in tribal ethnohistory. This history includes processes resulting in the rise of a self-interested worldview and the rise of a melancholic worldview. These experiences, one of pain and the other of profit, produced deeply contrary worldviews within the tribe. Citizen Potawatomi factions identify with either the pain or the profit in their tribal ethnohistory and have worldviews of self-interest or melancholia. This division in worldviews, values, and perceptions is apparent in the factional conflict. As we see in this chapter, due to the broad historic experience of the tribe, Citizen Potawatomis could portray themselves as members of a victimized ethno-political group or as members of an ethno-conglomerate of cunning small business owners. For participants in tribal politics, these worldviews are both challenged and reinforced daily. But how is it that Citizen Potawatomis select which worldview to embrace? The best answer is that each worldview is informed by more contemporary social and economic experiences borne in the stories that Citizen Potawatomis tell of family histories and through descriptions of their lived experiences, which are individual and recent—not collective and distant.

4.3 AMERICAN INDIAN NOSTALGIA: SELF-INTEREST AND MELANCHOLIA

Like most American Indians, Citizen Potawatomis recount family stories. Among the participants I interviewed, these stories are from the twentieth century. Rarely if ever is the nineteenth century discussed. No living Potawatomi remembers firsthand the last removal in 1861 from Kansas to Oklahoma. There are few discussions of any nineteenth-century removals told from the point of family memory that I encountered. In Citizen Potawatomi oral tradition, what could be their greatest grief is that the tribal homelands in the Great Lakes are now gone. The Citizen Potawatomis I interviewed only rarely mentioned cosmologies in the forms of religion, myth, or ancient belief as forming contemporary worldviews. A limited few Citizen Potawatomis might tend a fire and talk about spirits, but nearly all still in Oklahoma recount their family's relationship to the oil extraction in the early twentieth century. These stories revolve around oil victim and oil baron and seem to constitute crucial experiences in organizing their worldviews and making sense of and contesting their collective history. Oil on Citizen Potawatomi land, and the animosity it created, will be returned to later in the chapter.

The role that lived experience has in reflecting upon ethnohistory is not a novel observation or distinct to American Indians. Anthropologist David Graeber observed something similar when examining the role of personal stories and tragedies substituting for larger political ones. Graeber writes of stories told among the people of Madagascar, "[The stories told] were much more likely to be stories of personal tragedy—usually, framed as tales of transgression and retribution. This is significant because it was especially through the lens of such personal dramas that people thought about wider historical change" (2008, 175). Citizen Potawatomi stories also involve personal and collective transgression where meaning and sense are reflected between individual and group. This reflection is the centerpiece of the notion of nostalgia, which evokes the emotional attachment to what is remembered but yet is not present or retrievable.

It would be understandable for nostalgia to be a common sentiment in American Indian communities, which have lost immeasurably significant aspects of their previous lifeways.[2] Nostalgic sentiment involves a remembrance, which on the one hand infuses value to the past and on the other provokes a mourning of it. In the expression or recognition of nostalgic emotions or sentiments, our assessment of a loss has both a settling and unsettling effect. As with any type of fantasy, which nostalgia is, we project ourselves into this remembrance but do so without present or pending anxieties. For why fantasize but not escape anxiety? Yet with nostalgic remembrance, perhaps unlike other fantasies, what we pine over is an impossible past rather than a possible future.

In a study of rural Appalachian communities, anthropologist Kathleen Stewart identifies the settling and unsettling quality in nostalgia as involving a frame or understanding of meaning. Stewart suggests that this is an emotional commitment that "creates a frame for meaning, [and] a means for dramatizing aspects of an increasingly fluid and unnamed social life" (1988, 227). In times of change and loss, when anxiety is high, nostalgia is inspirational and structural. It gives order to an unclear present, even if this order is irrelevant to all but our own recent experiences and current needs. To Stewart, nostalgia is an intermediary between imagined history or experience and sense of contemporary loss: "[Nostalgia] becomes the very lighthouse waving us back to shore—the one point on the landscape that gives hope of direction" (1988, 229). Time and its continuity are also in jeopardy. In an effort to rearrange what is perceived as fractured time, which is distorted by traumatic events, Stewart, who examines the expressions of nostalgia among Appalachian coal miners, posits a double vision quality to nostalgic expression:

> The search for a past and a place [that] leads them to reconstitute their lives in narrative form, a story designed to reassemble a broken history into a new whole. The world created there is a world unnatural and unreal; it resembles fiction or dream. They create an extreme subjectivism, an insatiable will to meaning. . . . They see themselves doubly—as they construct themselves in the local talk (and this is itself already masked and metaphoric) and as they are imaged by the distanced surround of "America" (whether nostalgically, as our "contemporary ancestors" or, in the ideology of "profess" and the "need to be realistic").

Stewart explains further,

> In the daily, lived conflict between what is and what might have been if people had not lived the lives they were forced to live or chose to live, there is a *double vision* of two lives (caught and free, *used to* and *anymore*, the city and home) differentiated by a lived experience of loss and the dream of redemption. (1988, 236)

In Stewart's double vision, nostalgics search for meaning in "a past and a place," the first criteria, and weave their contemporary lives into these larger, more distant times. Primordial identities are found in individual subjectivities that search for a sense of belonging, stability, and order in larger communal histories and meanings. Recent and individual memories become ways of ordering the past and communal unknowns, which are then interpreted as derivative of tribal values, preferences, and worldviews. In this perspective, individual life stories shape group meanings.

Nostalgia has a second duality in addition to this double vision. Though nostalgia is generally thought to create community unity, the subject of that nostalgia is potentially divisive to those managing the same polity. Comparative literature scholar Svetlana Boym, in her analysis of post-socialist Eastern Europe, describes the divisive potential of nostalgia as having two forms: restorative and reflective. Each of these nostalgias has a different provenance and motivation that are potentially contradictory. As Boym describes, "Two kinds of nostalgia are not absolute types, but rather tendencies, ways of giving shape and meaning to longing. Restorative nostalgia puts emphasis on *nostos* and proposes to rebuild the lost home and patch up the memory gaps. Reflective nostalgia dwells in *algia*, in longing and loss, the imperfect process of remembrance. The first category of nostalgics do not think of themselves as nostalgic" (2001). If the Citizen Potawatomi development and self-interested faction were placed into Byom's nostalgic categories, the faction would share considerable characteristics with the restorative nostalgics. This faction seeks to move forward and rebuild what was lost in the Great Lakes ancestral lands in the Oklahoma reservation. Contrast restorative nostalgias' attachment for rebuilding with reflective nostalgias' desire for remembering. Boym claims, "Restorative nostalgia manifests itself in total reconstructions of monuments of the past, while reflective nostalgia lingers on ruins, the patina of time and history, in the dreams of another place and another time" (2001, 41). Shall the tribe mourn its losses at the risk of never healing? Or forget these losses at the risk of never mourning? These normative questions, though beyond the aim of this book, are still worth acknowledging and are central to the politics of traumatized communities.

Reflective nostalgia is close to the memory and longing of the Sacred Heart Citizen Potawatomi and melancholic worldviews. As demonstrated by the Sacred Heart Potawatomis, and even more apparent in chapter 6 on the Rosebud Lakotas, reflective nostalgia "is a form of deep mourning that performs a labor of grief . . . through pondering pain" (2001, 41). Those who take their reference points in this form of affect are susceptible to melancholic worldviews and bind their mourning to contemporary identity through attaching meaning or significance at the individual and collective level.

The coming section seeks to explain the origins of these factions and divergent forms of nostalgia that make Citizen Potawatomi politics so acrimonious to each other.

4.4 POLITICAL FACTIONS IN THE CITIZEN POTAWATOMI NATION

To Tecumseh and Shawnee residents, tribal factions are understood as something akin to a family feud. Politically active Citizen Potawatomis are divided into two factions that often split around family or clan designation. The majority of the Citizen Potawatomis sympathize with current tribal chairman John Barrett. This faction's self-interest worldview frames the tribal collective mostly in terms of economic development, social services, efficiency, and the utilitarian aspect of American Indian rights and tends to focus on the future with regard to what projects are to be materially built, such as stores, businesses, and clinics. These future-oriented projects include larger warehouses, commercial offices, residential housing projects, and casinos on ancestral homelands. If one believes in such distinctions between culture and economic projects, which are contentious concepts in Indian country, one could characterize the Barrett faction as progressive.

Nominally and ancestrally part of the same tribe, the Sacred Heart Citizen Potawatomis dissent to the direction the tribe has taken since the early 1980s when the Barrett faction came to prominence. The Sacred Heart faction takes its name from the township of Sacred Heart, which is now abandoned, and is the more traditional tribal group. This area was settled first by Citizen Potawatomis when they migrated from Kansas, and shortly afterward the Sacred Heart Mission School was constructed. Multiple informants suggested that the Sacred Heart faction accounts for about 20 percent of the local, politically active Citizen Potawatomis. In their opposition to the direction in which Barrett has taken the tribe, Sacred Heart Citizen Potawatomis emphasize Potawatomi culture and religion, consensus-based politics, and restoration of the past. For the Oklahoma Potawatomis, politics seems to be a dialogue between two worldviews unaccommodating to each other, originating from two separate

TABLE 4.1 Differences in motivations and frames among other political characteristics in Barrett and Sacred Heart factions

	SELF-INTERESTED DEVELOPMENTAL BARRETT FACTION	MELANCHOLIC GRIEVANCE SACRED HEART BAND
Characteristic		
Organizing political principle	Collective revenue; identity pooling; service delivery	Relationships between clans
Leadership background	Local business	Local clan leaders; academia
Racial difference		
White–Potawatomi racial distinctions (similar or different)	Whites and Potawatomis are similar.	Whites and Potawatomis are different.
General White–non-Potawatomi Indian racial distinction	Seen as different; Indian lives with "pain"	Seen as different; Whites "material"; Indians "spiritual"
Citizen Potawatomi–other Indian distinction	Seen as different; Potawatomis are "pragmatic"	Seen as similar
Potawatomi migration history	Entrepreneurial triumph	Betrayal; broken treaties; Trail of Death
Worldview	Potawatomi survival and triumph through utilitarianism[1]	Continuity between Potawatomi experience and larger indigenous loss; absolutist[2]
Subjectivity	Indistinguishable between individual and communal economic activity; success through profit; greater community through social services	Links individual pain in the form of recent personal poverty or family oil exploitation to the need for community therapy and recognition of colonial wrongs
Negotiating logic	Cost-benefit	Rights-based
Formalized political expression	Tribal newspaper	Slander/news websites and blogs
Between era of colonization and contemporary era	Seen as broken; two different times	Seen as continuity; same colonial dynamics of extraction and exploitation

1. Belief that the right course of action is the one that is selected from an array of the alternatives that produce the most good (welfare/wealth/material goods) for the most people.
2. Belief that there are certain actions that we must not pursue even if pursuing them would produce the most good (welfare/wealth/material goods).

contemporary selections of older tribal experience, one corporate and the other communal.

4.4.1 SACRED HEART CITIZEN POTAWATOMIS: THE MERGER OF INDIVIDUAL AS COLONIAL EXPERIENCE

The Sacred Heart Citizen Potawatomis contend that the Barrett faction is desecrating the past. This perspective both makes their lives painful and is the result of painful lives. As the developmental faction has forwarded tribal enterprises over the last twenty years, exploiting special economic rights, such as gaming monopolies, it has minimized important forms and organizations of indigenous culture. As described in chapter 1, contemporary indigenous economic enterprises often require negotiations with the state and federal systems that ask for concessions. These concessions come in the form of relinquishing land claims or paying gaming revenue percentages.

Barrett's economic activity is an affront to Sacred Heart Citizen Potawatomis in two ways. First, Barrett negotiates with outsiders who ask him to relinquish land grievances in Kansas and Indiana, and, second, by doing so, he pushes the tribe away from its central cultural imperative and toward economic development projects. As one Sacred Heart Citizen Potawatomi declared to me, "A tribe is more than a fucking casino" (Informant 2007). As these profit-seeking activities transgress notions of identity, the sense of betrayal is profound, for it is experienced as a tribal rebuke of the Indian, whose identity is often shaped by personal and family experiences with loss and exploitation.

One could call the Sacred Heart faction more "traditional," which was a common response from the Citizen Potawatomis when asked to describe the group. People say "traditional" with greater comfort in Indian country than "progressive" or "modern." The Sacred Heart Potawatomis often use "traditional" when asked what differentiates them from non–Sacred Heart Potawatomis. When I asked to define what "traditional" means to them regarding tribal identity, a characteristic response was, "It is about belonging, belonging in a network of relationships. These relationships are historical and have importance to you and who you are" (Informant 2007).

Sacred Heart Citizen Potawatomis, like other groups who describe themselves as traditional, find solace in being Indian. It is clear to those who talk with the Sacred Heart members that, whereas indigenous heritage brought suffering in the past, it now seems to provide an opportunity for healing as well. Sacred Heart Citizen Potawatomis bracket their socio-emotional lives with a sense of belonging, mutual caring, and ethnofraternity. Lives are linked through friends, clans, and kinship, and it is in this communal model that their individual hopes and losses gain greater significance. Despite aspects of this healing, resounding pain and melancholy surround it. There is a strong, almost obsessive relationship with loss and pain.

In interviews there was greater proclivity by Sacred Heart Citizen Potawatomis to intertwine nostalgic solace with pain. A pronounced feature of melancholia that separates it from nostalgia or mourning is the attempt to recapture previous loss through unsuccessful grief. The Sacred Heart Citizen Potawatomis often express a deep sense of nostalgia and remorse simultaneously. The faction's members lead lives in cultural and historic tension. In the recounting of life stories that conveyed meanings of lived experiences, these informants seem to make interchangeable the individual and the collective indigenous experience. For instance, a clear analogy emerged in many of my interviews with the Sacred Heart Citizen Potawatomis that revolved around giving and taking, or generosity and greediness. As one Sacred Heart Citizen Potawatomi told me, "My mother told me that I was a giver and that is going to make my life difficult. You end up with a lot of takers in your life, son. That is why you've had a difficult road. Those takers latch on to you and pretty soon you're empty" (Informant 2007). Such reflection is a fusion of the individual experience with the colonial and collective dispossession. Perhaps greater meaning is discovered in the individual's lived experience, sense is made from complexity, and confusing behaviors are explained. In such stories, we are soothed and saddened by placing ourselves in larger narratives—ethnic or otherwise—of justice and pain.

Despite the gained meanings from the recounting of loss and abuse, this modern ritual is not without liability. These feelings may cease, but in framing the world in these terms indignation and pain is nearby. In interviews, the Sacred Heart Potawatomis use words such as "religion," "culture," "lifeways," and "sacred"—words we would expect from more traditional Indians, but ones that express notions similar to communal affect. Yet words of indignation, injustice, grievance, exploitation, and pain follow or are intertwined with this affect. My impression from hearing conclusions after the recounting of lived experiences is that the Sacred Heart Citizen Potawatomis feel profoundly depleted through interaction with the outside world. Life is an uneven exchange or a struggle against the materially self-interested. This depletion is spiritual, psychological, financial, or physical. Far more frequently than in conversations with the Barrett faction, the Sacred Heart faction included unsolicited information about health problems such as diabetes, cancer, death, and addiction. Yet in expressing senses of fellowship and belonging, the Sacred Heart Citizen Potawatomis also show for each other and their tribal identity emotions and expressions of joy, love, and hope for a less painful world. Joy seems disappointingly fleeting, and, once pleasure is identified in the current moment with the recognition of togetherness, it then serves as a prologue to evoking negative feelings and the articulation of loss, depression, isolation, and abuse. In this way, the conversation oscillates between Indian decency and white exploitation, with each experience setting the stage for the next. Justice and injustice emerge as personal and indigenous issues, embedded in recounting the paths of the ancestors and one's own journey. The Sacred Heart Citizen Potawatomis approach the larger tribe looking to express these feelings and feel robbed—yet again.

4.4.2 BARRETT AND THE SELF-INTEREST FACTION

The majority of politically interested Citizen Potawatomis support the current tribal chairman, John "Rocky" Barrett, whose tenure dates back to 1984. This faction of Citizen Potawatomis and its supporters prioritize development and the communal economic relationship between tribe and member. As tribal chairman, Barrett is the chief administrator for the tribe. This position is powerful; it is both a managerial and policy-making position. Barrett can terminate employees, set agency goals, and negotiate for the tribe with outside governments. It is difficult to separate Barrett's bureaucratic authority from the personal authority he has amassed after twenty-five years in office. After being tribal chairman and guiding the Citizen Potawatomis to relative economic successes, Barrett walks through the headquarters with a self-awareness that is neither exactly menacing nor benign.

The Citizen Potawatomi tribe is a comparatively successful tribal government if such achievements are measured economically. In John Barrett's tenure as chairman, tribal enterprise has expanded significantly. As of 2014, the tribe was the largest employer in the county, with business revenues in excess of $100 million and nearly 1,400 employees. It is clear that the Citizen Potawatomi orientation prioritizes economic development. Some local people attribute this success to genetics. One Shawnee resident told me that business is "natural" to the Potawatomis. The Citizen Potawatomi economic fortune is a recent phenomenon, only dating back to the 1980s. Federal government reform in the Reagan administration sought to downsize the Bureau of Indian Affairs (BIA). Believing the tribes would administer Indian program funding more efficiently than the BIA (which would remain as a supervisory agency), the federal government dispersed funding directly to the tribes. Tribal funding was less than $50,000 annually in the early 1980s. The former Citizen Potawatomi headquarters, before the current building was constructed in the late 1980s, was an old trailer. As Barrett describes, "It had a phone and desk, but that was about it" (2008). In presentations, Barrett shows a photo of this trailer in the 1980s to emphasize the economic change of the last thirty years.

Substantially greater wealth came for the tribe in the mid-1990s, when gaming revenues reached into the tens of millions of dollars annually. Tribal funding was generally from federal grants when Barrett took office and from the mid-1990s casino boom, when gaming facilities became a major economic development strategy for tribes. The meaning-making associated with large economic transitions is receiving greater focus from scholars. Anthropologist Jessica Cattelino's work on the Seminoles, for instance, suggests that the cash distributions from casino revenues have become new cultural spheres (Cattelino 2006, 2008). Money then creates geographical spaces that are transformed into new cultural centers. Citizen Potawatomi social services have become cultural spaces for members, paralleling what Cattelino describes regarding Seminole economic enterprises such as alligator wrestling. Housing and health grants supported a tribal apparatus that became increasingly adept at finding more federal grants. Elders have food provided free of charge in dining halls. Indian children play in day care subsidized by casino profits. According to many I spoke with, these interactions through programs are an important part of the Citizen Potawatomi community.

The economic story of the Citizen Potawatomi tribe is not particularly different from that of many other Oklahoma tribes. Gaming revenue supplied the capital for business enterprises in the mid-1980s throughout many Oklahoma tribes, with a significant increase in revenue occurring in the late 1990s during the national economic upswing and second wave of gaming expansion. Along with two casinos, the Potawatomis own multiple housing developments, numerous farms, a mansion built by a local oil-wealthy family during the Oklahoma oil boom, a rock quarry, a concrete fill company, a grocery store, a petroleum station, a smoke shop, a golf course, and a radio station. Showing a somewhat detailed knowledge of the economic activities and successful rents, Barrett-led Potawatomis will tell you that these enterprises vary in profitability with the tax collected at the grocery store. Among all of the tribal enterprises, the radio station generates the least revenue.

The Citizen Potawatomi Business Committee, which serves as a representative body for the tribe and oversees part of tribal operations, is comprised of mostly local business owners who are elected to four-year terms. As of my writing in 2012, of the five members of the committee, three own local businesses. A fourth, Citizen Potawatomi Nation vice chairwoman Linda Capps, taught business at a Tecumseh high school (Capps 2007). The fifth member worked in the marketing department of a local bank. During meetings of the business committee that I observed, the Barrett faction, which holds all the seats on the committee, discussed tribal services and earnings from various business enterprises. Human issues, such as the social needs of members and communities, are also addressed, but significantly less so than income. It is clear that the calculus of the leading members of Barrett's developmental faction is not that of empathy or Marxian fellow-feeling, but the logic of businesspeople or possibly social workers and community regulators. "Does he work? Is he reliable and clean?" Barrett asked the tribe's housing director, trying to solicit a trailer for a golf course employee and member who was living in the course's maintenance shed (Informant 2007). More often than not, tribal charity and social services are extended to citizens who demonstrate responsible behavior.

It is difficult to gauge the degree to which the Barrett faction is guided by American Indian cosmology or primordial sentiments. During Barrett's tenure, the tribe has built and funded a tribal cultural center and museum. The Citizen Potawatomi Heritage Center, which opened in 2005, facilitates cultural programs for the young and elders and offers language programs. Culture is relegated away from the attention of the tribal council to less central institutions that build monuments to Potawatomi history. Though a Pueblo Indian informant from the Southwest told me, "Real Indians don't need museums" (Informant 2007). These types of projects include a small ceremonial podium near a man-made lake where, if Citizen Potawatomis wish, they can be given Indian names. Neither American Indian religion nor traditional spiritual values were discussed at the Citizen Potawatomi Business Committee meetings I attended. Larger meetings incorporate a Potawatomi prayer, and a ceremonial pipe is smoked. Traditional fire-starting, which is difficult but may be the most sacred Potawatomi political tradition, is occasionally done at the large clan gatherings. Barrett and other officials partake in this activity; however, a Sacred Heart Citizen Potawatomi mentioned that "Barrett can never get the fire started when others are watching" (Informant 2007).

The Citizen Potawatomi Business Committee was most comfortable speaking about economic activities during interviews. Committee members showed me rental properties that the tribe built or purchased to lease to Citizen Potawatomis at subsidized rates (the tribe subsidized part of the costs and employed programs such as low-cost housing, elder meals, fitness centers, and childcare with Department of Housing and Urban Development grants). The tour also featured two large stone estates (that used to be oil mansions in the first half of the twentieth century), which the tribe purchased recently, garnering significant criticism. One Sacred Heart Citizen Potawatomi said, "That was a foolish idea," and another more suspicious Potawatomi said, "Rocky just bought those because it made his land nearby more valuable" (Informant 2007). There were also modest and middle-class homes that were rented to tribal members at a below-market rate after being subsidized by the tribe. The tribe also helps local Citizen Potawatomis finance their homes with funding from the federal government and tribal business enterprises.

Citizen Potawatomis associated with the Barrett faction imply that they are unlike other Indians and that this racial or ethnic distinction lies in both preferences and capacity. They promote a sense of Citizen Potawatomi exceptionalism. In this perspective, other Indians do not engage in economic activities as well as do the Potawatomis and are "weighed down by their emotions," according to a Potawatomi who supports Barrett (Informant 2007). According to those who support Barrett, I was told over and over in interviews that the Potawatomis have always been "businesspeople." Another common characterization is that other Indians make mistakes that the Potawatomis do not. The Citizen Potawatomis "see opportunities all the time," an informant explained in a discussion over lunch at the casino buffet (Informant 2007). One story came to light about the Sac and Fox Nation, whose reservation is also in Shawnee. In the mid-1990s, the Sac and Fox tribe had purchased land in downtown Oklahoma City. The tribe was attempting to place the land into trust status. This would allow the Sac and Fox Nation to operate a casino in central Oklahoma City, which would have been exceedingly profitable, as revenue is typically contingent upon proximity to a large population. The Sac and Fox Nation was unable to successfully negotiate the BIA criteria for the land transfer. I was told, "They [Sac and Fox Nation] got pissed off and quit at the first barrier" and "We [Citizen Potawatomis] wouldn't have done that" (Informant 2007). When asked why the Sac and Fox tribe quit, the interviewee told me, "Because they had some bad experiences with business, like a clothing manufacturing plant that failed, and thought that was going to happen again" (Informant 2007). Now that high-stakes gaming is a polarizing issue, there is little chance that the property the Sac and Fox Nation owns in Oklahoma City will become a casino. This is not to suggest that the Potawatomis hold other tribes in low regard; they see themselves differently than other Indians, as "more successful" (Informant 2007). The Citizen Potawatomis who identify with Chairman Barrett would reflect upon their position as an island of industriousness in a sea of missed opportunities and pity. As a Barrett supporter told me, "We aren't really like other Indians; we are the type of people who are looking for more" (Informant 2007).

4.5 CITIZEN POTAWATOMI CONFLICT CHARACTERISTICS

Citizen Potawatomi conflict has three characteristics: (1) the lines of conflict are pronounced; (2) the division between ideologies is broad, with little common ground; and (3) the animosity is strong. Potawatomi factions are relatively highly organized and cohesive. Like other groups examined in this work, the Citizen Potawatomis have two factions, but these factions are more explicit than those found among other tribes such as the Pueblos or Rosebud Lakotas. There is little dispute about the existence of Citizen Potawatomi factions. These factions are ordered by family with last names to distinguish membership—not only because they are identifiable with names but also because they have found steady mediums through which to express their ideas. The Barrett faction controls the tribal newspaper, the *HowNiKan*, which angers the Sacred Heart Citizen Potawatomis and inspires them to use websites and blogs to publish their opinions. These sites, however, are usually eventually shut down and restarted under new addresses. According to a Sacred Heart Citizen Potawatomi, these shutdowns result from lawsuits by individuals associated with John Barrett.

The Citizen Potawatomis aligned with Barrett interpret the difference in worldview as a family feud, possibly due to the group's interest in minimizing the impact of the disagreement. This interpretation is partially true. The hostility is between families and clans. Yet the acrimony results from how Potawatomi families experienced the twentieth century differently, with one group gaining economic prominence and the other dealing with dispossession.

For the Sacred Heart Citizen Potawatomis, votes on economic activities are interpreted as erosive to social relationships. When the Barrett faction attempts to sanction cultural or religious events, it is regarded as a mockery of the deep, spiritual aspects of American Indian cosmology and religion championed by the Sacred Heart Citizen Potawatomi faction. To Barrett's self-interested faction, the Sacred Heart group's remonstrance undermines tribal progress without purpose. Lawsuits and accusations of corrupt elections, which happen nearly every election cycle, embarrass the tribe and potentially tarnish the image of Potawatomi exceptionalism.

With communal goals producing conflict at every stage, these schisms prove more significant than policy. Quarrels are not only broad but also vehement. Intratribal rage originates from more than policy disagreements, though those are catalysts. The anger in the polity is connected to the fact that American Indian politics is personal and involves individual identity and lived experiences, which in turn create worldviews that frame tribal political life and ethnicity itself.

Identity-based political discourse raises two questions that link self to worldview: What are Indians? and, often asked anxiously, Why am I an Indian? It is both the group and individual experience that make this conflict broad and intense. For example, the Citizen Potawatomi population has multiple worldviews that embrace divergent moral outlooks that are appropriate for their lived experiences. The more important and essential question probes the personal and family histories that construct individual subjectivities, and examines what informs an individual's selection of a worldview and subsequent faction.

The personal nature and subjectivity in this conflict are apparent to see and also easily confused. The animosity between factions is severe because it is personal and about the individuals themselves but relates to ethnohistory from their lived experiences (two important and recent works that draw upon lived experiences in debates about belonging and membership are Dennison 2012 and Strum 2002). This animosity gives local conflict the appearance of a family feud, but it is the class differences that ushers families into tribal factions. Political attacks are mixed with personal accusations and often include short stories about the rival's family history, pointing to subjectivity. "They are just angry at all of us that their grandfather was put in jail sixty years ago by mine"; "His father was a white man who just married an Indian to get his hands on Indian oil; that's something you need to know about him"; or "his father was a drunk" (Informant 2008) are sentiments expressed about rivals' contemporary ancestors. All of these statements, interestingly, cast the rival as either entrepreneurial to the point of engaging in sexual colonialism or as bitter, resentful, and chained to the past.

These are personal battles between individuals, but also between individuals and themselves. Personal identity and the attention given by American Indians to their individual pasts infuse a deep bellicosity into the communal debates. This conflict is not solely over worldviews but is over the experiences that form decisions about worldview selection. These conflicts are not just about tribal and Indian identities. They are also about the values that individual participants have regarding the interpretations of their own history that merge with the groups' and larger worldviews.

4.5.1 FROM TRAUMA TO TRIUMPH: CONFLICT IN THE REFLECTION OF POTAWATOMI POLITICAL FORMS

As claimed earlier, these disparities between the Sacred Heart and Barrett factions represent deeper schisms in approaches to Indian or tribal identity, not simply family feuds or random community strife. I suggest that Citizen Potawatomi factions display a higher degree of conflict around three cultural markers: (1) political forms; (2) Potawatomi identity (understandings of what it is to be Potawatomi contrasted with other ethnic and indigenous groups); and (3) Citizen Potawatomi history.

Before constitutional reorganization in the twentieth century, the tribal government consisted of a large general council called the Fire Council. Decisions were made at these types of councils for many tribes. Though exact methods varied, villages were under part of a confederation and sent representatives to the council, which deliberated tribal decisions. Starting in the late nineteenth century, during periods of reorganization, this form of deliberation generally disappeared. The factions have contrary interpretations of the Potawatomi government during this time. The Sacred Heart Citizen Potawatomis describe political decisions being made at the Fire Council, something akin to a general council of politically interested Citizen Potawatomis. The meetings sought consensus among members with special status for elders. "Meetings lasted days and required people to agree on the important issues," one Sacred Heart informant explained (though it should be noted there was divergence on the degree of "consensus" by the

Sacred Heart informants) (Informant 2007). Potawatomis associated with the Barrett faction hold starkly different opinions of the general council. One Potawatomi, who described himself as a "mostly" Barrett supporter and who was old enough to see the Fire Council when he was a young adult, described the meetings:

> A mess best described it. Nothing got done. People were just shout-ing at each other, nobody was in charge, and many people were talking about something that had nothing to do with the meeting. People just went on and on and told you about what they had for lunch as a kid. It was no way to run a tribe. Maybe it was like long ago but it wasn't working well for today's world. (Informant 2008)

Barrett conversely places the historical roots of current Potawatomi polit-ical strife in these meetings. Contrary to the goal of consensus, I was told by Barrett that the "general council started so much acrimony in the 1970s; I think it probably led to the attempted tribal takeover in 1984" (2008). The claim that consensus should determine tribal decisions was also ques-tioned by Barrett: "The pure democracy that the Fire Council was is not traditional. Thirty or forty are not a majority, the Sacred Heart ran the general council [referring to Fire Council]" (2008).

The Fire Council was replaced in the mid-1970s via the passing of constitutional amendments, which were highly contested by Sacred Heart Citizen Potawatomis who openly protested the election as "fixed" and the amendments as violating Potawatomi custom (Barrett 2008). Challenges to Barrett leadership stem primarily from Leon Bruno, the Sacred Heart faction's leading political figure who was tribal chairman before Barrett (2008). A widespread conceptualization among those associated with Barrett, when asked about Bruno's administration and earlier leaders, was that it was "inefficient" and rife with "missed opportunities" (Informant 2007). The language used in describing the current administration mostly, if not exclusively, echoes that of a business plan. Spirituality and religion are rarely raised to the level of categories of Indian expression or as criteria for tribal expectation.

Barrett himself has much to say about the way the tribe was run under his predecessors. His comments do not probe the personal characteristics of Bruno and other rivals, but Barrett observes that times have changed for the Potawatomis and leaders need "business judgment" (2008). In my interview with Barrett, he suggested that "if the Sacred Heart took control of this tribe, we could probably go bankrupt. There are a lot of good things about Potawatomi and capable people out there, but you need to know something about business in this age. . . . It is a different time" (Barrett 2008).

4.5.2 MIGRATION HISTORY AND DISAGREEMENTS

The most hostile feelings between Citizen Potawatomis and Sacred Heart Citizen Potawatomis are saved for discussions of their ethnohistory, which includes removal and migration. Depending upon who is asked, the tribal migration from Indiana to Oklahoma seems either an indigenous escape from genocide or a march of small businessmen to gaming monopolies. As one Sacred Heart Citizen Potawatomi said while discussing the nature of Citizen Potawatomi migration in an interview, "Our history was as bad as any tribes' [history]. We were moved violently during a two decade period of horrible bloodshed in America that was as awful, as bad as any time. Then they did it again. The [U.S.] government betrayed our people at every turn. In Indiana, then Iowa, then Kansas. It was awful, our people died in incredible numbers. We were given nothing they promised" (Informant 2008).

The migration, or removal, is often referred to as the Trail of Death, a play on the Cherokee Trail of Tears. To the Sacred Heart Citizen Potawatomis, the removal represents the climax of an era of betrayal. By placing the Citizen Potawatomi history into grander stories of general American exploitation, the Sacred Heart members move and understand themselves as compatriots in loss with other tribes, such as the Lakotas or Cherokees.

The Barrett Potawatomis hold a different interpretation of the migration. This faction's stories are of survival and Citizen Potawatomi exceptionalism compared to other North American Indian groups who suffered:

Potawatomi were always pragmatic people and our history shows we were. We weren't treated well, I'm not saying that. The [U.S.] government put us with other groups like in Kansas. Those things didn't work out, we were different than them. The other Indians wanted different things, they were, you know, kind of more traditional and wanted to do things the old ways. We Potawatomi were always looking for a new place and new opportunity and that is how we ended up in Oklahoma. (Informant 2008)

From this perspective, Citizen Potawatomi transitions involved opportunity. Colonialism's pernicious and unhelpful legacy is absent in many appraisals of Citizen Potawatomi ethnohistory. Ancestors not only were advanced by the removals but also welcomed later removals. As one Citizen Potawatomi described the Kansas to Oklahoma removal, "We wanted land we could own and that was hard in Kansas because it was trust land. They [those who became Citizen Potawatomi] jumped at the opportunity to come here [Oklahoma] and have our own land" (Informant 2008). This Citizen Potawatomi's framing of the tribe's ethnohistory and provenance is at odds with that of the Sacred Heart faction's in nearly every sense. For the developmental Barrett faction, trauma is inverted into economic triumph or appropriated into the faction's sense of exceptionalism. The era of trauma ended, something the Sacred Heart faction disputes. As a Barrett supporter who worked for the tribe told me when I asked him what an Indian is in America, "An Indian walks in America with a heavy heart. They are in a lot of pain and carry it deep. They seem stoic but deep down they're feeling a lot" (Informant 2008). I then asked if that described him he said, "No, not really" (Informant 2008).

Indeed, Citizen Potawatomi history is complicated enough to accommodate these different perspectives. Prominent Potawatomi historians R. David Edmunds and James Clifton appreciated the dual and conflicting nature of the Potawatomi experience. Edmunds and Clifton recognized that the migration from the Potawatomis' ancestral home on the Indiana shores of the Great Lakes to Oklahoma took multiple decades and included both episodes of survival and of demise (Clifton [1977] 1998; Edmunds 1987). Yet the disparities of interpretations are vastly more extreme than the ambiguity of the events. If there were a truth to Potawatomi migration, or at least a great clarity to its character, both positions of opportunity and death would be incorporated. Particularly emblematic of this period in

Potawatomi history is Chief Abram Burnett's cane. Burnett lead part of the tribe during the removal period, and his cane, displayed in the cultural center, is clearly fashioned to a nineteenth-century businessman's up-market taste. It has a silver knob handle and a black finish but also conceals an eighteen-inch knife within the shaft to deal with the violence associated with Indian status in the nineteenth century. A remembered figure among Citizen Potawatomis today, Burnett is recognized less for his acts as a chief during the Jacksonian removal period than as an object of curiosity—his physical stature was so substantial (i.e., obese) that it required his burial in a wooden box originally constructed to move a piano.

With exceptions such as the Isleta Pueblos, who are the subject of the next chapter, American Indian peoples are geographically situated differently than during pre-colonial times. The growing demand for land in the Great Lakes region by Euro-American settlers during the nineteenth century increased the premium for Potawatomi land. Indian groups in these regions were forced to relocate elsewhere during these expansions, which exacerbated the alliances among Indian groups. The Great Lakes removal of the mid-nineteenth century, it has been argued by historian Keith Drury, has not received similar attention as the Cherokee removal, a contemporary plight (2007). Further, the Great Lakes removal and the conflict surrounding it have been overshadowed by the Great Plain wars following the American Civil War, leading to an underappreciation of the violence in this region. Historian James Clifton identified the 1830s as a period when the Potawatomis faced intense pressure from newcomers that was "only increased by the hordes of new settlers pouring into Michigan and Illinois, now made easier and cheaply accessible from the east by the opening of the Erie Canal" ([1977] 1998, 238).

The aggression from settlement reached its apex in the Black Hawk War. Spurred by removal and white geographic encroachment, the allied tribes waged war against settlers. Led by the Sauk leader Black Hawk, Potawatomi warriors fought settlers, militias, and the regular army. As for most American Indian groups in the old Northwest, the war and the removal were deadly. Yet this work is concerned with contemporary tribal political culture and its link to this painful past. There are no personal or family stories from either the Indian or Kansas removals. Yet some

Potawatomis identify grievance, loss, and abuse as the primary lens in understanding the indigenous experience.

Like discussions of Indian identity, what is worthy of attention in competing historiographies among the Potawatomi factions, beyond solely the identities themselves, is that these could reflect how identity is framed. However the collective ethnohistory makes sense, Potawatomi identity is likely arranged or made congruent with more recent social and economic lived experiences that the sub-tribal group (often family or clan) encountered. The businesspeople of the tribe who hold office, like Barrett, see themselves in the Potawatomi story of migration through a pursuit of increasing economic opportunities. The framing of ethnohistory in this way only became possible after these business classes were created through encounters with the petroleum industry in the mid-twentieth century. Further, in the tribe's history, the establishment of casinos also resonates nostalgically with the entrepreneurial class's interpretation of the forced relocations and migrations. The Citizen Potawatomi telos is reached, and the migration gains greater significance and purpose than that of historical happenstance. The Sacred Heart Citizen Potawatomis' interpretation of history differs from the Barrett-led Citizen Potawatomis'. The Sacred Heart Citizen Potawatomis connect oil theft and poverty as a continuation of the abuse at the hands of non-Indians during the removals sanctioned by the American government.

The self-interest and business interest that lead the tribe now under Barrett are the same motivations that led to the dispossession of the Potawatomi homeland. This is intensified in the perspectives of the Sacred Heart Potawatomis, who understand themselves as the traditional leadership class sent to Oklahoma to make a path for later groups. The families who identify most with the Sacred Heart faction claim to reside in the earliest Citizen Potawatomi settlements on the reservation according to maps found in the Citizen Potawatomi cultural center. The towns of Shawnee and Tecumseh were settled later in the more contemporary remote regions of Pottawatomi County (alternative spelling for *Potawatomi*), but no clear or vetted history has been written on the Kansas to Oklahoma migration. No one disputes the Sacred Heart group's claim to have arrived earlier than other Citizen Potawatomis, but their claim to have been the original leadership clan is not accepted outside of their faction. More meaningful than the historical record, perhaps, is the way in which the Sacred Heart Potawatomis talk about the land in Oklahoma.

Many contemporary Citizen Potawatomis no longer own title to the land allotted them. This is true of the Sacred Heart region of the reservation. From the stories the Sacred Heart Potawatomis tell, they seemed to have lost the land in the last sixty years and moved to other locations within the county. This local, recent loss is compounded by its projection into larger grievances, and the reverse is equally true.

Ceremony is a significant part of Sacred Heart Potawatomis' communal life. Unlike most Citizen Potawatomis, they practice ritual sweats. This is a space of death in many ways. In these lodges, death both brackets and encompasses the experience. With only darkness between dirt and blanket, the dead march often in the minds of living. Prayer conducted in pitch darkness and hot steam makes the gauging of time difficult (which is probably an intended effect). Within an hour-long rite, perhaps half of the time at the beginning and end of the ceremony is used to pray for the deceased and sick. Death seems to be in the forefront of the participants' minds. They told me of missing those who had passed. "I'm still affected" or "recovering" were phrases mentioned often (Informant 2008). In American Indian communities it is difficult to differentiate between what is therapeutic mourning and what is melancholia.

There were no Potawatomi massacres by U.S. troops in Oklahoma unlike there were in the conflicts of the old Northwest, Black Hawk War, and Jacksonian removal. There were, however, instances in which government negligence created causalities during the migration from Indiana to Kansas, and the Sacred Heart Citizen Potawatomis talk about this often. On the two-month march from Indiana to Kansas, the Citizen Potawatomis sustained a high death rate. Between September 4, 1838, and November 4, 1838, the migratory population lost approximately 5 percent of its people to death (Drury 2007). In addition to these documented deaths, another 10 percent of the migration party went missing. The presumption is that many escaped custody and fled to be Indians without a tribe (Edmunds 1987, 244).

When the diminished Citizen band arrived in Kansas, the land was held in trust (Edmunds 1987). The Citizen Potawatomi Band spent close to two decades in Kansas and was grouped with the Prairie Band Potawatomis (a separate tribe within the larger Potawatomi cultural group). During the time in Kansas, federal Indian policy changed. The desire for Indians to assimilate to Euro-American society gained popularity, and the protection of Indian cultural distinctness lost favor with federal Indian advocates. Criticism of the Kansas Potawatomis as unproductive resulted in a proposal to remove trust land status from portions of the Kansas reservation (Clifton 1987). Among tribal members, there is a sense that non-industriousness is a vice—or, to put it in different terms, there is an apparent resentment of those who are capable of economically contributing but do not do so, citing tradition as a reason. Citizen Potawatomis, usually developmentalists, will slander idle tribal members with the term "blanket-ass-Indians" to refer to Indians who do not work but sit on blankets panhandling or selling jewelry (Informant 2008). It is specifically reserved for Indians who trade on ethnic images of "full-time cultural Indians" (Informant 2008).

Disparities in landownership and being grouped together with a different tribe made for awkward economic and cultural conditions for the Potawatomis in Kansas. The developmentalists believe that this led the Citizen Potawatomis to search for new lands. Sacred Heart Citizen Potawatomis claim that the railroad lobbied the federal government for the Citizen Potawatomi side of the Kansas reservation, becoming the impetus for the second removal. The remaining allotted lands in Kansas were becoming increasingly valuable for two reasons. Eastern Americans were starting to migrate toward this farmland. Additionally, rail companies were expanding westward and found the Prairie and Citizen Potawatomis' Kansas reservation geographically and legally ideal. Land was approved to be opened in Oklahoma in exchange for portions of the Kansas reservation. The families that chose to leave in exchange for the new allotment lands in Oklahoma became the contemporary Citizen Potawatomi Nation.

4.5.3 SURVIVAL AND VICTIMHOOD IN POTAWATOMI IDENTITY: EXCEPTIONALISM OR ABUSE?

The Trail of Death, the twenty-year period in Kansas, and the removal to Oklahoma make Potawatomi history complicated enough to satisfy both factions' contemporary worldviews. Historical experience has produced two features for contemporary Citizen Potawatomis: (1) it has given them a varied historical and economic background from which to draw meaning that is often contradictory (economically enfranchised or geographically disposessed, for instance); and (2) the historical experience has material legacies that impact how Citizen Potawatomis frame both their individual lived experience and their collective ethnohistory.

The multiple migrations were acts of entrepreneurship, survival, and endurance, as the Barrett faction believes. The decision to leave Kansas was likely for economic gain but perhaps was only out of a context of economic desperation. The Sacred Heart Citizen Potawatomis see the last migration, from Kansas to Oklahoma, as a result of having their land seized by the expanding railroad. After the historic reality that both narratives could be true, the question becomes, how did the Potawatomis choose between these narratives? When asked about how Potawatomis are similar or dissimilar to other Indians, two types of responses emerge. Sympathizers with the development faction are quick to place the Citizen Potawatomis as something exceptional in the American Indian world. "[The Citizen] Potawatomi are different, we are a more pragmatic people [compared to other American Indian groups]," I was told by one Citizen Potawatomi. Other descriptions, including "problem-solving," "good at business," and "assimilated," were also used to describe Potawatomi uniqueness (Informant 2007). When asked about what difference there was between Indians and whites, one interviewee who sympathized with the Barrett faction said, "Whites and Indians, there isn't any real difference. Everyone is trying to get ahead in this world" (Informant 2007). Consensus was not achieved among the Barrett development faction over the differences between the Indians and whites.

In an interview with a college newspaper, Vice Chairwoman Linda Capps discussed her experience dealing with racism: "My family suffered economic barriers. They could have been contributed by being an Indian, but it took a small part. . . . I would like to think that I have overcome that [discrimination] in my lifetime and if I did ever meet it, I did overcome it" (Elliott 2004). Capps is unwilling to fully attribute racism as a cause to her poverty and is hesitant to say it was a factor in her life's trajectory. This stands in contrast to the frame that the Sacred

Heart Citizen Potawatomis hold of racism and greed as causing continual exploitation over centuries.

The Sacred Heart Citizen Potawatomis see greater distinctions between whites and Indians and greater commonality between the Citizen Potawatomis and other Indians. "We are supposed to be just like other Indians," was one explanation (Informant 2008). The brisk answer was quickly followed by a certain resentfulness by the same interviewee, "Yeah, but other Indians are laughing at us. They think it's hilarious what the tribe is doing" (Informant 2008). When I asked the interviewee to clarify, the response was, "We look greedy, like white men, trying to get as much as we can" (Informant 2008). Another response to the question about white and Indian differences was, "Indians are suppose[d] to be more spiritual. And we are. We believe in sacred things and relationships between each other. That is very important. We care for each other more than whites" (Informant 2008). Among Sacred Heart Citizen Potawatomis, it seemed that there was some consensus that a difference existed between whites and Indians. The Barrett development faction understood the primary difference as being between themselves and other Indians who were less adept at business.

4.5.4 CLASS FORMATIONS IN THE POTAWATOMI TWENTIETH CENTURY

Compared to the other tribes in this book, the Citizen Potawatomis are relatively diverse in terms of economic class structure and historical memory repertoires. Ethnographic accounts of their conflict also make them the most openly fractious polity in the book. Pervading these dynamics is the experience the tribe had with Oklahoma oil extraction during the nineteenth century. The presence of oil and the ability to take advantage of this resource was a seminal event in the formation of contemporary Potawatomi politics, though it goes unrecognized by Potawatomi historians, so our analysis relies upon historians of other tribes. It is nonetheless striking that the most vocal participants in bellicose politics are those families that were shaped by twentieth-century oil. The Barrett faction was the beneficiary of oil revenues, and the Sacred Heart faction carry the deep belief that they were cheated out of oil.

Historian Terry Wilson's *The Underground Reservation: Osage Oil* examines oil exploration and wealth in early twentieth-century Oklahoma (1985). Oil extraction explains the new forms of cleavages within the Osage tribe that were not present earlier in the Osage tribe's history. Even on trust land, which much of the Osage Reservation was, it could be assumed that the benefits from oil would be dispersed throughout the tribe. Wilson claims that the oil boom in the region produced something else. Significant pressure from inside and outside the tribe to divide the lands into individual allotments resulted in the creation of intense pockets of wealth and Indian oil barons. After oil was discovered, only a signature was required for drilling rights to be exchanged. The price of rights to speculative drilling reached as high as $1,300,000 in 1928 to drill on a 160-acre allotment (Wilson 1985). As one might imagine, wealth became tremendous and uneven. My grandmother lived on the Osage Reservation until a teenager while her father was a sharecropper for an Osage oil well owner. She described Osage wealth during this period in this way:

> The little [Osage] girls had beautiful clothes. At school they would wear white rabbit coats that were so soft. I still remember. My sisters were jealous of me that I had Osage friends because they would take me out every day for ice cream. [My grandmother describes herself as "chubby" until she finished school and no longer benefited from the free ice cream.] My father farmed for the Osage on their land. The old Indian man, who owned the land, would drive up to check on the farm every week. He arrived in a white limousine driven by a black man who would translate for him, he didn't speak English. It was a sight. (Lickliter 2007)

A black limousine driver translating between Osage and English for a white sharecropper and a minor American Indian oil baron in the 1930s is a stretch to our sense of class and race. Division within the Osage tribe occurred from the presence of wealth. Osages referred to membership in a way that was not present before: "the haves" and "the have-nots" (Wilson 1985). And the Osage polity suffered from this extraction and the uneven economic landscape it created.

Oil also brought a new interest in American Indian women of this region. In the rush to secure oil royalties, whites descended upon the Osages not only with contracts but also as suitors. White men sought to marry Osage women to gain advantage with the tribe over drilling, which became a long pattern of resource exchange between American Indians and outsiders. Particularly telling of how oil genetically "polluted" the tribe through self-interest is what some Sacred Heart Citizen Potawatomis claim about Barrett's family background. I heard multiple versions from Sacred Heart Citizen Potawatomis, usually holding in anger with limited success, of Chairman Barrett's father only marrying an Indian woman "to get his hands on Indian oil" (Informant 2008). Sacred Heart Potawatomis infer that tribal women were pillaged as was Potawatomi land, and that these exploitations were not centuries ago but occurred as recently as the mid-nineteenth century. It is a vivid grafting of a narrative of mineral pillage to sexual pillage and, by extension, to wombs. Chairman Barrett, in the perspective of certain members, one supposes, is even genetically tainted by this oil exploitation.

No work on Citizen Potawatomi oil has yet been published similar to Wilson's book on Osage oil. What was sought in this chapter was to consider how oil, wealth, and dispossession frame Citizen Potawatomi discourse on identity and worldview. Based on how informants frame ethnicity, motivation, and history, it is not inaccurate to assume that the Citizen Potawatomis had a similar experience as the Osages, though on a smaller scale. When asked about oil, a Sacred Heart Citizen Potawatomi told me, "Those oil companies robbed us. They paid us only a fraction of its worth. My grandfather was a good man, he thought you could take people by their word" (Informant 2008). In a January 18, 2004, *Time Magazine* article on the *Cobell v. Salazar* litigation, a class-action lawsuit around mineral royalties and government negligence on Indian trust land, a Potawatomi from the Sacred Heart township recollects:

> Ruby remembers the happy days she spent as a young child on her grandfather Moses Bruno's 80-acre homestead near Shawnee, Oklahoma. There the extended Bruno family, members of the Potawatomi tribe, tended large gardens of vegetables and fruits and raised chickens, hogs and cows. On Sundays the whole family

attended the Sacred Heart Catholic Mission just down the road. But all that changed soon after oil was discovered on the Bruno property. Lease agreements were arranged with oil producers, wells were dug, and pumping began in 1939. But family members say Grampa Bruno never knew how much oil and gas were being taken out of his land or how much money he was due from their sale. (Michaels 2004)

The Potawatomis' past transpired not just on the ancestral Indiana shores but also in sacred pre-oil, bucolic Oklahoma. Swindled of both ancestral lands in Indiana and grandparents' lands, the Sacred Heart Citizen Potawatomis who identify with the exploitation of oil extraction have an understandable sense of grievance. It is this experience, not a profound cosmological or primordial one but a recent historical one, that may help frame the tribal political world through narratives of larger grievances. Recent loss sees a pattern in human behavior and works retrospectively into the past. In the Sacred Heart Citizen Potawatomi case, worldview is a function of recent early-to-mid-twentieth-century experience. The Oklahoma oil injustice is a close reminder of distant pain. Each faction frames the temporal world differently. For the Sacred Heart Citizen Potawatomis, the contemporary world is not a departure from the past but a continuation without break of both colonialism and healing. For Citizen Potawatomis who associate with Barrett and worldviews of self-interest, the contemporary world is a departure from the past. The pain is behind, not around, them.

For the families that have aligned themselves with the Sacred Heart faction, the oil theft pushes for communion with pain and the powerful pan-ethnic Indian narrative that links land loss to contemporary impoverishment. As one Sacred Heart Potawatomi told me, "We didn't get good things growing up. We didn't have cars, we didn't get money to go to school. I feel we would have been much better off had we gotten what we deserved from our oil" (Informant 2008). Another Sacred Heart Citizen Potawatomi explained in an interview, "We are trying to get back something, something that is ours to begin with. My grandfather was a good man. He was honest and did things honestly. He was taken advantage of and we think that is wrong" (Informant 2008). To him, his grandfather was "the American Indian" and his grandfather's land his own removed "homeland."

When a factional group's frame is that greed and self-interest violated sacred social and political institutions such as a tribe, the presence of a self-described "oil man" and "son of an oil man" as tribal chairman is a challenge to political consensus. John Barrett was reluctant to discuss his family when asked. What I was able to gather from others who knew him was that Barrett was the son of a prominent local oil rig owner. Barrett grew up in an expansive stone home—even in the age where scale is distorted by the presence of "McMansions"—that was situated behind a large iron gate. Barrett attended Princeton University and then returned to organize oil rigs for his father and the tribe. An experience with oil wealth undoubtedly frames his world in a markedly different way than Potawatomis who gaze upon it from bending wooden shacks with burning potbelly stoves.

4.6 CONCLUSION

It is clear to those listening to the Sacred Heart Potawatomis that the twentieth-century oil issue has activated deep senses of injustice. This feeling of injustice is similarly found among the South Dakota Lakotas yet is absent among the Isleta Pueblos, considered to have ethnohistories further from the trauma so salient to the Sacred Heart Citizen Potawatomis. All tribes have conflict, though few have as great difficulty finding things about which to agree. The Pueblos, despite the presence of religious and political divisions, do agree on their cultural authenticity over other American Indians. The Citizen Potawatomis and Oklahoma tribes have wide ideological, financial, and emotional disparities between factions. These groups are deeply wed to opposing worldviews, thus facilitating a vicious competition over control and direction.

CHAPTER 5

Blood / Fear / Harmony
Pueblo Politics

5.1 INTRODUCTION

Few North American communities can claim continuous confinement to a single mud village for eight hundred years. The Isleta Pueblos, a tribe in New Mexico, is one such community. The village—*pueblo* means *village* in Spanish—is not entirely a solitary community, but, unlike the Citizen Potawatomis, who rarely regulate outsiders' presence on the reservation, the Isletas allow only outsiders who are spouses to reside permanently on tribal lands. Semi-temporal isolation is a community feature; what we might call material or visual *modernity*, and what consumers might call *conveniences*, are present but typically in incomplete forms.

A reservation resident described the presence of technology this way: "We have cars, trucks and we drive them. Now and then people ride horses but that was given up as a way to get around maybe fifty years ago. We have washing machines, but no dryers, we never used them before and don't really think about getting them" (Informant 2007). In such arid regions, there exists a perfunctory form of dry cleaning. Certainly, the vivid sunlight in the high desert deals with the moisture from recently laundered clothing, but soil debris—either left in your clothing from cattle kicking dust during ranching or added by the breeze that moves over vast amounts of exposed dirt before sweeping the laundry line—endows dried clothing and the final product with a rigidity that makes starching and ironing more than unnecessary.

The Isleta Pueblo is typically dusty and calm; tumbleweeds move across the fields when not lying low in ditches. Unlike conversations I had on other reservations on which I conducted fieldwork, Isleta conversations were held in their native langue, Tiwa, and not in English. Despite the bucolic feel and sense of isolation, only a fifteen-minute drive separates the reservation from Albuquerque, the largest city in New Mexico. Isleta feels little like the sprawling track homes that house most of the Southwest's population. Isleta tribal members mainly live in either the village proper or in two- to three-bedroom houses attached to small three- to ten-acre farms. The village proper is adjacent to the Rio Grande, which divides the reservation geographically. Running parallel to the river are railroad tracks from the Santa Fe Pacific line and Interstate 25, which, according to a 1998 road atlas, starts in El Paso, Texas, and ends in Buffalo, Wyoming.

In comparison to the Citizen Potawatomis, the Isleta Pueblos are less integrated into the non-Indian world. The Spanish initially colonized the Isleta, whose name originated in Spanish and means the "little island." Despite what was undoubtedly brutal religious assimilation that accompanied Spanish rule, the Isleta village and community remained geographically in its precontact location. Massacres such as those inflicted upon the Citizen Potawatomis did not happen in Isleta. There were no wars between Isleta Pueblos and the U.S. government. Spanish colonization of what would become New Mexico began in 1598 with Juan de Oñate leaving the mission at Santa Barbara. Colonization by Mexico ended (ten years after the Citizen Potawatomis' Trail of Death) with the 1848 Treaty of Guadalupe Hidalgo, which ceded the territory to the United States as a Mexican-American War concession. Spain was an atrocious colonial hegemon, whose repertory of oppression was as abundant as any that operated in the New World and restraint as little. The Isleta Pueblos were comparatively fortunate, given what could have been taken from them, and they survived Spanish rule speaking their native language and continuing to dwell in the same village that they started it in—a rare outcome among Indian communities in the Americas.

———

To illustrate the communal life, the role of rumor, and the high value appropriateness has among the Isleta Pueblos, let me start with a story of a funeral told to me.

A friend, also Isleta, married a white woman who was Hispanic, too. You know, Spanish not Mexican. Her mother died a few weeks back. She was pretty old . . . like in her eighties probably. He [the Isleta husband] wanted to make the casket. He made a beautiful casket, wood with a nice finish. Only problem he made it eight feet long by maybe four feet in width. It was enormous and she was a little old lady. They told me they looked it up on-line to get the standard dimensions; I don't think they got it right. So I went to the funeral and some church workers there, who had seen lots of caskets before, were kinda measuring it with their hands from a distance when it was in the front. They were talking about how it was too big. You could tell by looking at them use their hands [the church workers]. You know caskets are supposed to be kinda the same size. After the funeral was over they took the hearse to the graveyard. Well, this casket was so big they couldn't shut the back doors of the hearse. They had to keep the doors open and drive with it sticking out the back of the hearse. Well when they [the funeral party] got to the grave, they tried to put the casket in every which way, but it wouldn't fit. There was no way it would fit.

The woman whose mother had died, the wife of my Isleta friend, told them to make the hole wider. The people with the machines to dig had gone home. The funeral manager, or the foreman, told my friend's wife that they could make the hole bigger but they would charge them for it and bring back the crew. This woman got mad, oh she got mad and started cussing. It got ugly. She and the person in charge were going at it for a while. She wasn't going to pay whatever it was to make the hole bigger. I can't believe what happened next. So some of the guys pried the casket open and rolled the old woman into the hole. Man, the woman had been dead for a week. Then they had a truck of cement that they are supposed to pour over the coffins. They backed it up and poured it over the mother right there in the grave with her at the bottom. No dirt, just cement first. Can you believe it? What a way to go. (Informant 2007)

We might all do better to leave stories like these untold. Yet we are fasci-nated by the macabre they contain and by the frequency with which these stories get told in our communal lives. This tale is one of stellar indignity: pried from the coffin, the body of a woman, in her eighties, rolled into her grave and submerged in cement, limbs likely now akimbo forever. This constitutes a rather powerful image. However, the story is more than one of a local burial gone badly. It is a story of a local non-Indian burial done poorly.

Tales like this one are commonly told among New Mexico Pueblos. They follow a pattern: the poor behavior of non-Indians and non–Pueblo Indians (particularly the Navajos, their ancestral enemies) can invoke disaster. Consider carefully who did what in this story. The Isleta cherished his mother-in-law and caringly built a casket. His Hispanic wife fought, cursed, and had her mother rolled from her coffin into her grave. The cemetery workers (whose race is unspecified, but likely not Indian) poured cement on the corpse. The only participant in this story who behaved with appropriate respect for the deceased was the Isleta husband. Of course, he built too large a casket, but his was a transgression produced by inexperience, not by defect of character. This story was about Pueblo Indians honoring that around them and non-Indians doing the opposite.

This chapter is organized into four sections. The first provides a brief historical background to the Isleta Pueblo, addressing its geography, history, and contemporary conditions. The second section describes the types of conflicts that exist between tribal members and examines the dynamics of Isleta political conflict. The third section describes the social mechanisms of communal affect, which I argue is the organizing logic of the Isletas. This section also addresses the Isleta society's conventions for the suppression of openly expressed acrimony, which includes harsh perceptions of judgment by peers, rumors, and even accusations of witchcraft. The fourth and final section considers speculation, based on observations, for change by the Isletas.

In 2008, after a long period of relative economic seclusion, the Isleta Pueblos built a luxury resort to accompany their casino. Along with the jobs provided by the casino, the resort created high-salaried positions that may likely lead to future class divisions and greater differentiation among the Isletas, placing significant strain on the social logic of communal affect. These jobs will produce economic winners and losers (see Gonzales 2003 for discussion of "winners" and "losers" in economic development around casino gaming), previously absent at such a large scale among the Isletas, and create fissures similar to those found among the Citizen Potawatomis resulting from the petroleum industry. More salient intratribal rivalries may appear as some Isletas identify with and advocate for a self-interested worldview and others identify with resentment and a melancholic worldview. As melancholy and self-interest share social and political spaces uneasily—as examined in the Citizen Potawatomis in the previous chapter—these new worldviews may heighten a sense of difference and instigate sharper community acrimony and the development of more organized, formal political factions. The future of Isleta politics may be one of greater factional divides and resultant tribal infighting as the casino sharpens economic differences. These factions could be entirely new or be absorbed into smaller fissures around existing formations who support constitutional government or religious societies.

The conceptual framework for this chapter is shaped by an inquiry into what facilitates the interplay of the forces of *integration* and *differentiation* among the Isleta Pueblos. These terms, borrowed from the work of Emile Durkheim, aid in gauging social processes as experiences that produce greater communal affect or integration than differentiation, which was described in the previous chapter as the rise of self-interest and melancholia through variance in lived experience with oil wealth and loss within the Citizen Potawatomi Nation. Whereas the Citizen Potawatomis had intense and multiple experiences of differentiation, the Isleta ethnohistory has comparatively fewer of these experiences and less contemporary community fragmentation.

5.2 ISLETA PUEBLO: GEOGRAPHIC AND HISTORICAL BACKGROUND OF AN EIGHT-HUNDRED-YEAR-OLD MUD VILLAGE

Not only has the Isleta Pueblo stayed in one place for an inordinately long time, but even the non–American Indian institutions are unusually old in Isleta. Founded by the Spanish in 1612, the Isleta catholic mission, San Agustín de la Isleta Mission, is one of the oldest churches in the United

States (Isleta Pueblos claim it is the second-oldest). As the contemporary Isleta Pueblo world fuses a traditional village probably as old as any in the United States with a recently built five-star luxury hotel casino, reservation topography is distinctive and not easy to imagine. The clearest way to conceptualize the pueblo is to see it as dividing into five distinct geographic zones. Each zone has a spiritual, communal, or economic function that is distinguishable from the others. These zones are: (1) the central village; (2) the irrigated farmland; (3) the rangeland; (4) the Manzano Mountains; and (5) the resort hotel and casino.

5.2.1 THE VILLAGE

The village itself contains both major religious centers: the Catholic mission and the Isleta kiva. During religious feasts and holidays, the Isletas dance in the plaza between the kiva and the church. The modern post office and police station are just at the outer perimeter of the village. Buildings in the village center are made of adobe and terron bricks, and many of them are hundreds of years old.[1] Most of the brick used in these buildings was cut from the riverbanks using ancient construction techniques. About one hundred families live in the village.

5.2.2 THE FARMLAND

To the north and south of the village proper are bands of farmland. The Rio Grande twists slowly through this very shallow river valley. Historically, the Isleta Pueblos, like many of the Rio Grande Pueblos, were farmers. The silt deposited from the river left a fertile layer of topsoil. Alfalfa, beans, melons, and corn grow on these plots that generally range from three to eight acres in size. Due to the difficulty in finding open space to build homes in the village proper,[2] most Isleta families on the reservation live in small farmhouses and in new trailers on this band of farmland.

The Isletas still engage in irrigation-based farming, which has been their practice for hundreds of years. The major irrigation canals are three- to five-feet deep and follow paved roads. The tributary canals branch through the many plots of this farmland zone. If allotment checkerboarded American Indian Oklahoma lands as a product of colonial efforts of inclusion and exclusion, these ditches in Isleta dividing the Pueblo farmland are pre-colonial artifices.[3] Though older, this irrigation system divides the property, making contiguous landownership difficult. If Isleta families own more than one of these plots, they are generally scattered across multiples areas of this zone.

5.2.3 THE RANCHLAND

Communal ranchland, called "the range" by Isletas, is the third zone. It is on the far west side of the pueblo past Interstate 25. No one is allowed to live there, just cattle, or as an Isleta put it, "things that go *moo*" (Informant 2007). It is arid ranchland with black mesa rock and long-dormant volcanoes jutting upward into the landscape every now and then. The tribe separated this rangeland into twenty-thousand-acre segments. Four or five ranchers share such an allotment, each paying annually approximately ten dollars per heifer to the tribal government for grazing rights.

5.2.4 THE MOUNTAINS

East of the village are the Manzano Mountains. The Manzanos are still within the reservation boundaries, situated at the reservation's far eastern edge, and are uninhabited. The Isleta Pueblos like to tease and say that demons live in the mountains and caution everyone not to go there at night. According to some Isletas, mountain monsters prefer plump children, but "will eat adults if they get hungry enough" (Informant 2007). The degree of seriousness with which this statement was asserted was unclear; it seemed at first that the Isletas were joking about believing in these monsters. The mountains are important for mostly spiritual reasons. Religious leaders often use the mountains to gather materials for religious ceremonies. Materials from these mountains are used because they are perceived as pure, owing to the lack of contact with people. I was asked by the Isletas not to divulge precisely what they take from these mountains for these purposes. The mountains were not portrayed as spiritually charged places or sacred sites, such as the Lakotas' relationship with the Black Hills (which will be discussed later). Secular or economic activities were absent in the Isleta-controlled part of the Manzanos. At most, game is hunted and trees are removed, but no systematic commercial enterprises operate in the mountain zone.

5.2.5 THE CASINO

The fifth zone is relatively new compared to the others. It is on the northern boundary of the reservation where Interstate 25 meets a major county highway. Most Isleta economic and political activities take place in this zone. The casino, hotel, golf course, bowling alley, arcade, recreational vehicle park, gas stations, and majority of the tribal government offices are in this area. Unlike on the rest of the reservation, there is traffic. The original bingo hall was built in the late 1980s when high-stakes bingo operations were popular among Indian nations. This bingo hall was first upgraded to slot machines and then replaced by a more modern casino in the late 1990s. This original bingo building is now the Isleta Fun Center and houses a bowling alley, arcade, and laser tag operation. In 2008, revenue from the Isleta casino grossed approximately $38 million (Informant 2007).

5.3 FACTIONS IN ISLETA

Unlike with the Citizen Potawatomis, there are no formally organized Isleta political factions. Political groups are, at best, loosely organized. Who may take what side of an issue can be unpredictable. As I was told by one Isleta, "It is hard to tell how someone is going to react to politics, or an issue. You just don't know who is going to support what. It is hard to know" (Informant 2007). Despite the greater sense of tranquility in open politics compared to that of Citizen Potawatomis, there is a noticeable lack of apparent structure to Isleta politics. Whereas the Citizen Potawatomis have established political factions and know the political channels to advocate particular preferences, the Isletas have difficulty selecting on the basis of ideology which council member will best secure the resources, such as jobs or housing subsidies.

Without clear ideological demarcation, Isleta politics is organized through family ties. When I asked how tribal members were elected to tribal council or governor (the Pueblo equivalent to tribal chairman), the responses were often, "They had a large family who votes for them. That's how they got to be there" or "Yeah, that person is not really that qualified, they just got elected because of their family" (Informant 2007). Of the tribal council, I was told that only three or four of the twelve members had been elected without gaining solid support from their large families. These individuals had to "get votes that no one else [other candidates] wanted to get" (Informant 2007). If families are the primary units of the Isleta political landscape, they are not ideologically divided units. On the subject of family difference, one Isleta told me, "[Isleta] families don't have big differences in what they think in terms of politics. Maybe some are more conservative but issues aren't agreed upon in families. Some people in some families believe one thing and another other things, but they still get along. It isn't a big deal" (Informant 2007). Unlike the Citizen Potawatomis, the Isletas have neither wealthy nor deeply poor families because there were few resources or processes that supported the development of large-scale wealth or contributed to poverty.

So if there are ideological divisions within families, why do they still vote as a block? There are two main reasons for this: (*a*) the Isletas have had relatively few issues to vote upon thus far that could elicit dramatic political emotions; and (*b*) votes are allocated in a loose patronage method. Isletas vote to have a related tribal member on the council with the aim of securing resources, administering disputes between them and the tribal authorities, and maintaining—not changing—the direction of the tribe. Much of this chapter seeks to unravel why this relatively homogenous political dynamic exists in Isleta politics in contrast to the bitter conflicts among Citizen Potawatomis. In short, why is the political community of Isleta significantly less polarized compared to other tribes, such as the Citizen Potawatomis? Why have the forces of integration been so successful in preserving ideological and behavioral unity?

5.4 HISTORY AND NEGLIGIBLE DIFFERENTIATION: ISLETA AS A "COLD SOCIETY"'

Describing absence of change is problematic for the social scientist, whose field language and orientation is designed to recognize and to highlight the dynamics behind change. The Isleta Pueblos place emphasis on avoiding community acrimony and on the continuation of stability. This is not to suggest there is a total absence of dislike, change, anger, progress, or ill-will in Isleta. Claude Lévi-Strauss famously separated societies into two types or forms: hot and cold. *Hot societies* are "dedicated to rapid change and innovation," and *cold societies* "seek to remain static" (Pace 1983, 52). Within this Lévi-Straussian framework, the Isletas possess the character-istics of a cold society; appearing "satisfied with relatively low energy lev-els, they seek to prevent the formation of such internal differences" (Pace 1983, 52). Lévi-Strauss understood the difference between these two types of societies as that between stability and innovation (Pace 1983, 53). Isleta acrimony between members exists, but as in many relatively closed com-munities, the integrative forces go far in preserving cold societies.

Though change and political conflict exist among the Isletas, acri-mony differs from that of the Citizen Potawatomis. The Isleta Pueblos can be contrasted to the Citizen Potawatomis in four ways: (*a*) acrimony is socially constrained and punishable for the Isletas, whereas participating in conflict is a necessary initiation into Citizen Potawatomi politics; (*b*) political conflict is not systemic among the Isletas, and the conflicts that do develop are repressed or relegated to hidden arenas, such as the super-natural, whereas the Citizen Potawatomis elevate personal disputes into civilizational narratives; (*c*) the Isletas are unaccustomed to showing anger and have limited repertoires of conflict, whereas the Citizen Potawatomis are well-versed in and comfortable with displaying acrimony and creating conflict; and (*d*) the Isletas are less likely to expect emotional validation from the political aspect of their community than the Citizen Potawatomis, who use politics and economic development projects (whether advocating for or against them) to posit and reinforce indigenous identity.

To put the conclusion first: what explains the difference in political character between the Isleta Pueblos and the Citizen Potawatomis is the fact that the former community has encountered significantly fewer drastic historical processes, and has therefore experienced less differenti-ation within the community, than the latter. The older methods of social cohesion remained unchallenged and intact, as there were few processes that created economic or historic differences within Isleta society. Social innovation among the Isletas is strongly discouraged by social judgment. The Isletas are defined in many ways by what they did not experience. There were no removals or trails of death. Though the Spanish controlled and periodically brutalized Pueblo society for over two centuries and

built Catholic institutions, the traditional Isleta kiva remained and functioned like much of Isleta life. Except for the area around the government
buildings and casino resort, the various Isleta geographic zones described
earlier have changed little in eight hundred years: the village is in the same
place; the native language, Tiwa, is still spoken in regular conversation;
crops are still grown in the same fields; clan groupings are still observed;
and ceremonies are still taken seriously. Isleta Pueblo history is not filled
with forced relocations, wars against the United States, economic booms,
or massacres carried out by colonial powers.[4] As a result of this lack of
traumatic historical processes—pain and profit—the Isleta economic
class structure is much less varied than that of the steeply divided Citizen
Potawatomis. Factional development is limited, not so much due to the
power of traditional institutions, but rather because of the weakness of
new challenges to the established order. The Isletas, in a way, are a counter-
example of the classic political science adage that older political orders
fail as a result of lack of sufficient number of political friends rather than
from having too many enemies. Older Isleta institutions have encountered
disruptors from the outside, but those have been meek compared to the
Potawatomi relocations.

Communal affect persisted in the case of the Isleta Pueblos. Compared
with the other tribes examined in this project, the integrational Isleta institutions survived mostly intact—especially when compared to those of the
Citizen Potawatomis. Social integration is a concept identified with Emile
Durkheim, who described industrialization as producing sociological
differentiation within a society (Durkheim 1966, 1976, 1997). Durkheim
points to industrialization and the complication around modern societies
as the forces that create differentiation, and traditional social mechanisms
as the forces that sought to maintain collective order and integration. These
forces of differentiation and integration have moved from sociological theory to other fields, such as administrative theory in the study of division of
labor (Durkheim 1997). Administrative theorists Paul Lawrence and Jay
Lorsche describe these concepts: "Differentiation is defined as the state of
segmentation of the organizational system into subsystems . . . [and] integration is defined as the process of achieving unity of effort among various
subsystems" (1967, 3–4).

In *Big Structures, Large Processes, Huge Comparisons*, sociologist Charles Tilly provides a sociological perspective on processes of differentiation and integration. Tilly describes integration as keeping "a sense of likeness, shared belief, respect for authority, satisfaction with modest rewards, fear of moral deviation—essentially a set of habits and attitudes that encouraged people to reproduce the existing structure of rewards and authority" (1984, 4). Differentiation was "at the small scale, popular violence, crime, immorality" and "at the large scale, popular rebellion, insubordination, class conflict" (Tilly 1984, 4). However, modernizing forces such as "increasing education, the expansion of markets, occupational specialization, and other forms of differentiation would cause these dangers as well" (Tilly 1984, 4).

Integration and non-differentiation are not identical social forces. Generally integration and differentiation are forces that work against each other once social change has been put in motion. These pressures to change and to remain the same (maintaining similarities or creating differences) coexist. If the gravity of differentiation is stronger than that of integration, an existing order will change. The Isletas are unusual as their history is one that allowed the survival of older forms of integration (rumor, accusations of witchcraft, strong social norms, and so on), which will be discussed later in this chapter. Their history was also absent of differentiation forces that pressured them to change. These historic dynamics work in conjunction.

The degree of agency exercised by tribes or any community is unclear; it is not that Isleta integrative forces were so omnipotent as to keep differentiating processes outside the reservation. If the U.S. military had been ordered to remove the Isletas during the nineteenth century, such as the cases of the Lakotas and Potawatomis, or if oil had been discovered in the rangeland, the Isletas would likely hold different worldviews than those found on the contemporary reservation. The strong presence of rumor and social pressure independently would likely have been unable to protect Isleta society from change. Fortune, or misfortune, has played a part in the absence of transformative experiences that could have led to greater division in Isleta. Geographic remoteness, few identifiable resources, and the lack of a population for the Spanish to enslave (as they did in much of Latin America) spared much of the indigenous Southwest from the exploitative colonial processes of dispossession and massacre during the early colonial period (pre-nineteenth century). In the later colonial period (post-nineteenth century), the Southwest was not a desirable homestead location, for there was little arable farmland.

5.4.1 CLASS IN ISLETA EVERYDAY TALK

When asked about economic class differences in Isleta, one respondent said, "There are some people [Isletas] who use the range and make a little extra money" (Informant 2007). A rancher told me about income from thirty head of cattle (the average on the communal rangeland), and explained, "In a normal year you get about $3,000 and in a good year you can get to maybe $5,000 . . . depends upon how many calves you have but no one is making big money" (Informant 2007). This rangeland rancher group (sometimes referred to as "the cowboys" by other Isletas) at best resembles a weak kulak class and constitutes the most identifiable tribal economic subgroup. However, when asked if this group wanted anything from the tribe, an Isleta told me, "They don't really want much. Maybe not to raise the rates [grazing fees] and not add too many people to the land" (Informant 2007).

Questions regarding class, wealth, and power were asked during Isleta interviews. No participant identified a reservation-based common economic class that regularly organized along particular interests. After extensive interaction with the Isletas lasting over five years, I have not identified any potent, politically active factions. There is only one Isleta who is considered by his peers to be wealthy.[5] This Isleta owns a construction business that works on municipal and state projects. There are Isleta committees that advocate certain forms of tribal policy such as a change in the blood-quantum requirements for membership. An Isleta tribal council member told me that there were no voting coalitions that were predictable beyond a single issue. "We don't have those types of people" (Informant 2007), one Isleta told me. "We are all pretty much the same economically. You know we all live in similar houses. Everyone has a house pretty much. Some of us got trailers, but they are new," was another Isleta's response (Informant 2007).

5.4.2 REGULAR CONFLICT IN ISLETA

Class or ethnic rage is not the only reason to hate a community member. Despite comparatively narrow class disparities, Isletas are neither consummately satisfied nor without anger. Conflicts, however, mostly start from fellow community members' incursions onto another's economic resources. These conflicts stay tied to these points of disagreement and are not organized around worldviews, life experiences, or values. When asked about recent conflicts, one Isleta told me a ranching story that involved his brother and himself:

> We bought a new cattle squeeze.[6] It was pretty nice. Well, he [the informant's brother] locked the squeeze at the end of the chute using a chain and big lock. The guys he was sharing [the parcel of] land with came to do some work on their cows. Because my brother had left it locked to the end of the chute and put a lock on the gates so it couldn't be operated, these guys couldn't work on their cows. They couldn't even attach their squeeze to the end of his because he [the informant's brother] locked it. So they called his house over and over again. We went out there to unlock it. Man did it get bad. Those guys were calling each other names. It almost came to blows. I think they were gonna do something, they had some wrenches and chains in their hands like they were going to start a fight. They were drinking too. We unlocked the lock but damn, I mean it wasn't fun. (Informant 2007)

In lieu of well-articulated narratives regarding the flaws of rivals' worldviews and ethnic authenticity—a theme in Citizen Potawatomi acrimony—the Isletas tell regular stories about tribal conflicts. I asked what "ugly" words were spoken and was told by an Isleta that it was profanity but the informant did not relate back to authenticity or accusations of ethnic fraud. These stories are what I call regular because they are shallow. Isleta stories of communal irritation and hatred are only rarely infused with the nature or meaning of colonization, ethnic or tribal identity, or themes of character.[7] In contrast, the Isletas invest in deeper meanings about colonization and sociopsychological character when comparing themselves with non-Isleta Indians or non-Indians than with one another. Among themselves, bickering seems to just be bickering. The ranching stories, and others like it, are not about the boundaries of indigenous ethnic, cultural, or moral authenticity. Though the stories they tell of one another are often grim and deeply unflattering, the Isletas do not feel compelled to associate the motivations, moral outlooks, worldviews, or character of fellow Isletas—even the ones who have cheated them—to larger historical processes. Isleta conflicts arise from communal irritation, and these conflicts remain about communal irritation, not historical processes.

Disputes between Isletas about water and grazing are common. And the narratives surrounding property loss are dissimilar to those of the Citizen Potawatomis. Isleta property and land grievances are less intense and certainly not cosmological in the way that the factional groups of the Citizen Potawatomis describe the nineteenth-century Great Lakes and twentieth-century oil dispossessions. Isleta property disputes and loss mostly revolve around ill-behaved livestock and are similar to the ranching story just related.

The more dramatic intratribal conflict stories I encountered during fieldwork research involved minimal infighting about property and livestock and were mild when compared to the bitter rivalries of the Citizen Potawatomis. Though most livestock are raised on the range, the interior farmland is mixed-use with cattle, horses, pigs, and even alpacas. Often these livestock escape their enclosures and graze in neighbors' fields. Occasionally a story is told of an Isleta who intentionally lets his animals graze his neighbor's alfalfa:

> I went out one night during the summer, it was late maybe after 1 A.M., and I saw these shadows on my field. I got close and these shadows were horses. My neighbor's horses eating my alfalfa. I went over to see how they got in and his gate was open. The next night the same thing. So the next day I told him not to do it again. He said his horses weren't on my field. I took him to court and judge told me that there was no proof. So I told him, this is what I told him, "Next time I see your horses in my field, this is what I'm going to do: I'm going to shoot both of them and you can come out and we will see whose field they are in." (Informant 2007)

Threatening to gun down a neighbor's horses is a creative solution—dragging a dead horse to one's own land to falsely incriminate someone is a near physical impossibility. The horses subsequently stopped grazing in the wrong field. But the key aspect of this story is that the Isleta's analysis did not lead to anything beyond a neighbor engaging in hay theft and equine death threats. I asked about what deficiencies the neighbor possessed in letting his horses graze. "I don't know, maybe didn't want to buy them hay, I guess," responded the Isleta (Informant 2007). Unlike conflicts among the Citizen Potawatomis, there was no speculation on whether the neighbor was a "bad Indian" or a fraud or emblematic of what is worst in colonial processes. Local grievances between Isletas are not framed within global narratives of loss and abuse. It is certainly possible that if the dispute had been over a different matter, say tribal government and leadership, that these disagreements would not be regular but would resemble conflict between the Citizen Potawatomis. With the Citizen Potawatomi, rarely were disagreements kept or made regular, and rarely were conflicts dramatized among Isleta members.

5.5 POLITICAL ISSUES AND CONFLICT SUPPRESSION

Political issues were not catalysts for intratribal political struggles in Isleta. Issues such as financing a new casino or resort, which have created severe strain among the Citizen Potawatomis and included allegations of corruption, did not seem to rupture politics in the Isleta Pueblo. Only two significant issues—one political and the other economic—came before the tribal council during my time speaking with Isletas, which spanned approximately two years. The Isleta response to these two issues is emblematic of a group unconditioned by historical intratribal conflict and of a community with a prevailing logic of communal affect.

Revenue from the Isleta Casino and Resort is approximately $40 million per year. It is the primary source of revenue for the tribe (Informant 2007). The Isletas are in a crowded gaming market and have to compete with two other Pueblo casinos that are within twenty miles of Albuquerque. Since the early 2000s, Isleta casino revenue has been declining in comparison to their two major competitors. It was thought that the absence of a luxury resort hotel to accompany the existing casino was responsible for this decline in competitiveness. The Sandia and Acoma Pueblos both have resorts of between three hundred and four hundred rooms attached to their casinos. To pay for the resort expansion, the Isletas would need to borrow just over $100 million (Informant 2007). At the time of the creation of these plans, much of senior casino management was non-Isleta. One of these senior managers was selected to negotiate the loan as the individual had a professional background in finance.

Without informing the tribal council, this manager designed the loans for the resort expansion using revenue as a criterion for determining the interest rate of the loan. As an Isleta who worked for the casino described the loan to me, "The interest rate of this loan depended upon how much money the slots were making. The interest was tied to the cash we had coming in. Rates would be lower if we made more money, but if we didn't the rates would get really high" (Informant 2007). This employee also said that the revenue information that the finance-trained manager gave the banks was different from that given to the tribal council. That Isleta employee told me, "The slots had never generated this type of revenue before [he inflated the numbers]. He for some reason made the loan this way and hid it [the correct revenue that the slot machines generated] from the tribal council. The council also thought they were making more money than they were because [the manager] had given them inflated numbers to make him look better" (Informant 2007). "They [the tribal council] couldn't understand the loan papers and he told them that it was a good deal. Well, when [the bank] called about the interest rate rising because of low revenues, it was amazing. The tribal council and Isleta found out that they had to pay an extra $10 million, maybe $20 million for the loan due to the interest" (Informant 2007).

As a non-Isleta casino employee recounted the day the Isletas were told of the unfavorable loan details:

> I've worked in hotels and casinos a long time. I've seen executives be escorted to the door right there on the spot for much less. You can't lose $15 million of the tribe's money and keep your job right? I couldn't believe what happened. I spent the whole day waiting for

[this manager] to be walked out by security. He screwed them so bad and nothing happened. The only walking that took place was him walking right into the tribal council and start talking about fishing, that is what I heard, and they did nothing. Not a goddamn thing. (Informant 2007)

For understandable reasons, the terms and particulars of the loan were unavailable for me to examine. Individuals working in close proximity to the tribal government and the casino and hotel told similar stories. Another informant verified the event and the loan conditions. The total costs are ultimately unverifiable from the perspective of an outside researcher, but some informants stipulated that the extra interest payments will cost the tribe between $10 million and $20 million, which is between one-fourth and one-half of annual casino revenue (Informant 2007).

The tribe eventually opted not to renew the manager's contract, which expired six months after the loan debacle. A few Isletas told me that the members of the tribal council, which makes the major decisions for all tribal businesses as well as staffing the executive positions of tribal businesses, were afraid of the manager. "They didn't want to get the guy mad; they didn't know what to do," an Isleta continued. "You see, the manager was able to bully the tribal council. They [the tribal council] asked him about it that day. He told them not to worry about it. [Changing the subject], then he told them that no one had caught a $10,000 prize fish in the lake next to the RV park.[8] They just sat there" (Informant 2007).

Tribal members knew they had been fooled. An Isleta told me, "We found out but what could we do?" (Informant 2007). One would imagine that the Citizen Potawatomis would have moved seamlessly into malicious politics. What happened, or rather did not happen, resulted from a mixture of the commitment to preserve harmony and the lack of lived experience of the Isleta leadership in high-stakes conflict. It was apparent to those who witnessed what happened that the tribal council knew that the manager had taken advantage of the Isletas, confident that they would do little to punish him. It was also made clear to me by the people I interviewed that many of the tribal council members spoke about the failure of their peers to reprimand the manager or organize an effort to get rid of him.

Ultimately, the Isleta tribal council did terminate the contract, but did it by letting it expire—achieving the desired outcome via the route of least friction. Before the expiration of the contract, the manager took a position at a casino elsewhere.

5.5.1 SPANISH GOLD, INDIAN MOUNTAINS

Being at a loss in difficult political situations is nothing new for the tribal council. An Isleta recounted a similar incident that took place in the 1980s and centered on the presence of buried treasure in the Manzano Mountains. There was a long-standing legend that the Spanish had hidden treasure in the mountains during the Pueblo Revolt of the 1680s. The story claims that the Spanish were in a rush to leave and decided that it was safe to hide the Spanish Crown's gold and silver in the mountains rather than to risk the journey south to El Paso then to Mexico City. As an Isleta told the story:

> It was a meeting maybe in the late '80s. This white guy walks in with his lawyer and has a contract. He goes before the council and says that he found a treasure map to this gold, and if they [the council] sign the contract and let him search for it then we can have half the gold he finds. They [the council] didn't know what to do. So they asked him to leave for a little while and sit in the hall. They decided that the guy should give them 80 percent of the gold. I don't know where they came up with the number. They guy told them that he was going to go outside and talk with this lawyer about it. I guess he [the gold hunter] didn't like it so he said, "Forget these guys" and bolted. No one at the council thought to get his name or investigate who he was. People think that he already had the gold but felt bad for taking it from them so came in and tried to make it right. (Informant 2007)

I asked the Isleta who told me this story why the council was not able to either detain the treasure hunter or accept the contract. They said, "Nobody knew what they were doing. Yeah, it was a strange thing to have a guy like that show up, but you got to do better than that. It was out of their league, I think" (Informant 2007).

The Isletas are a people unaccustomed to open conflict. They watch other people fight but generally seem uncomfortable creating or participating in human acrimony, particularly in front of outsiders. The Isleta history of the last three hundred years is one of low intensity compared to other North American indigenous groups. They have not had cause to form harsh worldviews. The Isleta interest groups are underdeveloped compared to the Citizen Potawatomis', making them ill-prepared to elect leaders and lacking in available candidates able to deal with groups who now come before them with sizeable interests and complex proposals.

If the class background of the Isleta Pueblos had been peppered with periods of differentiation around pain and profit, would this event in Isleta political economy have ended differently? Would the Isletas respond differently to conflict? The theory advocated in this work suggests that the Isletas would have responded differently to pending conflict, and it would have certainly changed political behavior and political outcomes previously described. If the historic trajectory of the Isletas had created various classes, such as had happened to the Citizen Potawatomis, the Isletas would have been accustomed to this type of conflict. Among the Citizen Potawatomis, market incorporation has created a group of small and medium business owners who are drawn into tribal politics and who might have foreseen this problem and been prepared to undermine the manager and the leadership for allowing such an undesirable outcome.

5.5.2 CAGED ACRIMONY

In less political forums, the Isletas have an unusual relationship with conflict. An Isleta invited me to attend a cage fight to be held at the casino auditorium. I sat near the tribal council members, who were given preferential seating. Men fought with near bare knuckles twenty feet in front of us for two hours. Fighters of many racial groups choked one another in a cage. Cage fighting is a hybrid form of pugilism. In something between wrestling and street fighting, participants—in this case both local amateurs and professionals—choked and beat one another until one fighter surrendered or the referee interrupted in the interest of safety. Though stereotypes of the stoic Indian have been exhausted, the tribal council sat still and quiet through the entire match.

In front of the tribal council sat two boys, maybe eight and ten years old, with their mother. The family had black T-shirts in support of their father, who was fighting that night and who had advertised on the back of those T-shirts what appeared to be a local training gymnasium. The father's match was particularly brutal and long. The father, Hispanic, was a local amateur. He fought a semiprofessional black fighter from Detroit. Cage fighting generally has three rounds that last around five minutes. The nature of this type of fighting creates a pattern for each round. During the first thirty seconds, opponents jab, kick, and box. Usually, this precipitates one trying to take down the other, with both fighters ending down on the mat wrestling. The fighters then wrestle between ten and thirty seconds to establish position. After a fighter gains an offensive position, the remaining four minutes of the round is the second fighter torquing his (or her) body to avoid face strikes or wrestling holds that might either cut off the supply of air or blood to the head or tear an arm from its socket.

Each round of the fight involving the father of the family in front of us and the semiprofessional from Detroit took place in the corner of the ring closest to our section. The father engaged in extreme forms of genuflection in order to block the elbows sent to break his nose. He was only moderately successful. Often he struggled to breathe while being choked. By the end, blood peppered the lightly colored apparel of those spectators in the closer rows. Both sons, one in a wheelchair, were crying slowly toward the end of the match. I have seen cockfighting in the southern Philippines and have witnessed reluctant children break the necks of the losing fighting birds they had raised, but this unsettled me even more. In such a powerful human scene, with children and wives watching their fathers and husbands fight in a cage, their blood on the floor, I wondered what my Isleta host thought of what was happening around him. I leaned in to ask and was told, "Gaw, Raymond, these people like to fight, and these other people [motioning to the crowd] like to watch" (Informant 2007).

Of course, my Isleta host was right. People like to fight, and those around do like to watch; some people even like to spend years researching it. In his perspective, Isletas would not participate in the conflict and would spend much of their energy avoiding it. Non-Isletas, however, do. And, one imagines, America has inundated the insular Isletas, like much of the rest of the world, with visions of life as belligerency.

5.6 THE PERSISTENCE OF COMMUNAL AFFECT AND THE MECHANISMS OF SOCIAL UNIFORMITY

The Pueblo communities in the Southwest have an unusual history. Compared to other North American indigenous groups, the Pueblos were generally less disturbed, as stated earlier. "The sense of unbroken cultural continuity, from prehistoric peoples to the present-day Puebloans," according to Trudy Griffin-Pierce, "is a major part of what makes Pueblo societies so strong and vital in today's world" (2000, 33). Archeological studies have also furthered the sense that Pueblos were able to maintain cultural and material traditions in the face of Spanish and American colonization (Wilcox 2009). The Isletas' five geographic zones were mostly physically unchanged over the years until recently (Sando 1992). There was the addition of the church in the seventeenth century and the introduction of Catholicism. The kiva, a traditional religious building, still stood at the center of the village, and Catholicism was grafted onto Isleta culture. The basic lifeways of the Isletas did not change as they did for others during removal. Both material and ideational systems have changed little, I was told (and from what I have experienced there, I tend to agree with the perception of minimal change in a relative sense). The evidence is abundant: the irrigation ditches are mostly the same as the ones from hundreds of years ago; the Isleta clan system is still intact; the medicine men practice their arts; and, though some Isletas are buried as Catholics, many more are buried in their tradition. There is less corn grown and fewer baskets woven than when the entire adult population was agrarian, but, until the recent addition of the casino resort, living patterns had a rare historic continuity for the New World.

As discussed in chapter 2, sensitivities vis-à-vis research topics vary. There are those who would object that the portrayal of Pueblo communities as an ancient and unchanging group is deeply passé. The arrangement between what is new and old for those who study indigenous peoples is a hazy and contradictory one (see the controversy of Alfred's *Peace, Power and Righteousness* [1999] or over Hanson's "The Making of the Maori" [1989]). What we might describe as being—or not being—socially constructed is an issue that elicits some sensitivity. There is a desire to reclaim the past and demonstrate the cultural survival of our abused communities.

See the efforts at language, cultural, or religious revitalization, for instance, in the premium placed on older or ancient knowledge. Certainly, the past is important and to be emphasized, but we must be careful not to cast indigenous peoples as retrograde or unable to adapt. Yet most social scientists consider ideas, identities, culture, and values to be socially constructed. An excellent study of this is found in Jeffrey Shepherd's analysis of Apache nationhood (2010) or Sebastian Braun's work on economic development and its incorporation within traditional Lakota values (2013). Of course, casting indigenous peoples as highly socially constructed and malleable, rather than inherently conservative, is rather uncomfortable. I hold these commitments awkwardly, especially when considering the immense destruction and loss in Indian country and its potential in creating contemporary identities, worldviews, and preferences.

The classic debate over the nature of indigenous minds in contemporary anthropology is that between scholars who see their subjects as rational/strategic adapters and those who see them and their worldviews as artifices shaped by ancient cosmologies. A well-publicized dispute between Marshall Sahlins and Gananath Obeyesekere over the killing of Captain Cook by the Native Hawaiians captured this central fissure and is worth repeating (Perlstein 1995; Pinney 1995). When Cook arrived in 1778 in what Europeans then called the Sandwich Islands (now Hawaiian Islands), he was greeted as a figuration of the Hawaiian god Lono and was eventually sacrificed/killed. Sahlins interprets the Native Hawaiians' actions as deeply a product of their existing cosmology. The Hawaiians believed that Cook was attached to a deity (Sahlins 1976, 1987, 1995). To Obeyesekere, Sahlins's interpretation negated the Native Hawaiians' agency to interpret Cook outside their cosmological boundaries. Obeyesekere's *The Apotheosis of Captain Cook* suggests that the Native Hawaiians interpreted Cook as a rival chief, not a god, and made a political calculation to dispose of him accordingly. The Native Hawaiians thought practically about Cook in "the process whereby human beings reflectively assess the implications of a problem in terms of practical criteria" (Obeyesekere 1992, 19). In his retort, *How "Natives" Think: About Captain Cook, for Example*, Sahlins remorselessly—and rather convincingly—accuses Obeyesekere of removing the very voice of the Hawaiians he sought to grant agency to and of substituting their beliefs with his own calculating rational perspective (1995).

The distinction between the Sahlins and Obeyesekere approaches to the Native worldview is a seminal distinction in the social sciences and one worth more honest inspection by American Indian scholars. Cosmologically driven motivations and strategic, rationally driven motivations are not always one and the same. American Indian scholarship has conducted its analysis holding both the Sahlins and Obeyesekere views but fails to realize, or does not wish to realize, that those views are more mutually exclusive than we would want. In essence, to the question of whether American Indians are similar to or different from non–American Indians, "Both" is a correct but unhelpful answer. Rather, more meaningful questions are, What do these differences and similarities look like? and What are the origins?

When considering the Isletas within similarity and difference, it is, or should be, striking, how different their context is from most Native communities in the United States. Few North Americans live in 800-year-old villages and 400-year-old homes and attend 350-year-old churches. While it is true that all communities and worldviews change at least in some respect, at issue is a matter of degree. And, as it pertains to the Sahlins and Obeyesekere debate, though some social scientists would still argue that Pueblos, like all people, are radical and strategic adapters, this misses the point that the Isletas and their politics take the shape they do because the Isletas are atypical in comparison to the rest of American society. The Isletas are also distinct from many other American Indians as they have not had to adapt following either traumatic events or radical economic changes as these exclusionary and inclusionary events did not happen to the degree they did elsewhere.

What explains the characteristics of Isleta politics is the absence of major historical change that would have formed polarized/interested groups and divergent rationalities or logics. This absence has two effects: (1) the absence of experiential divergence between members who promoted worldviews other than communal affect; which in turn (2) allowed mechanisms of Isleta integration to persist over the presence of only weak forces of differentiation.

5.6.1 SOCIAL FORCES OF INTEGRATION AND UNIFORMITY

While we shoveled gravel to make concrete one day, an Isleta asked me
what the other tribes I studied were like. I told him about the Citizen
Potawatomis and the degree to which the community bickered. He gave
the customary and prolonged "gaaawwww," which is what the Isleta men
and women do when they hear something they think is strange or outland-
ish. I asked him why he thought that "Oklahoma Indians"[9] fight as much as
they do. He told me, "Those Indians learned how to fight from white people. . . . White people got to them like that, you know?" (Informant 2007).
He told me, "White people fight like that, not here. People would think
something is wrong with you if you acted like that. You would be kinda an
outsider" (Informant 2007). It is a striking contrast between the two American Indian communities—to create or engage in conflict in Isleta would
make a member a political and social outsider, whereas, within the Citizen
Potawatomis and Sacred Heart Potawatomis, to engage in this conflict
makes one a political participant and member of a sociopolitical group.

Scholars have observed that the Pueblos are secretive societies regarding their own affairs (Pritzker 1999, among others). The Pueblos possess
an unusual uniformity as framed in the perspectives of early twentieth-
century anthropologists (Pritzker 1999; Suina 1998). Anthropologist Ruth
Benedict concluded that the Pueblo commitment to secrecy and boundaries separated them from other North American indigenous groups, who
"seek to attain in [their] most valued moments escape from the boundaries
imposed upon [them] by [their] senses" (1989, 79). Benedict suggested
that the Pueblos were one of the few North American indigenous groups
that could be placed in the Nietzschean category of *Apollonian*, instead of
Dionysian, due to cultural features that taught restraint and communalism
through the subordination of the individual (1989, 79). According to Benedict,

> Apollonian institutions have been carried much further in the
> pueblos than in Greece. Greece was by no means as single-minded.
> In particular, Greece did not carry out as the Pueblos have the
> distrust of individualism that the Apollonian way of life implies,
> but which in Greece was scanted because of forces with which it

came in conflict. . . . [An] Apollonian is embodied in the common tradition of his people. To stay always within it is to commit himself to precedent, to tradition. Therefore those influences that are powerful against tradition are uncongenial and minimized in their institutions, and the greatest of these is individualism. It is disruptive, according to Apollonian philosophy in the Southwest, even when it refines upon and enlarges the tradition itself. That is not to say that the Pueblos prevent this. No culture can protect itself from additions and changes. But the process by which these come is suspect and cloaked, and institutions that would give individuals a free hand are outlawed. (1989, 79–81)

The suppression of individual desires for the benefit of group unity and harmony strongly suggests that communal affect has been—at least at the time Benedict conducted fieldwork in the early twentieth century—a pervasive and long-standing logic among the Pueblos. This pressure to emphasize communal accord is still strong in the twenty-first century. Fear of rumor and judgment seem to still occupy the individual Isleta in the contemporary Pueblo tribe.

After hearing many Isletas tell me about how people are judged, I asked a younger tribal member if he could provide a description of an ideal Isleta that would satisfy the demands of the community. This Isleta described what one would need to do in order to not violate norms:

To be well liked [in Isleta], you have to act like you are beaten down and humble. Not be perceived as wanting too much. You live in the same manner. You have a job that pays, but they know you are not making too much money. You're a good person for doing that. If you are trying to be too successful, lawyer, doctor, or own [a] business it is difficult. No way someone like that is going to come back and talk about their lives and share. They [other Isletas] are going to think that they are successful and only interested in making money and that they have a lot more than the rest of the community.

It is important that you are not seen as being power hungry or greedy. You are not trying to be better than them. They like it when you are being complacent or living within manufactured housing and listen to them. You have to humble yourself, listen to a lot of their bullshit, and pretend to pay attention. You get a job there and work with people. You don't try to engage the world in any way. . . . That is fine with them. If you are seen as trying to do too much for yourself, that is when the anger comes. If you want to be successful, you want to kick ass, you can't be there [Isleta]. You are one or the other [professionally aggressive or living in Isleta]; there is nothing in between. It's a strange choice between [the two]. The costs are high if you don't want to be like them. (Informant 2007)

I asked this Isleta what the minimum behavioral requirements were for community members:

You need to have a job, not be an alcoholic or [have a] big drug problem would be good too. Essentially you need to not subsist off another person. But even if you don't have a job or have a lot of problems you can still be socially successful if you are heavily involved in the religious activities. They are comfortable with that because it is theirs [Isleta]. They never think you are uppity even if you are trying very hard in religious ceremonies. Because they [those heavily involved in traditional religion] are never seen as hypocritical by the community even if they are bad people. They are never accused of showing off in religious activities even if they are way into it to the point of making others look bad. (Informant 2007)

What this Isleta said supports Benedict's perspective of the Pueblos valuing community harmony and control over the individual expression of their members. The desire of the community to preserve order and control over innovation harkens back to the cold societies forwarded by Levi-Strauss (Benedict 1989, 79–81). Desiring and seeking a life different from that of their peers would result in social wrath. Bunzel describes the complicated relationship a Pueblo has with ambition:

In all social relations, whether within the family group or outside, the most honored personality traits are a pleasing address, a yielding disposition, and a generous heart. All the sterner virtues—initiative, ambition, and uncompromising sense of honor and justice, intense personal loyalties—not only are not admired but are heartily deplored. The woman who cleaves to her husband through misfortune and family quarrels, the man who speaks his mind where flattery would be much more comfortable, the man, above all, who thirsts for power or knowledge, who wishes to be, as they scornfully phrase it, "a leader of his people," receives nothing but censure and will very likely be persecuted for it. (1932, 480)

The price of harmony in the pueblo is high for its inhabitants, and institutionalized passivity often comes in the form of repressive communalism. They must keep their ambitions hidden or face community censure. The contemporary Isleta who described his community as one that required its members to remain consummately humble is very similar to what Bunzel describes in the early twentieth century. Communal affect and its mechanisms of enforcement seem to have persisted through the twentieth century and into the twenty-first century. The potential for resentment seems high among the Pueblos, but it is important to keep in mind that this resentment is directed toward fellow Isletas and not against non-Natives. Communal affect has an element of torment, and perhaps even violence, to it. Though possibly a more subtle form of human organizing, it is arguably still in control.

5.6.2 BEHIND PUEBLO SECRETS

Pueblos are well recognized for holding secrets, and there are multiple approaches to explain why they are so guarded. The first is a material approach with an economic anthropological perspective that suggests a stable food supply facilitated less interest and necessity in trade. A stable food source also discouraged immigration as each Pueblo, tied to the same river, had similar harvests. This is in contrast to hunter-gatherer food sources, which were highly flexible, producing abundance and scarcity that might have varied between tribal groups in the same region. The result was a social system that allowed for taking in starving groups but also for expecting to be taken in when under duress. Irrigation-based agricultural groups like many of the Pueblos (Suina 1998) did not experience multiple periods of starvation, and therefore were less likely to integrate geographically or demographically with other groups to survive.

There was only one major adoption of an outside group by the Isletas. In 1880, the Catholic Church gained influence in the Laguna Pueblo, which is approximately fifty miles from Isleta. A group of Lagunas fled to Isleta. These Lagunas are permitted to stay in Isleta and still live there today. The descendants of the Lagunas hold separate feasts and religious events and reside in a housing complex on the edge of the village (though many have integrated into the tribe through intermarriage). A stable food source meant that the Isletas did not need to rely on outsiders for food, trade, or potential relief from starvation.

Another possible perspective on the origin of Pueblos' closed societies is the history of relations with the Navajos. Telling the story of the Pueblos without reference to their regional nemesis would rob the reader of an important instance of historic intertribal acrimony. The strife and hatred between these groups is legendary in this region. The Isletas only recently stopped (in the late 1990s) taking out Navajo scalps from the kiva and chewing on them during ceremonies to soften what I hesitate to call the *leather*. For hundreds of years, there was near-constant and bloody low-level warfare. The brutality was extreme, as are the contemporary Pueblo jokes at the expense of the Navajos. One story an Isleta told me about the Navajos is indicative of this suspicion:

> My great grandfather told me this story. He saw it with his own eyes. A little over a hundred years ago [late nineteenth century] these Navajo came to raid the village. They were always trying to do that. We saw their fires in the distance, so we knew they were coming. So what we did is wait for them and we killed them all. Except for this little boy, you see. He went with them on the raiding party.... I guess the Navajo bring their kids up that way.... We got that little boy and we took him to the village and we tried to bring him up but he kept biting people. He was like an animal, ferocious like a Navajo. I guess we killed his father.... So they tied him to a stake in the village. He tried to run away and so we broke his legs so he couldn't. People would come through and look at him as a Navajo. He would spit and growl. Then when this boy got old enough we let

him go. He ran off into the desert. I guess he went home . . . I don't know. (Informant 2007)

Navajo raiders certainly loom large in Pueblo stories. It is possible that the prospect of Navajo raids created the Pueblo wariness toward all non-Pueblo outsiders. An important point to address is that, though the Isletas experienced conflict with the Navajos, it does not place Isletas into the high trauma category. The Navajos were certainly a serious nuisance to many Pueblo peoples, but these raiders, like the Spanish, did not destroy Pueblo communities. Despite the horrific realities of stolen food, children, and women, and the occasional murder, the raiders did not burn villages to the ground. The entire community was not shackled or relocated; certainly, individuals were, but this problem was not a categorical form of trauma. No doubt, as the story of the enslaved Navajo boy indicates, the Isletas gave as good as they got in these exchanges. Though friction still exists between the Navajos and Pueblos, it now mainly comes in the form of endless bombardments of ethno-tribal jokes. For instance, Pueblos may refer to Navajos as "gut-eaters," and the Navajos call the Pueblos "Gallup-ass-Indians" behind each other's backs.[10]

5.6.3 CULTURAL EXPOSURE

Though the Isleta Pueblos are outside the high trauma group as it is defined in this work, the Isletas have historically experienced forms of cultural trauma as a result of the exposure of sacred information. Beyond the raiding by regional groups, the Isleta sensitivity to outsiders regarding their culture may originate from a particular twentieth-century event. This cold society, as seen from the perspective of Levi Strauss, might be exacerbated by the publishing of *Isleta Paintings*, a book that depicts secret Isleta Pueblo religious ceremonies. In the early 1930s, under the guidance of Elsie Parsons, anthropologist Esther Goldfrank paid an Isleta artist to paint various religious events and explain their significance. The Isleta, Felipe (a pseudonym), was willing to help Goldfrank, though with some reservations. Felipe describes his motivations in the Isleta Paintings foreword: "I have no way of making a living, no farm. . . . If I had some way to get help in this world I would never have done this [depict the ceremonies]. I expect to get good help" (Goldfrank and Parsons 1962, 1). Felipe was aware of his part in this cultural transgression as well as how its rarity made it monetarily valuable to anthropologists:

> These drawings you will never see anywhere because no one [else] could do them, it is too hard. They are afraid to die if they do them. I don't want any soul to know as long as I live that I have drawn these pictures. I want good satisfaction because they are valuable and worth it. They [the subjects of the pictures] are most secret. No one can see them but Indians who believe. (Goldfrank and Parsons 1962, 1)

The Isletas still speak about the *Isleta Paintings* book. A few Isleta households I visited own a copy. When I asked one Isleta whether all adult Isletas know about it, I was told, "Yeah, everyone knows about it. The older people would talk about it when you were little. Not like a story, but to say what a bad person [the artist] was for doing it [painting the pictures and selling them]" (Informant 2007). Apparently, "[The community] found out who it was and he moved from the village" (Goldfrank and Parsons 1962, 1).

Felipe's fear also touches a little-discussed but fundamental part of Isleta sociopsychology and a mechanism of combating differentiation on the reservation. He leaves it vague, but Felipe is afraid of some type of retribution, "They [other Isletas] are afraid to die if they do them [share the ceremonies]. I don't want any soul to know as long as I live that I have drawn these pictures [of] them" (Goldfrank and Parsons 1962, 2). Understandably, fear and judgment by his peers concerns Felipe. Yet judgment and fear have central roles in the Isletas' sustaining communal affect and are common themes within their stories.

Felipe is actually afraid of two semi-related things. He is afraid of social and religious ostracism. When he says "They are afraid to die if they do them" (Goldfrank and Parsons 1962, 2), Felipe may be implying that even the suspicion that he shared ceremony will result in the medicine men denying him proper burial rights, resulting in his spirit never finding peace and being forever stuck in this world. He is also afraid of something more sinister. If he is found out, witches, in Felipe's perspective, will hex and curse him. The resulting blights may take the form of illnesses or of accidents that may bedevil or kill him.

Citizen Potawatomi politics exist as open, elaborate, and organized and are disseminated via tribal newspapers and websites. Isleta political culture is ostensibly the opposite. Though they may sue one another, I never got the sense that the Citizen Potawatomis cared about what was said if it reflected poorly on their character. In interviews, not once did a Citizen Potawatomi express concern about his or her community standing. The Isleta Pueblos are entirely different in this regard. I began interviews with an opportunity for participants to ask me questions, and most Isletas asked variations on the questions, Who have you talked to? and What did they say about me? They expressed disappointment at participant confidentiality rules that bound me from answering these questions.

Almost paradoxically, in Isleta the most intense form of sociopolitical conflict comes in the suppression of sociopolitical sentiments. Though in many ways the Isletas are a comparatively harmonious indigenous group, their social concord might be kept or reinforced via socially clandestine methods. Judgments, rumors, and fear are the primary sociological forces that suppress Isleta acrimony. Tied to the dynamic of fear is rumor, which is one of the other methods for communal solidarity. Rumors in Isleta reach from the banal, such as neglecting one's cattle, to extreme cases, such as accusing someone of practicing witchcraft. These mechanisms of integration, along with the history of class-based politics, produce the tranquil and static character of Isleta political life.

5.7 COMMUNAL AFFECT: FELLOW FEELING, FELLOW JUDGMENT, AND FEARFUL FEELINGS IN ISLETA

To reiterate, much of this chapter has described the Isletas as a rather culturally intact and conservative group. The Isletas minimize community conflict and describe serious disagreements as the influence of non-Isleta community power. Minimizing conflict makes Isleta political culture distinctive from that of the Citizen Potawatomis. Conflict among the Isletas is not historically shaped in the sense of contrasting worldviews as it is among the Citizen Potawatomis, which infuses Citizen Potawatomis' conflict with nearly intractable and ever intense contestations. All polities have communal conflict and so do the Isletas, as the grazing and ranching stories demonstrate, but narratives around these conflicts do not seem to incorporate elaborate narratives around ethnic authenticity or colonial processes. While the Citizen Potawatomis were eager to draw conclusions about the negative nature of their rivals through conflict, the Isletas—even when it was suggested they could have done so had they cared to, without judgment by the interviewer—were uninterested in drawing similar conclusions. Explaining the lack of apparent organized or intense political conflict in Isleta could end here by noting the absence of divergent material, emotional interest groups, and tribal historiographies, but there are still conflicts and politics in Isleta.

In the Polanyian triad, the Citizen Potawatomis and factional Sacred Heart Citizen Potawatomis encapsulate two distinct worldviews that were forced into one tribe. The melancholy of the Sacred Heart faction and the self-interest of the Barrett faction created tribal disharmony. Yet, if the triads created are based on each faction, the factions represent the logics of the adopted historic experiences of each group. The Isletas, due to the lack of major experience with trauma or development, have a motivational logic that has shifted little over time and remains largely one of communal affect from previous centuries, as described in figure 5.1.

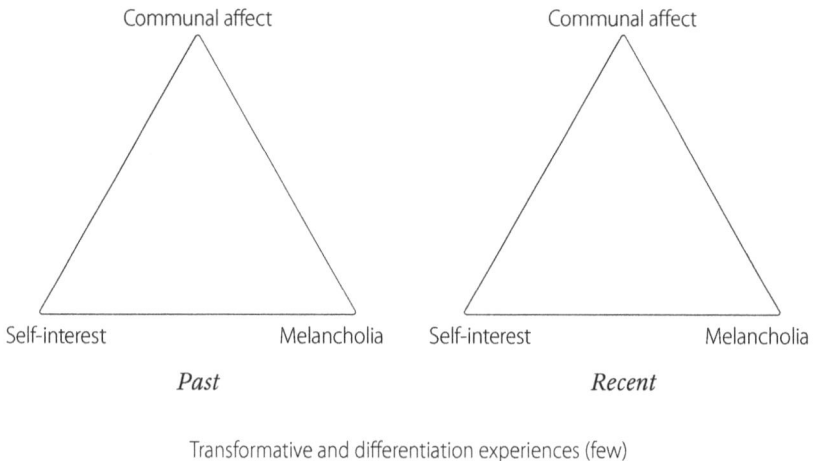

Transformative and differentiation experiences (few)

FIGURE 5.1   Absence of change among Isleta Pueblos, and the persistence of communal affect

The logic of communal affect goes far in explaining the emphasis that Isletas place on distancing themselves from serious conflicts, through positing these conflicts as the ugliness of the non-Pueblo world. It also explains the Isletas' reluctance to hypothesize into rival tribal members' character flaws in the stories they told me. Whether the Isletas' preference regarding acrimony is that it is suppressed or that there is a communal proclivity to greater harmony is unclear—a question not needing total resolution. Some Isletas no doubt are born more individualistic or cantankerous than others and find little release for their aggressive nature and individualism within the context of culturally induced sociopsychological suppression. Other Isletas appear so deeply steeped in communal affect that they seem to outwardly manifest internal harmony. It is safe to conclude that the Isleta community has a history and culture that stifles the individual's demand for autonomy; it sets the price high for such demands. In the case of the Isletas, the lack of differentiating experiences and an intact traditional culture of integration are two forces mutually reinforcing one another.

The emphasis here on communal affect is not meant to suggest that the Isletas are naturally prone to like one another or to agree. Their differences are less organized or shaped by ethnohistorical experience, hence there are fewer ideological grounds for them to clash over. The logic of communal affect prioritizes order over conflict. Such an order can exist because there is an absence of processes that create contrary worldviews and ideology. There is also an absence of the same organized interests groups that pursue differing ideological commitments. Finally, the Isleta Pueblos' past has a different kind of power from that of the Citizen Potawatomis, which differentiated the tribe. Social mechanisms that emphasized integration such as taboo and suspicion survived in a way not present for the Citizen Potawatomis.

A reader inclined to Rousseauean images of American Indians might interpret the Isletas as having avoided modern forms of greed and as living in harmony with each other and the past (Pueblo groups and their coherent social organization were the bases for Indian Affairs reformer John Collier to reorganize tribal governments in the 1930s and 40s). This harmony is somewhat accurate compared to other tribal polities. Despite not having intense points of disagreement, such as within the Citizen Potawatomis, the Isletas are possibly aided in reducing conflict and projecting harmony through the heavy presence of social anxiety and certain traditional mechanisms for the social suppression of communal aggression. Isleta social cohesion is also reinforced through strong forms of social censure—from the circulation of rumor about greed to participation in witchcraft. The next section describes the image of the limited good found in agrarian traditional societies, which contributes to the prevalence and severity of rumor.

5.7.1 THE POLITICS OF SECRETS: IMAGE OF THE LIMITED GOOD

Nietzsche suggested that who we allow to judge us reveals volumes regarding our inner lives and the society in which we dwell. Whether implicitly or explicitly determined, who people deem worthy to judge them will reveal a great deal about their psyches and societal orders. Those who allow themselves to be judged by strangers are more likely to live in a society that lives between shame and honor; to be judged by a god, a religious society; to be judged by elders, a gerontocracy. For individuals to create their own mores and judge themselves would indicate a society that is highly individualistic and liberal—compared to those that listen to priests, for instance—and that tends to be corporatist and communal.

Examining who judges does not merely produce vague impressions of societal characteristics; it is a critical indicator of the allocation of normative power in societies and the internalization of this power. Nietzsche framed the understanding of the relationship between freedom and power as one of judgment and allowing judgment. As Nietzsche's biographer, Rudiger Safranski, describes the centrality of Nietzsche's conception of judgment to our lives, "The battle in morality boils down to the power of definition. It is ultimately a question of who allows himself to be judged by whom" (2003, 302).

Who we reference in the normative evaluation of ourselves very much impacts our decision-making process. It indicates as well the deepest level of sociopsychological penetration by a system of thought, or inculcation into that system. Similar to any other group, American Indians have a multiplicity of potential sources from which to project casting of judgment. If American Indians are to be judged by others, they can look to their peers, their ancestors, or future generations. If looking for nonhuman judgments, American Indians can look to religion, spirituality, or the environment.

American Indians often talk about three temporal groups as arbiters of a correct course of action: ancestors, peers, and future generations. Past, present, and future were distinctions made often by the American Indians I spoke with on reservations. Of the three tribes with whom I did direct ethnographic work, each tribe seemed to posit greater weight for the judgments of certain temporal groups over other groups. The Rosebud Lakotas—whose politics will be discussed in the next chapter—more often cite their ancestors' opinions over those of contemporary or future generations as having saliency in their major political decisions. The Lakotas are cautious not to act in ways that violate the wishes of past generations that suffered with great significance. The Citizen Potawatomis split along factional fissures in their decision making, with the developmentalists thinking of future generations and the Sacred Heart Potawatomis emphasizing those who have already passed. Compared to these groups, the Isletas are concerned with what members of their community know about them in the present. If the Isletas are suspicious of outsiders, they are still more suspicious of each other. This concern comes from the anticipation of harsh verdicts from other Isletas. The pervasiveness of judgment between Isletas makes everyday politics an exercise in subterfuge. I was told that such deceptions were key to mitigating future rumors. An Isleta explained her strategy and motivation behind deception: "You have to hide things as much as you can. It is important to control what other people know about you. They are always trying to find things out then hold it against you" (Informant 2007). I asked if the interviewee could elaborate on why it was necessary to hide so much, to which she replied, "We are strange people. Always trying to get something on you then tell someone else. They try to subtly make you look bad if you cross them" (Informant 2007). On the Isleta Pueblo it is, as another Isleta put it, "like a game of espionage and counter-espionage" (Informant 2007).

Anthropologist George Foster examined the dynamics of rumor-based peasant communities and explained the origin of this form of social relation as a result of the "image of the limited good" (1965). Foster suggested that these communities understood "good" or "desired" things as being in finite quantities. As Foster states about origin of the concept of the image of the limited good,

Broad areas of peasant behavior are patterned in such fashion as to suggest that peasants view their social, economic, and natural universes—their total environment—as one in which all of the desired things in life such as land, wealth, health, friendship and love, manliness and honor, respect and status, power and influence, security and safety, *exist in finite quantity* and *are always in short supply*, as far as the peasant is concerned. (1965, 296)

The Isleta Reservation has similar dynamics. Isleta farmland was finite and non-expandable. It has become increasingly limited as the population has grown. It was repeated that land even outside the village was only rarely for sale.

The image of the limited good presents a zero-sum game as "An individual or a family can only improve a position only at the expense of others" (Foster 1965, 296). Under these perceived conditions, individual ambition is a communal problem: the "apparent relative improvement in someone's position with respect to any 'Good' is viewed as a threat to the entire community" (Foster 1965, 297). There are constant accusations that a member is using greater resources than they deserved to the harm of others.

Isletas perceive envy and jealousy as strong emotions of their peers. "You have to watch out, people are always looking at what you are doing. I don't drive my new car to Indian doings because I don't want them thinking we're rich" (Informant 2007), was what one Isleta said about judgment. Social relations in communities like Isleta are "an interpersonal combat fraught with anxiety, uncertainty, and aggressive potentials" (Foster 1965, 301). Social as well as material resources are highly scrutinized. An Isleta told me that his mother chided him for serving an honorary position twice in his lifetime. According to this Isleta, "I was acting like a big man doing this community services, she said 'stop showing off like a big shot by cleaning those ditches'" (Informant 2007). I asked him if he was serious and was told, "Yeah, she was really angry at me and held it over me for months" (Informant 2007).

Other Isletas made similar statements about the nature and power of rumor in the tribe. One said, regarding what constitutes rumor, "Anything really. People here [Isletas] just don't have much to do. You don't want people knowing too much about you because they can use it against you later on" (Informant 2007). Often I asked what the cost was for rumors against them. Would it cost them jobs? Or influence with others? Standing in any clear sense? Not one Isleta I spoke with identified a clear personal cost to rumor. Isletas repeated variations on, "You just don't want them to" or "It is upsetting and pisses me off" (Informant 2007). The most clearly articulated cost was an Isleta who seemed to imply that social life consumed a great deal of her energy already and that controlling possible rumors, despite the initial concern, meant less work in the long run. As this Isleta put it, "It is easier to have them know nothing about you than deal with what happens when they do" (Informant 2007).

Echoing the Isleta who complained about his community's desire to see him "beaten down," Foster says, under these circumstances,

> The ideal man strives for moderation and equality in his behavior. Should he attempt to better his comparative standing, thereby threatening village stability, the informal and usually unorganized sanctions appear. This is the 'club,' and it takes the form of gossip, slander, backbiting, character assassination, witchcraft or the threat of witchcraft, and sometimes actual physical aggression. . . . Concern with public opinion is one of the most striking characteristics of peasant communities. (1965, 305)

The Isletas show similar patterns in their worldviews as the peasant societies that Foster describes with his limited good theory. They, as do Fosters' peasants, frame individual advancement as a threat to community cohesion and equality, and as an attack on the resources of those left behind—and they utilize rumor to express dissatisfaction with those who puncture the social equilibrium.

5.7.2 DESERT WITCHES: DIVISION AND FEAR FOR SOCIAL COHESION

One subset of general rumors in Isleta is that of witchcraft. In this work, the decision whether to discuss accusations of witchcraft and the presence of witch hunts in Pueblo politics was a difficult one. As an important feature of Isleta Pueblo politics and a mechanism of communal integration, I deemed that accusations of witchcraft merited inclusion. Pueblo accusations of witchcraft have been written about before (see Bunzel 1932; Dozier 1983; Leighton and Adair 1966 for discussion of Pueblo witchcraft) and should therefore be no secret for those who are familiar with indigenous polities or peoples. Details on the actual hunts and accusations are intentionally omitted. Indeed, no Isleta provided me with any significant details on particular ceremonies, rituals, or specifics of these events. I was only able to ascertain that accusations of witchcraft, and community responses to these accusations, occupy some portion of Isleta cognitive terrain. Put simply, there are Isletas who believe in witchcraft and other Isletas who have to deal with those who believe in witchcraft, and vice versa. This division makes witchcraft salient to political and social life in the village.

I was visiting Isleta in springtime and had to make an early afternoon trip to nearby Albuquerque. Telling an Isleta about my scheduled journey, he informed me that I would not be able to come back to the village until the evening, as the streets would be blockaded. Asking why the Isletas were doing this, he said it was because of a religious ceremony. I asked another Isleta about what type of ceremony was in progress, and was told, "It was to chase out bad spirits from the village, to purify it" (Informant 2007). Satisfying the stereotype of a nosey outsider in Pueblo communities and worldviews, I asked about what went on during the ceremony, to which an Isleta replied, "It is a hunt for witches" (Informant 2007). And when I attempted to return to the village, police and community members blocked the roads and only allowed Isletas through.

There are sensitivities around the subject of witchcraft in American Indian communities, and few write about supernatural beliefs in contemporary American Indian studies and politics. This sensitivity takes the form of being concerned about witchcraft, and of being concerned about the opinions of outsiders who discover this belief in witchcraft. I asked those willing to discuss witchcraft whether it should be written about. A few Isletas were concerned that they would look "foolish" to outsiders. "I don't want people to think we are crazy or fools," an Isleta said (Informant 2007). Most told me that writing about Isleta society and politics would be incomplete without at least mentioning it. As one Isleta man told me, "You can't talk about this place and what goes on here without understanding that [the role witchcraft plays in Isleta life]" (Informant 2007). I asked an Isleta who was more forthcoming about witchcraft about how many Isletas believe in the presence of witches on the reservation and was told, "Probably half of the people here believe in witchcraft doing something around here" (Informant 2007). I asked this same Isleta to estimate what percentage of Isletas he knew well who thought that witches were the most pressing issue on the reservation, and he said, "About twenty percent of those guys really think witches are controlling a lot and make a lot of the bad things happen here. Yeah, one in five maybe think it is the biggest issue" (Informant 2007). Some Isletas ridiculed others' belief in witchcraft. One Isleta sarcastically called the members who participated in the searching for witches "the ghostbusters" (Informant 2007).

5.8 CONCLUSION: RECENT CASINO WEALTH AND THREATS TO COMMUNAL AFFECT IN ISLETA

To say that the religious and secular authorities get along well would miss a form of Isleta's hidden bellicosity. Moments of conflict came about during my interaction with Isletas that indicated a division between the religious authorities (American Indians' religion) and the business and political leaders. I was told that religious leaders were upset that the casino was not shut during the witch hunts and had scolded the governor when he arrived to take part in a purification ritual during the hunt.

The casino and this economic development created a mild issue during the witch hunt, though this rare instance of communal conflict might foreshadow more disagreement to come in Isleta politics. Processes that lead toward greater differentiation are becoming more powerful in Isleta. The degree of homogeneity may be more difficult to sustain in the future, and there will be a rise of self-interest and perhaps of melancholia among those alienated from economic gains but subject to witnessing it in others. "The casino pays really well for around here, much better than the alternatives" (Informant 2007), said an Isleta who worked at the casino. Pay varies significantly by position, and salaries for mid-managers at the casino can be as high as $75,000, which is a considerable income for the area. The casino hires non-Isletas but strongly encourages tribal members to apply and also provides these members with preferential treatment. One Isleta said, "They want to hire us [Isletas] and pretty much do if we are qualified at all over other applicants" (Informant 2007).

However, not every position is highly paid. "All they are qualified to do is push a broom," is what a younger Isleta professional told me about fellow tribe members who have not had the similar benefit of a formal education (Informant 2007). I was told that the class difference seems to be growing and so is resentment—especially from those Isletas unable to be hired by the casino due to failed background checks. An Isleta describing the growing inequality and community dynamics resulting from disparities in casino employment remarked, "There is a lot more snickering these days by people [tribal members] who get big jobs about those who don't get them or can't. There is a lot of anger from the second bunch" (Informant 2007). Another informant observed that "religious and senior people [in the tribe] end up doing crummy jobs at the casino and don't like having younger bosses tell them what to do" (Informant 2007).

The casino positions are also eroding Isleta respect for gerontocracy. Younger Isletas have significantly greater access to educational resources compared to their elders. As a result, younger cohorts are more highly represented in upper-level managerial positions. Walking the casino floor and the hotel in Isleta are younger tribal members in business suits, managing older members, who are more directly related to customer services, such as food and housekeeping. This trend of the young managing their elders is not unique to the Isletas but is a developing one in Indian country. When I asked about the difficulties of managing older tribal members, an Isleta said, "Yeah, it is pretty weird. It is awkward and nobody feels good about it. You see these guys as important members of the community outside the casino, then you are asked to boss them around in the casino" (Informant 2007).

The new form of employment and diversification of employment (manager against non-manger, salaried against hourly) as a result of the establishment of the casino hotel is encouraging variation in Isleta that challenges the mechanisms of Isleta integration and their communal affect worldview (see figure 5.2). The enforcement of cohesion and similarity may increase as a response to this change with harsher slander and censure.

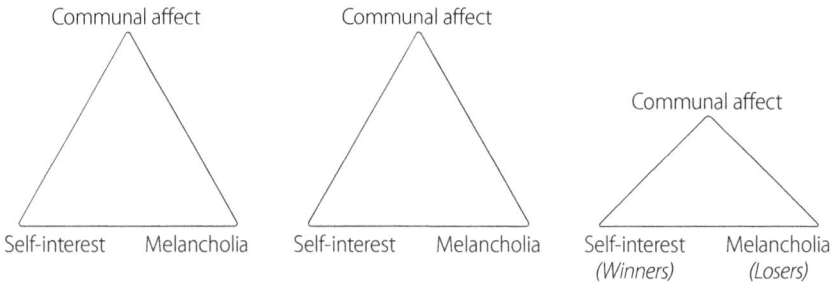

Casino / resort jobs may create class differences and resentment in Isleta.

FIGURE 5.2 Potential for change among Isleta Pueblos from casino development

Among those placed to do well, we would anticipate a rise in self-interest, but, for those left out of this system, there could be a form of melancholia and nostalgia for a past where power and value was arranged differently.

There is a strong possibility that the Isletas may develop an organized factional system due to immersion in casino-driven class formation. The logic of communal affect will thus be harder to maintain. Communal affect's diminishment was noticed by some Isletas on the reservation. As one Isleta told me, "People used to watch each other's kids. They would have something to do and the kids would come by for a little while but not anymore. You don't have that, people got jobs. There isn't the same community; it started changing fifteen years ago. The res [reservation] is a little different" (Informant 2007). The development of casinos has certainly been recognized as creating or exacerbating tensions inside communities. Angela Gonzales (2003) provides an exacting analysis of the rise in tension around membership and of what is now at stake when tribes become vehicles of economic development. Along with Gonzales's work on casino-related conflict is that of James Fenelon, whose work on gaming suggests that further conflict is likely as a result of clashes in traditional values and new values (2006), which increases the potential for intratribal conflict (2000). Though not explicitly about conflict, Jessica Cattelino's work also addresses social tension generated from economic change (2006, 2008). Through the pain and profit approach, what is claimed in this work, or is made more explicit, is that wealth not only changes the nature of tribes to profit-making ventures but alters their values toward self-interest.

The increase of class differentiation among the Isletas is far from the level seen within the Citizen Potawatomis. There are no internal groups among the Isletas strongly advocating changes that either facilitate or drastically mitigate economic development as there are within the Citizen Potawatomis. The casino is still an outside force—though owned by the Isletas, it is certainly not a traditional Isleta institution or one compatible with harmony. It has yet to create strong polarized groups or elite rivals who organize those groups, though one has the sense that this might change.

CHAPTER 6

Melancholic Logics
and Communities of Survival
The Rosebud Lakotas and Their Loss

"The heart of Indian country is here in the Plains."
— Rosebud Lakota Tribal Member

"People here [South Dakota] think that we are the most
Indian because we suffered so much."
— Rosebud Lakota Tribal Member

"Man, the bravest of animals and the one most accustomed
to suffering, does *not* repudiate suffering as such; he *desires*
it, he even seeks it out, provided he is shown a *meaning* for
it, a *purpose* of suffering."

— Friedrich Nietzsche,
On the Genealogy of Morals

A caveat is necessary at the beginning of this chapter. The following pages tell a story of one of the most abused groups in American history and do so through a provocative lens that might strike some readers as uncharitable. The Rosebud Lakotas, and the Lakotas in general, are strong and remarkable people who have endured hardships far beyond what any group should. This story focuses on their traumas (past and current) and, in doing so, is difficult and painful to tell and hear. Intensifying this already-difficult story of genocide, this chapter uses Freudian

and Nietzschean analytical lenses that are often unflattering and discomfort-
ing. Associated with twentieth-century fascism, the work of Friedrich Nietzsche
induces unusual angst and apprehension in scholarly communities. Freudian and
Nietzschean themes are developed here not to make a point about the literature
but because these lenses shed light on the interplay among anguish, melancholia,
worldview, and behavior. Consequently, many readers might object to this analysis.
However, it is my belief that this aspect of Lakota, American Indian, and human life
in general—that of possible self-exploitation and melancholic fatalism—needs
expression through these sociopsychological concepts. Anguish and sometimes
ill-fated human responses are a part of our lives, whether we wish they were or
not. I apologize in advance to those who might take offense, but I am hopeful
that some who read this story and my interpretation find the telling powerful and
necessary. One hopes that, particularly in dire situations, clarity of vision can be
valued as a prerequisite for positive change.

6.1 INTRODUCTION

To state that the human psyche has a peculiar relationship with the phenomenon of loss would be to underestimate the price of higher consciousness. Loss, for instance, looms heavily in our calculations of risk (see the
seminal work of Tversky and Kahneman 1991 on "loss aversion"). Loss and
pain, generally linked, hold significant weight in our sense of the world's
potential and can, for lack of a better word, *sear* us in the places where
we encounter loss. This is one of this work's common secrets. This chapter
engages the social and political effects of loss, pain, and trauma and their
role in shaping the worldviews of the Rosebud Lakota community in South
Dakota. More than those of the Citizen Potawatomis or Isleta Pueblos, the
Lakota worldviews I encountered while conducting research for this book
were the nearest to melancholic.

Forced removal and massacres took much from the Lakotas and other
Sioux groups of the Great Plains in the late nineteenth century. Court
cases, history books, and family stories document these losses and suffer-
ings. Though not as brutal as the nineteenth century, the twentieth century was not gentle to the Lakotas either. Social pathologies of alcoholism,

drug abuse, and suicide—all uncomfortable topics—slowly diminished the Lakota hope for a more generous future. What previous abuses might also have robbed the Lakotas of is the ability to easily hold an orthodox perspective of the world if that perspective is organized by material self-interest.

The Rosebud Lakotas' reservation encompasses approximately twenty communities, with the tribal headquarters located in the town of Rosebud, South Dakota. The towns in the reservation are small, with a gas station and a few government buildings that either are owned by the tribe or are administrative offices of the Bureau of Indian Affairs, which has a branch in Rosebud. The residential villages have small track homes built by the tribe or federal government. Each village has approximately twenty to thirty homes that are often painted brightly and sometimes have rusted playgrounds in their backyards. Thickets and brush cover the rangeland between these small towns and villages.

The Rosebud Lakotas are descendants of the Sicangu (Burnt Thigh) band of Lakotas, who are a Siouan-speaking group and part of the larger Sioux cultural and linguistic group. The American Indian population on the reservation was approximately ten thousand, according to the U.S. census in 2010. As the Rosebud Reservation is full of life and hope, it is equally full of death and despair—individual and collective. Unemployment among Rosebud enrolled members on the reservation is around 75 percent (U.S. Census Bureau 2000). The economic conditions on the Rosebud Reservation place this community in the low economic development category. The U.S. national suicide rate for teenagers is approximately 10 per 100,000 (Borowsky et al. 1999). Among young men on the Rosebud Reservation, the suicide rate is 200 per 100,000 (Borowsky et al. 1999). According to Robert Moore, a public health professional, in his testimony to the U.S. Senate's Committee on Indian Affairs, the "suicide rate is 200 per 100,000 for males ages 15 to 24, which right now puts us as having the highest suicide rate in the world" (*Youth Suicide* 2009, 18). The life expectancy for Rosebud males is in the upper forties, lower than that of men in Haiti and sub-Saharan Africa; Rosebud women have a slightly higher life expectancy (White 2013).

Within this context of fatalism realized, the Lakotas of the Northern Plains have refused to accept more than $1,200,000,000 in funding as of

2010 (Giago 2010). In the nineteenth century, along with other Lakotas, the Rosebud tribe sued for the illegal acquisition by the U.S. government of the Black Hills region, which extends from present-day western South Dakota into Wyoming. The Lakotas so revere the Black Hills area that they take offense to it being called "the Black *Hills*" and ask that it be referred to as the "Black *Mountains*," or "Paha Sapa" in Lakota, to give it proper respect. Proper respect and honor, particularly for geographic spaces, is a reoccurring theme among the Lakotas. Though the Black Hills settlement and the degree of abuse in many Lakota communities have been understood as distinct issues, this work treats them as intertwined phenomena, not only as problems and solutions but as reinforcing expressions of a similar logic.

By allowing settlers onto treaty-protected land in the late nineteenth century, the U.S. government violated a provision of the Fort Laramie Treaty of 1851. The Black Hills were permanently taken from the Lakotas after a series of wars to defend their homelands from settlers. Awarded approximately $104,000,000 in 1980 from the Black Hills court case brought in 1922, the Lakotas have not signed the papers releasing these funds. In a community that desperately needs economic and health development capital, why would the Lakotas not accept the money?

Focusing on the political culture of the Rosebud Reservation in South Dakota, this chapter analyzes the origin of the Lakotas' worldview, which prohibits the acceptance of economic development offers even in such dire circumstances. This chapter is divided into three main segments: (1) a brief outline of the Lakota's historical experience since the mid-nineteenth century and the social statistics of pathos on the reservation; (2) an analysis of the creation of a deontological and absolutist political culture from a dominant melancholic logic supported by traumatic historical experiences and intense social pathologies; and (3) an analysis of theories of value formation, rationality, intergenerational trauma, and what I term the *politics behind the geographies of exploitation.*

A theme in this chapter is a potential origin of the Lakota worldview (though I recognize that there is not one worldview but many, the dominant worldview will be discussed as it informs decision making and political behavior). It is often argued that the Lakotas are a warrior society (see Hassrick 1964 as one of many examples) and that this aspect of Lakota society informs their deontological perspectives and political behavior. As Lakota scholar Royal Hassrick recalls a Lakota saying, "It is better to die on the battlefield than to live to be old" (1964, 32). This chapter partially accepts the analysis that warrior values are translated into contemporary political culture but additionally posits that some manifestations of contemporary culture are a result of the melancholic logics stemming from Lakota trauma and poverty. Just as the horse intensified nomadic buffalo hunting among the Lakota, so too has trauma intensified the moral outlook and worldviews associated with their warrior society.

6.2 ROSEBUD HISTORIC AND SOCIOECONOMIC CONTEXT

The Greater Sioux (i.e., Lakota) Nation covered 48,000 square miles in the mid-nineteenth century (Kingsbury 1915, 1248). Traditionally organized into political subunits known as the Seven Council Fires (called *oceti sakowin*), the Lakotas functioned as a military alliance. The contemporary federally recognized Lakota communities are divided among nine reservations in South Dakota, two in North Dakota,[1] one in Montana, five in Minnesota, one in Nebraska, and one in Wisconsin. Lakota communities are also found in the Canadian provinces of Manitoba, Alberta, and Saskatchewan. *Lakota* or *Teton* Sioux refers to the Lakota groups who live on the Great Plains. The particular community with which this study is concerned is the Rosebud Sioux Tribal Nation (henceforth the Lakota or Rosebud tribe), whose reservation is in southwestern South Dakota. The reservation is adjacent to the Pine Ridge Lakota Reservation and South Dakota's southern border with Nebraska.

6.2.1 NINETEENTH-CENTURY LAKOTA HISTORY

Like many tribes that became dominant regional powers during the early colonial period (pre-eighteenth century), the Lakotas' ability to acquire rifles and horses through extensive trading networks helped secure their hegemony on the Great Plains (Blackhawk 2006). These trading relationships between Europeans and American Indians became networks intertwined with violence in the form of kidnapping and slavery (Wishart

2007, 4). At this point, the Lakotas found themselves in a strategic relationship within these networks and surrounded by American Indian
populations greatly weakened by plague. (Sedentary populations that
were denser than those of the seminomadic Indians were more susceptible to the spread of pathogens such as smallpox). Equipped with new
guns and horses, the Lakotas reduced their dependence on agriculture,
which required a sedentary presence, in favor of hunting buffalo (Wishart 2007, 4). During this early colonial period and before direct contact
with Euro-America, the Lakotas were able to expand their territory
significantly at the expense of American Indian groups unable to secure
European guns as easily (the guns primarily originating from the Spanish
along the Rio Grande) (Blackhawk 2006).

6.2.2 LOSS ON THE NORTHERN GREAT PLAINS

During the last half of the nineteenth century, the Lakotas defended their
territories with decreasing efficacy. The Lakotas are placed in the high
trauma category in this study as they were relocated, militarily defeated,
and massacred (and in the low development category due to widespread
unemployment). A series of wars with the U.S. military starting in 1854 and
ending with the Wounded Knee Massacre in 1890 reduced a people proud
of conquest, freedom, and independence to a geographically bounded
class with only memories of conquest, freedom, and independence in a
contemporary context of subjection, dependence, and poverty. As a result
of these experiences of American Indian resistance followed by poverty,
the Lakotas stand as an important group in the American imagination. The
Lakotas represent contemporary America's classical ideal of the Indian in
two important ways: (1) they are the horseback warriors of the roman-
ticized nineteenth-century Indian resistance; and (2) the Lakotas form
many of the images of the poverty-stricken reservations of the twentieth
century. It is these extremes, the warrior and the defeated pauper, that
breed confusion on the nature of contemporary Lakota life and its origins.

Though the Lakotas are a martial or warrior society, it is also possible
to understand that their moral outlook, which refuses needed aid, does
so from a merger of Freudian melancholic sociocultural attributes and
Nietzschean value hierarchies of *ressentiment* and *slave moralities*. It is

plausible that experience, as much as ancient cosmology and myth, has created this Lakota worldview. The Lakotas are deeply proud on one level and deeply ashamed on another, and they live with difficultly possessing both of these extremes.

Lakota military hegemony came to a close after the U.S. Civil War, and the substantial territorial Lakota gains turned into powerful Lakota losses. Western land became a desirable commodity to eastern Americans in post-bellum America. Manifest Destiny drove this western expansion, which already half a century earlier had removed groups such as the Potawatomis during the Jacksonian land disputes (Rogan 1975).

At first, the Lakotas faced the problems not of permanent settlers but of waves of migrants moving westward through the Great Plains. The first Treaty of Fort Laramie signed by the Lakotas and U.S. government in 1851 sought safe passage for travelers on the Oregon Trail through Lakota territory after a number of conflicts erupted between Indians and settlers. The Lakotas agreed to not impede settlers traveling through Indian territories and to allow the United States to build forts in their territory. The treaty required the Lakota, Cheyenne, Shoshone, Crow, Arapaho, Assiniboine, Mandan, Hidatsa, and Arikara Nations to maintain peaceful relations. In return, these nations were assigned geographic boundaries and assured $50,000 annual payments for fifty years. American Indians understood the tribal lands to be held in their possession for perpetuity.

In 1863, gold was discovered west of Lakota territory in what became Montana. Prospectors and those who profited from them, such as equipment dealers and blacksmiths, flooded through Lakota lands again. The Powder River country, the area occupied and traveled by prospectors, was an important hunting ground for the Lakotas. As the prospectors disrupted this area and its resources, the Lakotas retaliated under the leadership of Red Cloud. Red Cloud's War (1866–68) consisted of a series of skirmishes between the United States and Lakotas in which the U.S. cavalry was ill prepared for Red Cloud's changing tactics (Barrett 2007, 188). The U.S. military defeats resulted in the country offering initially generous terms to the Lakotas in the second Treaty of Fort Laramie in 1868, which established the Greater Sioux Nation, encompassing the Black Hills segment of South Dakota.

Gold was discovered in the Lakota Black Hills in 1874. As historian Carole Barrett describes, "Gold Seekers flooded into *Paha Sapa* (the Black Hills)—a clear violation of the 1868 Fort Laramie Treaty—forcing leaders such as Crazy Horse and Sitting Bull to defend Sioux territory" (2007, 188). Wishing to avoid another war as well as to regulate the prospectors, the U.S. government offered payment in exchange for the Black Hills. It was an unpopular offer among the Lakotas, and they rejected it. Many reservation-based Lakotas then joined Sitting Bull outside the reservation boundaries in defiance of an army order that all Lakotas physically report to local agency headquarters. In May 1876, the army launched an offensive to force rogue Lakotas back within reservation boundaries. Possibly the most famous military engagement of the American West was fought during this campaign. The Battle of the Little Big Horn in late June of 1876 resulted in a stunning military defeat of the U.S. military under Custer.

These Lakota successes were short lived. Unwilling to sustain a military campaign during the winter, the Lakota resistance divided into small groups and dispersed. Barrett writes,

> After this victory, the Sioux and their allies fragmented into small bands and dispersed. The army initiated a winter campaign and relentlessly hunted down those bands that had not returned to their agencies. In May 1877, Crazy Horse surrendered at Fort Robinson, Nebraska; he was killed four months later, reportedly while trying to escape. Sitting Bull fled to Canada with as many as two thousand followers. In retaliation for defeat at the Little Bighorn, Congress annexed the Black Hills from the Great Sioux Reservation on February 28, 1877. (2007, 188)

The loss of the Black Hills, though described impersonally and dispassionately in the previous quotation, has had enormous consequences for succeeding generations of Lakotas. The appropriation of this sacred place has created a melancholic attachment among the contemporary Lakotas. Terming the Black Hills an object of melancholic attachment is not intended to undermine the significance of the loss or to treat this sacred space as a geo-cultural accessory but, rather, to point out that this mourning has not stopped and, in the psychoanalytic perspective of Freud ([1923] 1971), has become engrained as cultural melancholia.

Lakota military defeats by the U.S. army shortly turned into the massacre of Lakota women and children at Wounded Knee. In 1889, Congress dissolved the original boundaries of the Great Sioux Reservation and created individual reservations with little geographic continuity. Many Lakotas refused to honor these newly prescribed boundaries. Around this time in the late 1880s, desperation inspired the adoption of a militaristic version of the Ghost Dance religion among the Lakotas. Originally, the Ghost Dance movement was a salvation-based, nonviolent doctrine for clean living created by Jack Wilson, a Nevada Paiute religious leader. The salvation promised by the Ghost Dance philosophy was the disappearance of European Americans and is considered by anthropologists to be a revivalism movement (Kehoe 1989). The Ghost Dance was adopted in such a desperate context that it was even hoped and believed that the dance would make warriors immune to the effects of bullets (Kehoe 1989).

In late December 1890, the last major violent confrontation between the U.S. government and the Lakotas took place at Wounded Knee, South Dakota. On that day in December, there was a brief battle followed by a long massacre. The Wounded Knee Battle, which lasted a few minutes, killed a few dozen Lakota braves. The Wounded Knee Massacre of women, children, and elders lasted hours. By the end of the massacre, it is believed that nearly three hundred Lakotas were killed (Kehoe 1989). This moment in Lakota history is remembered well, is recounted often, and forms a core narrative of these communities. It looms large in national American Indian life and has been a source of meaning for the Lakotas. Like no other event in Indian country, the Wounded Knee Massacre is emblematic of the loss, pain, and victimization of the brutality inflicted by colonization. And it is in this context of pain, removal, and loss in the late nineteenth century that much of Lakota life has since taken place. I asked a Rosebud tribal member if the massacre stopped that day and was told, "It hasn't ever stopped" (Informant 2007). To a certain extent, the twentieth-century socioeconomic conditions of the Lakotas on many South Dakota reservations support the statement that the massacre has never ended.

Yet *who* are the agents of suffering and what are their motives? This is unclear and uncomfortable to ask. At the end of the nineteenth century, exploitation in the form of violent oppression was intercivilizational, *between* Euro-derivative whites and their governments and the Lakotas. In the first decades of the twenty-first century, intercivilizational exploitation still exists, but the geography of exploitation is now less clear. The term *geographies of exploitation* is intended to capture the tension and spatiality of where the concept of exploitation is allowed by scholars and non-scholars to be placed analytically (as discussed in chapter 2) and where exploitation might be argued to actually exist. Like the stoic philosopher, one might make the case that the most prevalent and real form of exploitation is a person's exploitation of himself or herself. Instead, I claim that by emphasizing the interethnic nature of exploitation we undermine its potential to operate intra-ethnically. The narrower the scope, the more the discomfort in the homo-perspective of exploitation (on the potential for sameness to exploit itself) is replicated and intensified. It, therefore, is easy to think about exploitation between civilizations and races or ethnicity, more difficult to accept exploitation within a single race or ethnicity, even more so to accept exploitation within a community, and most difficult to think about a single individual exploiting himself or herself. This is what I mean by the geography of exploitation—the space in which exploitation may be considered and how the distance between the exploited and exploiter is conceptually constrained and expanded.

6.3 POLITICS OF PAIN, LOGICS OF LOSS, AND RATIONALITIES OF MELANCHOLY

"The heart of Indian country is here in the Plains," one Lakota on the Rosebud Reservation told me in an interview (Informant 2007). If this statement is true, this American Indian heart might be broken, but it is a resilient and courageous heart.

The Lakotas often describe themselves in relation to Wounded Knee Massacre. The site of the massacre itself is on the Pine Ridge Reservation, adjacent to Rosebud. When people on the Rosebud Reservation inquired what I was doing there, I told them I was researching political culture and history. The Lakotas were quick to tell me that they themselves were descendants of survivors of the Wounded Knee Massacre. "My great-great grandmother who was a baby then was hid under a body and retrieved later at night," one respondent told me (Informant 2007). Another reported, "My grandfather's grandfather survived that [the massacre]" (Informant 2007). I never asked participants if their families were involved in Wounded Knee or any other massacre, but approximately a third of those I interviewed mentioned this lineage unsolicited.

Lakota journalist Tim Giago's "The Lakota Will Never Forget Wounded Knee" captures the essence of this memory and self-understanding among the American Indian populations of this region:

> December 29 was a day they [the Lakota people] commemorated every year since 1890. It was a day when nearly 300 of their relatives were shot to death in cold blood by the enlisted men and officers of the 7th Cavalry. Ironically, 21 members of the 7th Cavalry were awarded Medals of Honor for this horrific slaughter of women and children.
>
> White people ask why we Lakota still talk about Wounded Knee as if it was not ancient history. If something terrible happened to your grandmother—that's right, your grandmother—something so heinous that it became a part of American history, would you still consider that to be ancient history? I think not. A grandmother can never be ancient history or you wouldn't be able to ride over the river and through the woods to her house on holidays.
>
> Consider this. On December 29, 1890, my grandmother, Sophie, was a 17-year-old student at the Holy Rosary Indian Mission, a Jesuit boarding school just a few miles from Wounded Knee. She was called out with the rest of the students to feed and water the horses of the soldiers of the 7th Cavalry that had just rode on to the mission grounds chasing down survivors that had escaped the slaughter. My grandmother recalled seeing blood on their uniforms, and she overheard them bragging about the mighty victory they had just scored at Wounded Knee. ([2007] 2011b)

The Lakotas remember this massacre in other ways. Annually since 1986, the Chief Bigfoot Memorial Ride honors the victims and survivors of the Wounded Knee Massacre with a two-week memorial ride to the site of the massacre. The ride is carried out on horseback and often in the snow (Informant 2007). Wounded Knee memorial walls, museums, books, and websites mark this event among the Lakotas.

Like the Sacred Heart Citizen Potawatomis in Oklahoma, some Lakotas seem to have a proclivity to interweave stories of individual traumas with histories of group oppression under colonialism. Often these stories oscillate between family abuse and colonial repression. One interviewee on the Rosebud Reservation told me about his relationship with his father, his substance abuse, and the pain caused by his father's failure to apologize before his death.

> I came home from Vietnam to find AIM [American Indian Movement]. Howitzers were pointed against my people. I had a decision to make: Did I belong to the Lakota people or this man's army? I never regretted the decision I made. I was stationed at fort in Colorado.
>
> I took a bus to Colorado Springs. My friends met me there. We drove up. Tried to get to Wounded Knee, got caught, and they did a check and said this guy is AWOL. The MPs took me to jail, stockade for a week, and sent me back to my unit. I wanted no part in this white man's army. Kept on leaving till they court-martialed me. Sent me to prison but didn't want me there. Then tricky Nixon messed up, 1974, had to leave office. Gerald Ford became president, gave Nixon a full pardon. Those of us in prison were told that. Gerald said, "If you have no other offences, just this one, we give you a pardon; go home." A full presidential pardon. Said, "You know you will never be able to work for the federal government," and I said, "You keep your government. I am going home to my people." I've remained home with my people, except to travel.
>
> When I came back and stayed with my family, it was good, but also the most difficult of all of it was dealing with my father. He was around but not really around. We tried to have a relationship. He had a problem when I was younger, and he drank and left me and my brothers and sisters with our mom. We got sober together [he

and his father]. But when he [my father] died, I relapsed. It was that
I was so angry that he would not be able to apologize. That apology
was needed. I thought, "Why didn't he apologize?" It hurts and is
something I will have to carry with me. (Informant 2007)

The death of this respondent's father robbed him of an apology and recognition of the loss and earlier abuse. In the politics of traumatized communities and families, the last act of the abusers, from governments to poor
parents, to their victims is the difficulty these abusers add to their victims'
ability to grieve or mourn properly.

The Lakotas on the Rosebud Reservation seem to have difficulty maintaining awareness both of past losses and traumas and of the needs to compromise with and make concessions to outside governments for further
resources. In the psychoanalytic perspective, this attitude follows what is
understood about the relationship between mourning and melancholia.

When individuals experience loss, a subset of trauma, the object of that
loss can be either mourned or repressed. For those who mourn, grief, or
what we might call acknowledgment, offers the possibility of resolution
or at least a state beyond the trauma of the loss. Freud observed that, in
mourning, we "[find] that the inhibition and loss of interest are fully
accounted for by the work of mourning" (1971, 245). By "inhibition and
loss of interest," Freud means that the individual diminishes due to "what it
is that is absorbing him so entirely" (1971, 246). In melancholia, the loss is
still present, even if unknown. "Unknown loss," which to Freud is unrecognized and repressed—and therefore unable to be mourned—"will result in a
similar internal work and will therefore be responsible for the melancholic
inhibition" (1971, 245). The melancholic "knows *whom* he has lost but not
what he has lost in him" (Freud 1971, 245) and, therefore, distances the lost
from consciousness.[2] It is the persistence of, and obsession with, loss that is
the center of the melancholic worldview, whereby the world, political and
otherwise, is held in enthrall to the perpetually unsatisfied unseen.

The preceding quotation from the Lakota informant explicitly concerned fathers and children, but this story of apologies has historical relevance to what happened in the late nineteenth century. This story about
apologies came from an interview on the subject of communal politics and

Lakota history. The informant told a story not only of his lived experience but also of his tribe's ethnohistory and experience with colonial trauma and abuse. The lived experience between father and child, bridged by the informant's desertion during Vietnam and pardon by President Ford, stands as true and significant on its own. Whether the lived experience, that of family trauma, shaped the narrative of ethno-political trauma or vice versa is impossible to know and perhaps is unimportant in light of how these narratives increase the other's legibility and move toward a world-view that is logical and coherent.

6.3.1 POLITICAL AND COMMUNITY MEETINGS ON THE ROSEBUD RESERVATION

There occurred what a posted flyer described as "a lot" of suicides on the Rosebud Reservation when I was there. A tribal election was scheduled for later that month, which had residents talking about politics. I attended approximately half a dozen community meetings during this preelection period. Topics at these events ranged from teen suicide to elders' knowledge of the pre-constitutional government. Many meetings did not seem to have a clear purpose. I was told that community forums were arranged in order to serve meals afterward to people who did not have enough to eat that day. The only gathering advertised as a "debate," as described on the flyer, in the weeks before the election was on teenage suicide.

Tribal social and political events were often held in the Sinte Gleska University auditorium in the town of Mission. The room had seating for seventy. Generally, twenty to forty people attended, with some leaving early and others arriving during the event. The meetings usually lasted a little over two hours.

The debate on teen suicides most directly engaged contemporary political issues. It also seemed the most powerful and salient to the community. Approximately eight candidates for tribal council participated. During this discussion of young people taking their lives, there was only one mention of jobs and economic development or opportunities. Instead, the candidates attributed suicide on the Rosebud Reservation to cultural loss and, as a solution, proposed more Lakota culture.

The term *hope* and the lack of it in the community were rarely mentioned during the two-hour debate. All the candidates seemed obliged to spend most of their opening remarks talking about how "these days young people don't know the culture" and need to participate in religious rituals, to "get them involved with the sweats and the elders" (tribal council candidate, Rosebud political debate 2008). One candidate broke the general trend and said, "Let us be real. Each of these suicides had something to do with a girl." This statement demonstrated blunt disregard for what seemed to be a taboo perspective at the meeting. When he said this, audience members demonstrated disapproval by lowering their heads, a gesture by which Indian people simultaneously express and refrain from expressing disdain.

Most political candidates at this meeting thought that suicide was commonplace on the reservation because of a lack of connection and goals among teenagers. To those in the room, the cause of suicide was cultural loss, not economic or professional factors. Troubled Rosebud teens needed to feel as though they belonged to the Lakota spiritual community. A sense of the future was never addressed, nor were jobs given more than a cursory consideration compared to Lakota culture. One candidate suggested an internship program for teenagers, but that discussion was dropped after a few minutes.

A theme that appeared in most speeches and in the following discussions was "the old ways" and "getting back" or "going back" to the old ways. This return to older Lakota culture was the most popular solution to the problem of suicide. The theme held that culture, if recovered and transmitted, could help teenagers find purpose, meaning, and support during periods of sorrow. A consensus emerged among the candidates that "young people need the elders to show them the way," as a candidate put it to me afterward (tribal council candidate, Rosebud political debate 2008).

6.3.2 FACTIONS ON THE ROSEBUD RESERVATION

Factions on the Rosebud Reservation are not clearly defined and certainly not organized like those of the Citizen Potawatomis. Though it has a strongly grievance-based political culture, it would be incorrect to say that Rosebud is a community completely void of those interested in economic development. Some individuals interested in development projects get elected to tribal council or other offices but, once in office, fight uphill battles. As one Rosebud Lakota told me, "Yeah, we elect people trying to get businesses, but we throw them out fast, because people get upset at them when it doesn't happen like they said or as fast" (Informant 2007). At the meeting on teenager suicide, I asked a Lakota next to me what groups were most interested in economic development. The Lakota pointed to three men who were differently dressed than the other five candidates.

In communities that have unemployment rates over 70 percent, understanding what middle class means is difficult. Tribal members with economic security in the community seem to come in two types: those Rosebuds employed by the tribe or a federal government agency such as the Bureau of Indian Affairs, and a very small group of ranchers, who might be somewhat wealthier than federal employees. Those ranching in Rosebud were unusual. This group, mostly if not entirely men, dressed in similar fashion to Charlton Heston and Ronald Reagan in the 1970s and 1980s, with blue jeans, cowboy shirts, and bandanas tied around their necks. Of approximately fifteen candidates running for tribal council, there were two cowboy-dressed candidates. I asked a Rosebud if people on the reservation gained a lot of political power from their wealth. He answered, "In politics, it doesn't do much for them. Some people say that they can buy votes, and maybe they do. They don't seem to get elected very much. People resent them mostly. It is not good to have all that money and try to convince people you are an honest person. That is hard to do here when people have so little" (Informant 2007). This small group of cattle ranchers was politically inconsequential. The same respondent told me that, "even if they get elected, people vote them out real quick" (Informant 2007).

6.3.3 WARRIOR SOCIETIES AND MELANCHOLIC WORLDVIEWS

How are we to understand the political culture of the Lakotas? As mentioned at the beginning of this chapter, the Lakota tribe has been portrayed as a warrior society that values honor (Informant 2007). It is certainly true that the Lakota men lived by a code of honor. "Bravery, Fortitude, Generosity, and Wisdom—these were the virtues which all [Lakota] men were expected to seek," according to ethnographer Royal Hassrick, but "of the four great virtues, bravery was foremost for both men and women" (1964, 32). Lakota bravery was for the battlefields and beyond; it was

Pyrrhic bravery, as on many occasions it demanded "show[ing] deliberate courage in fighting the grizzly bear" (Hassrick 1964, 32). The second great Lakota virtue, fortitude, was associated with bravery. "[Lakota] fortitude implied two things: the endurance of physical discomfort and pain, and the ability to show reserve during periods of emotional stress," observed Hassrick (1964, 34). Like all virtues, bravery and fortitude needed to be demonstrated.

> The importance of the quality of fortitude was demonstrated again and again in the social conventions of the Sioux. Men on war missions or hunting expeditions were noted for their ability to suffer wounds unflinchingly, to experience long periods of hunger and exposure. Fortitude dictated the voluntary acceptance of physical pain during burial ceremonies, when the mourners were required to subject themselves to self-inflicted slashings on the arms or legs, or to endure the agony of tiny skewers inserted beneath their skin, or to cut off the first joint of their little finger—all in order to show respect for the dead. (Hassrick 1964, 34)

Bravery and fortitude combined in a set of ethics heavily invested in honor and the repression of pain through strength. These expectations certainly bound Lakotas to their present-day deontological moral outlooks.

On the Great Plains, honor and bravery were not distinctly Lakota virtues. Interested in the phenomena of hope in culturally ravaged societies, philosopher Jonathan Lear examines the practice of counting coup[3] and the power of demonstrating virtue and danger among the Crows, who shared a similar warrior ethos to the Lakotas. Lear notes, "In the paradigm act of counting coups, one hits one's enemy with one's coup-stick before harming him. This requirement suggests that the struggle is not simply for survival, but for recognition. The enemy sees that you are the victor before you strike him down" (2006, 16). Counting coup was about honor, but, according to Lear, this honor was motivated by the importance of geographical and physical boundaries.

> This is the paradigm act of counting coups, the establishment of boundary recognized by both sides. And this paradigm is itself

like a condensed version of the original act of the Crow warrior's planting a coup-stick in order to mark a boundary. Hitting him with a coup-stick is like first planting a coup-stick in order to mark a boundary; then one kills him because he has violated it. One can now see that all the other acts of counting coups are derivative from this paradigm. (2006, 16)

The context in which these honor or warrior societies functioned has been relegated to the past. The Lakotas do not hunt buffalo, live nomadically, or engage in long periods of explicit warfare. The assumption tacitly accepted by the neo-primordialist perspective (scholarship not inclined to analyze American Indians as socially constructed) is that American Indians' worldview, which supports such moral ideals as honor and dishonor, has survived throughout the centuries. To a certain extent, worldviews are shaped by and are products of previous worldviews. However, the Viking and Norse civilizations were honor and warrior societies, and we do not think of Scandinavian countries as having unusually strong honor- or principle-bound societies. These moral outlooks that see in absolutes of right and wrong or of honor and dishonor are foundational to Rosebud Lakota tribal identities. *Absolutist worldviews* (those unamenable to negotiation or utilitarian self-interest) are also exceedingly proficient in finding ways in which the world can disappoint and hurt those who possess them. *Justice* and *injustice* form a potentially more painful lens through which to see the world than do the concepts of profitable or unprofitable. As trauma informs contemporary Lakota worldview selection, these worldviews have a strong tendency to revisit their origins. In Lakota community culture, the boundary between melancholy and honor is thinner than those who think about contemporary Lakota culture want to believe.

It is no secret that American Indians suffer greater rates of environmentally induced psychological pathologies than the average American (Bassett, Buchwald, and Manson 2014, Manson 1996, Manson et al. 2005). Neither is it a secret that American Indians suffer from the condition known as post-traumatic stress disorder (PTSD). In Indian country, depression, suicide, alcoholism, and the sexual abuse of adults and children (Brave Heart 2000, 2007, Brave Heart and DeBruyn 1998) are compounded by a lack of access to mental health support. These critically important sociopsychological characteristics of American Indian societies are kept out of political analysis. Studies on the politics of indigenous communities that address these issues generally focus on delivering better treatment and improving policies. This focus is certainly needed, but to ignore the fact that approximately 75 percent of a community's citizenry might experience PTSD as children or adults (Robin et al. 1997) and that this situation does not influence political culture and decisions itself is a startling omission.

Scholarly work pays significant attention to the realities of American Indian mental health and the precarious conditions in which indigenous peoples attempt to maintain healthy emotional lives (see Morrissette 1994). These grim conditions generally are treated as pathologies and coping mechanisms often resulting from experiences of colonialism (Brave Heart 2003). There has been great reluctance to blur the boundaries between pathology, pathos, and culture. Indigenous scholarship tends to believe that trauma creates coping mechanisms, which is true, but this trauma is placed on the fringes of society and culture. In some instances, trauma among indigenous and colonized peoples needs to be placed at the core of societies because loss inextricably is part of human life itself. If we are socially constructed creatures, some of us are constructed in pain and loss.

An observer might posit that the Rosebud Lakotas are practicing human sacrifice of their children and themselves to extract meaning from the pain of previous generations. Children on the reservation, as a result of poor nutrition and access to nutrition, develop diabetes at astonishingly young ages (Baldwin et al. 2009). Possibly a result of lack of opportunities, the teen suicide rate is the highest in the country and likely among the highest in the world. In many ways, the genocide never stopped but only slowed, although the identities of the contemporary perpetrators are unclear.

In response to the suggestion that the Rosebud Lakotas are harming themselves by not accepting development funds, interviewees generally responded in terms of culture and dignity. A representative explanation of a Rosebud Lakota on why they oppose accepting the Black Hills settlement is that "it would betray our ancestors. We will never accept a settlement. They gave their lives for the Black Hills" (Informant 2008). The contemporary Lakotas' ancestors did die in protecting the Black Hills, but the ancestors lost, and the Black Hills are gone. Contemporary generations think that, with their sacrifices, they are protecting their ancestors. At this point in conversations with the Lakotas, the avenue is open to suggest that the Lakotas are still dying for the Black Hills, but it would have been impolite as a guest to give voice to that sentiment.

Why is it that this honor culture persists among the Lakotas in this region? The point is not to chide the Lakotas but to attempt to understand what conditions support a worldview that ignores aspects of reality (they will never get the Black Hills physically back and are still dying for them). If the standard interpretation of ancient worldviews does not fully explain the persistence or strengthening of absolutist and deontological outlooks, then how could the prevalence of high trauma and poverty explain the Rosebud Lakota moral outlook? By even asking this question, this work moves into uncomfortable territory for many who research American Indians.

6.4 LOSS, VALUE, AND ETHNIC DIFFERENCE

Among the Rosebud Lakotas, the historic battles with the Seventh Cavalry are mixed with battles of alcoholism, abuse, and premature death. As prevalent as pain and historical trauma is in this region, the people and communities are not unkind, without hope, or devoid of wonderful forms of humanity. Nonetheless, pain and loss are significant for the Lakotas not only in Rosebud but also throughout this area. For instance, men in the Pine Ridge Lakota Reservation adjacent to Rosebud, as mentioned at the start of chapter 1, have life expectancies of forty-five to forty-eight years (Schwartz 2006) and substance abuse rates even higher than those in Rosebud. Why then do the Lakotas refuse certain forms of help? In what ways have these extreme conditions of loss and poverty informed Lakota political culture in terms of its moral outlook, perceptions, and worldview?

At the outset, this work proposed a meta-theme of common secrets. One of these common secrets is the role of pain and loss in rationality, perceptions, and moral outlooks. The Rosebud Lakotas see the world differently than do the Isleta Pueblos or the business faction of the Citizen Potawatomis. The Rosebud Lakotas live in a pain-filled world created in a brutal history, but at least this history and world are clear. In contrast to the Isletas, who are often unsure of what decisions to make due to the absence of historically created interest groups and the presence of older religious cosmologies that do not easily accommodate contemporary decision-making situations, the Rosebud Lakotas derive clear meanings from their past. "Whites cheated us out of everything," said one Lakota, "the Black Hills, everything" (Informant 2007). The cosmology of binary oppositions outlined by Lévi-Strauss (1955) exists within Lakota narratives about values and ethnicity. "Honor" and "dishonor," "right" and "wrong," "give word" and "lie," "materialistic" and "spiritual," "respect" and "use," and "family oriented" and "individualistic" are systems of opposition that surface in Rosebud speech. Unlike the Isleta worldviews, many of the worldviews present among the Lakotas are in part responses to poverty, abuse, and loss, not a mandate from ancient worldviews.

Comments from informants on the Rosebud Reservation repeatedly indicate that melancholic worldviews inform how this group perceives the political world and frames its own decisions. The decision to reject the Black Hills settlement under conditions of extreme financial need and the high rates of depression and suicide seem to indicate a community in need of help but unwilling to accept or let go of the past in order to gain support for the future.

The previous chapter discussed the importance of peer judgment among the Isletas. The logic of communal affect strongly prefers unity and harmony to division. However, the creation of community harmony among the Isletas emerges from harsh peer judgment that enforces stern anti-individualism. Rumors of ambition and accusations of witchcraft were known to be traded as political and social commodities to reinforce strong norms of communalism. These measures, like all good forms of repression, generally functioned to preempt certain behaviors and expressions. Among the Citizen Potawatomis, the divisions between developmentalist/ self-interested and grievance/melancholic factions can be seen in different preferences of whether to honor past or future generations through the acknowledgment of historic losses that prohibit economic gains. Ancestors loom large in Lakota society. After I asked why the tribe would not accept funds over the Black Hills, one tribal member who described himself as "progressive" told me, "We will never take the money. It would be wrong. Our ancestors sacrificed and suffered for that land. We will never take the money. It would betray them" (Informant 2007). Of the many methods to honor those who came before us, two major categories can be teased out. Sacrificing is the first, and living well is the second. The Lakotas see sacrifice as showing respect for their ancestors, whereas most of the Citizen Potawatomis do what their ancestors could not: live well.

6.5 EXPECTATIONS AND EXPERIENCES

In *States of Injury*, political theorist Wendy Brown links Nietzsche's theory of value to political identities (1995). Brown says Nietzsche viewed "the substitution of reasons, norms, and ethics for deeds," and further, that "not only moral systems but identities themselves take their bearing in this reaction" (1995, 69). Painful memories create expectations and norms in communities and individuals regarding their own behavior and identity (see figure 6.1 for visualization of change from courage to melancholia). Put differently but with a similar sentiment, I heard that Indians are different from whites significantly more often and with greater clarity on the Rosebud Reservation than on other reservations. Other comments did not deviate far from one respondent who said, "We [Indians] are honorable people. We keep our word" (Informant 2007).

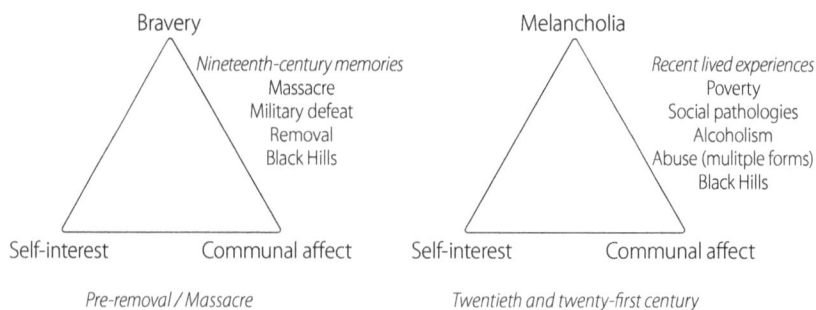

FIGURE 6.1 Shifts in worldviews and logics of Lakotas through ethnohistory and lived experience

Embedded in statements such as these is the assumption of racial differences in values—that whites are willing to break commitments, and do so at the expense of Indians. The historical experience of loss and betrayal by the federal government, generally associated with violations of the Fort Laramie Treaties, is a large part of the political culture on the Rosebud Reservation. It would be difficult for history not to be part of the Rosebud Lakotas' worldview as a result of what happened there. Resentment against these events runs deep and strong among the Lakotas. These community politics and identities of resentment both confront pain and are manifested in pain.

6.5.1 POLITICS UNDER PTSD

Trauma alters values and perception. Those who have been abused have a heightened sense of fear, particularly of future abuse. PTSD often results from severe exposure to intensely negative experiences; its symptoms vary (Bratton 1998). PTSD makes difficult future engagements with phenomena similar to that which initially traumatized individuals. Psychiatrist Mardi Horowitz explains that PTSD "characteristically includes experiences that in some way repeat the traumatic event, often as intrusive ideas accompanied by unbidden feelings" (1986, 244). Mark Bouton and Jaylyn Waddell describe PTSD as a condition of fear and suggest, "An organism learns to associate environmental stimuli with a frightening event, and those stimuli consequently evoke fear. Fear can be defined as a loosely coordinated set of physiological, behavioral, and cognitive responses that are designed to get the organism ready for a future aversive event" (2007, 41; see also Ehlers et al. 1998; Herman 1997).

Some individuals who undergo difficult circumstances are able to become highly durable. For others who undergo similar events, Horowitz points out, "preexisting neurotic conflicts may be impediments to processing stressful life events" (1986, 246). Horowitz outlines four ways in which PTSD can impact perceptions and attitudes:

1. Irrational but enduring attitudes that "Bad thoughts cause real harm," "Wishing makes it so," or "One must always be loved or protected by another in order to survive."

2. Active, incompatible, and so conflicted sets of wishes and values whose content is associatively similar to traumatic events.

3. Excessive preoccupation with fantasy-based reparations of deficits, involving fantasies related associatively to what was threatened by or lost in the stressful event.

4. Self-concepts and role relationship models that organize stressful information by the view that the self is bad, damaged, worthless or incompetent. (1986, 246)

Certainly points 1, 2, and 3 can be applied to the Lakotas' political culture and worldviews regarding the Black Hills dispossession and sensitivity to development offers. As one Rosebud Lakota who described himself as interested in economic development responded when I asked about the difficulty of bringing businesses to Rosebud, "It is tough. People here [Rosebud] see a contract and they think Custer is riding over the hill" (Informant 2007). This perspective, which sees impending harm, views outsiders as exploitative, and is constantly on guard resembles the psychological symptoms of PTSD outlined by Horowitz.

6.5.2 RAGE, HONOR, PAIN, AND ALCOHOL

Though reluctant to address a potentially sensitive issue in American Indian communities, I was compelled by the facts on the ground to write about the prevalence of witchcraft in Pueblo society. The prevalence of alcohol in Lakota Sioux communities is similarly as sensitive a subject. Substance abuse is understandably a charged topic; however, by not addressing alcoholism, I would be leaving out of this analysis an important sociopsychological community characteristic.

Conflict seems internalized among the Lakotas. In preparing to be hurt, they are remarkably apt at self-injury. They might state that the "world is good at hurting us," as it seems to according to ethnohistory, but neither the white world, as construed by them, nor that of outsiders engages in reservation pillaging or conducts raids on this community. Being hurt and getting hurt may work in conjuncture. On the Rosebud Reservation, violence is not organized by and among competing factions as it is in the Citizen Potawatomi polity. Conflict and violence, I claim, are often internalized among Lakotas in the region. Substance abuse such as alcoholism has contributed to a melancholic worldview similar to the Sacred Heart Potawatomi dyadic systems of oppositions. A physician working on the Sioux Cheyenne River Reservation, a community with similar socioeconomic conditions as Rosebud, observed:

> They are strangely silent. . . . This Indian passivity and silence, however, is deceptive. Mild alcoholic intoxication is all that is needed to allow the seething, repressed hatred and frustration to surface. Unfortunately for the Indians (fortunately for the white man) these hatreds, once unleashed by alcohol, are directed inwardly and towards members of the immediate family. Wife beatings by intoxicated husbands are common. Recurrent episodes of wild drunken driving, leading to serious injury and death, present this prevalent self-destructive tendency of the Sioux. In the younger age groups, especially among the dormitory students, suicidal gestures, breath holding contests, glue sniffing, and self-laceration are common. Only rarely, on the other hand, are epithets hurled at white people; even rarer are instances of Indian attacks on whites. (Prager 1972, 41)

The physician describes the prevalence of self-destructive behavior on the reservation, and therein lies the inverted nature of agony. The next Lakota generation engages in telling signs of intense self-directed anger such as "suicidal gestures, breath holding contests," and "self-laceration [now commonly referred to as 'cutting']" (Prager 1972, 23).

Residents on the Rosebud Reservation face strong pressures both to drink and to abstain. These two expectations are powerful themes on the Rosebud Reservation. Life on many reservations exhibits this paradox. Posters fill the reservation with descriptions of the debilitating results of alcohol, and as anthropologist Thomas Biolsi has described, the Rosebud Reservation has pursued multiple, unsuccessful legal strategies to remove liquor stores from Mission, South Dakota, the largest town on the reservation (2001).

Beatrice Medicine, who studied drinking among the Lakotas in the 1970s and 1980s, explains:

> There is a tremendous pressure from peers to drink alcohol. This is especially so for Lakota males to whom drinking means becoming

or being masculine. Most males drink to demonstrate their *bloka*
"character." *Bloka* can be translated from Siouan to correspond
to the Spanish macho or chauvinistic behavior. However, a more
appropriate English gloss is male superiority, a desirable character
trait among Lakota males. This is especially significant in opposition to the terms *winkte*, which not only means womanlike but also
commonly designates a male homosexual. In a culture that previously institutionalized male homosexuality, the term is now generally colored with ridicule and derision. Manhood is signaled by
bloka-ness, and current enactment of masculinity is demonstration
of the ability to drink. For a Lakota male to refuse a drink is a sign
of weakness and femininity and often results in teasing and verbal
abuse. The connotation of a dare is important here. One often hears
male teenagers being dared to "Be a Man! Have a drink!" All indi-
cations and inclinations are that it is normative for a Sioux male to
drink alcohol. (2006, 59–60)

Medicine's description of initiations into adult manhood and alcohol consumption and the link between drinking and masculinity in Lakota peer
groups are not, of course distinct to the Lakotas. As has been observed
in America (West 2001), the United Kingdom (Tomsen 1997), and Japan
(Shimizu et al. 2000), acceptance or rejection of alcohol as determining
maleness or femaleness is shared among cultures beyond that of the Lakotas. However, what is distinctive among the Lakota communities is the
prevalence of alcoholism and the fact that those whom it affects are not
fringe groups. Alcohol is both an indicator and a facilitator of more trauma
for communities. The Rosebud Lakota told me that alcoholism peaked in
the 1970s and 1980s (which coincides with the time of Medicine's fieldwork) and that levels of abuse have declined slightly since then. None of
my interviewees, however, suggested that alcoholism was not a significant
problem on the Rosebud Reservation.

Medicine describes a pattern not unlike regular cycles of human emotions concerning masculinity influenced by alcoholism:

There is, then, a definite pattern to drunken Lakota masculine
behavior. It begins by drinking a great deal of any available alcoholic

beverage. This is the feeling good stage in which talking, joking, and bragging—the telling of tales of daring and success—occurs. This is often referred to as a "laughing spell" by some males (Mohatt 1972, 274). It is followed by a period of maudlin reminiscences that often lead to tears. This is one of the few time when Sioux males resort to tears in public. This phase can be traumatic for young children who may be present. After this comes a stage in which bellicosity and belligerence dominate. Kutter and Lorincz (1967) indicate that drunkenness allows Sioux individuals to display aggressiveness that is under control when they are sober. This aggressive behavior often results in fights and acts of violence. The final state is complete comatoseness—called "passing out" by the Lakota in reservation vernacular. (2006, 60)

I avoided direct forms of participatory research with alcohol at Rosebud. Most nights, I ate dinner and spoke with people at a bar next to a public golf course on the edge of downtown Mission. It was similar to many restaurant bars in that region—loud, with an all-wooden interior and neon lights. The reservation does not have grocery stores and prohibits convenience stores from selling alcohol, so this bar was one of the few places in the county that sold alcohol. Much of its business was carry out, with customers coming in and taking out their beer. While dining at the bar, it was common for patrons to be approached by Indians asking for money to help them visit a sick family member. Crowds of twenty to thirty men, both Indian and non-phenotypically Indian, gathered outside the bar entrance often enough for the grass to have turned into a firm mud. The purpose of this gathering was unclear to me at first, until I was told that many of the men were looking for friends who patronized the bar and who would buy them the alcohol or share what they had purchased.

Families are sometimes included in drinking, and not shielded from it, on Lakota reservations. Kemnitzer observed drinking habits on the Pine Ridge Reservation, which are also true in the Rosebud Reservation:

Although the main environments for social drinking are homes, car parks and bars, in all of these the whole family is included. Small children are present at drinking parties, and infants are taken to

bars and there suckled, or beer and wine is mixed in their bottles.
Children under twelve play around the drinkers in bars, and by the
age of fifteen are in drinking groups of their own, but do not participate in public bar drinking until they are older. . . . The drinking
culture is also expressed in the play of younger children:

> Two young boys are playing with toy cars. They pretend to
> load the cars with people, drive the car to White Clay [off-res-
> ervation town] for wine, get drunk, and wreck the cars on the
> way home. Little girls playing with dolls make up a situation
> where the "parents" get drunk and fight. (1972, 139)

6.6 TOWARD THE POLITICAL BEHAVIOR OF TRAUMA

Do those suffering from PTSD, alcoholism, or depression vote in elections and participate in politics? Does that constitute what is claimed in
the Rosebud community: that politics has been "derailed" by abusers?
I do not think this accounts for how abuse changes community politics.
The influence is not that direct. Individual and family pathologies or even
pathos can set the tone for community culture and perceptions of the
world around them. However, pathos is both an indicator and facilitator of
drastic conditions.

The first impact of abuse and trauma on politics and decision-making
occurs through the altering of perceptions and values. It is presumed that
abused individuals see the world differently. The betrayed, for instance,
seek trust as a virtue and might search for trust but only see betrayal. Quick
to avoid a new, severe betrayal, as is common in traumatized individuals,
they might be inclined to exhibit paranoia, whether justified or unjustified. The result is a propensity to reenact hurt and to forgo opportunities
to experience something different (see Horowitz 1986 for the problem of
"new" experiences for the traumatized).

A context of abuse encourages perceptions of future abuse and mis-
deeds. The attempt to finance a tribal grocery store on the reservation
exemplifies the political decisions that result from the blending of honor or
melancholic politics and perceptions and predictions of future injury. As

of the fall of 2007, the Rosebud Reservation did not have a grocery store. The stores at which tribal members purchased groceries were in Valentine, Nebraska, and Winner, South Dakota, approximately sixty miles away from the center of the reservation. Capital is scarce, and financing difficult to come by for the Rosebuds. A tribal member told me that businesses regularly close. Drastic poverty and low wages means narrow margins among households and little disposable income. Consequently, prospective financiers see tribal businesses as a significant credit risk.

When I was engaged in fieldwork on the Rosebud Reservation, the Shakopee Mdewakanton Sioux (Dakota) Community in Minnesota offered to fund a $3 million grocery store on the Rosebud Reservation. The Shakopee Mdewakanton Sioux are Dakota Sioux, which means that they are Siouan peoples but woodland dwellers, not plains dwellers like the Lakotas. The wealthy Shakopee tribe outside the Minneapolis area owns a profitable high-stakes casino with annual revenue between $600 million and $1 billion (McNaney and Nahm 2010). Though not privy to the loan papers myself, I was told by tribal employees and council members that the Shakopees were willing to provide a $2 million loan and $1 million grant. Those would seem generous terms, given that a member had told me that few other financial entities had made offers to fund the tribal grocery store.

However, the Rosebud tribal council rejected the Shakopees' offer. A sitting tribal council member explained to me that he and many council members voted against it because "the Shakopee wanted the terms to say that if there was a dispute, the dispute would be litigated in Minnesota state court, not our tribal court on Rosebud. It was a bad deal" (Informant 2007). The councilperson who told me this described himself as on the more progressive side of the spectrum of tribal politics but still could not accept a deal perceived as insulting tribal honor. Another tribal member told me that, due to the jurisdiction issues, the deal was "an affront to our tribal sovereignty. We can't have another state's court tell us what to do" (Informant 2007).

The Rosebud Lakotas' responses to the loan terms indicate that they took offense to the issue of jurisdiction. Residents who knew about the terms felt that it was not only morally wrong to have the loan adjudicated outside their tribal courts but also an affront to their dignity as a tribe.

A $1 million grant and $2 million loan with few to no other offers seem fair given the dire circumstances of the Rosebuds. The Shakopees did not request that the disputes be resolved in Shakopee tribal courts but in Minnesota state courts. The Rosebud residents who supported a rejection of the financing never made clear to me what was objectionable about dispute resolution occurring outside their tribal courts, other than to say that it was an insult to their honor. "They are going to try to take advantage of us," one Rosebud resident said about the Shakopees. Another resident told me, "We would never accept something that dishonors our sovereignty like that. It has to be in our courts or else no deal" (Informant 2007).

The rejection of the grocery store loan does not seem to be an isolated instance of dignity hindering economic progress. A Rosebud Lakota told me that other stores had wanted to start franchises on the reservation.

> If you look around the reservation, what you see here is 139 years of acculturation. You don't see no industry here. It isn't because they won't come. No Wal-Mart, no McDonalds because we stipulate that, if you come here, you have to recognize we are sovereign nation and have to go by our laws here. Abide by Indian law, "No thank you," they say. So they don't come. So there is no industry here for our people. (Informant 2007)

The discussions of the loan to bring a grocery store quickly become visceral. So intense were the responses and emotional buildup that follow-up questions of whether it were unreasonable or unfair to expect the Shakopees to agree to adjudicating contract disputes in the court of the debtor seemed imprudent. There was little reflection on the interests of the Shakopees. Few of the Lakotas with whom I spoke acknowledge that part of the $3 million loan was a grant. The perceived injustice and indignity were what caught and very much held their focus. The Rosebud Lakotas look for dignity in a world short of such goods.

The perception of indignity in what is by business standards a fair contract illustrates how perceptions and values alter decisions. With gas stations serving as major food sources (foods made from refined sugars are inexpensive) for a community with a diabetes rate 800 percent higher than the national average (Manning 2005) and where type II diabetes has been diagnosed in a six-year-old (Informant 2007), healthy, non-junk food is a community necessity.

Why we are inclined to seek out our disappointments and frustrations is an interesting question. It is my opinion that it is worthwhile to ask or consider why a community, such as that of Rosebud, seems to instigate painful events, a severe form of disappointment and frustration. It seems possible that it is done to serve as a mirror into past trauma and past disappointments and frustrations. The Black Hills matter might concern honor, but the Lakotas, I believe, refuse to find closure and therefore continue at least some of the trauma of colonization. The grocery store controversy, whether the store ultimately is built or not, can be interpreted in a way that lets the Rosebud Lakotas reaffirm the injustice of the past even though the store may have nothing to do with their historical exploitation. A trend in Indian country is to re-create disappointment and frustration in inappropriate or unhelpful places. Sometimes an offer to finance a grocery store might be just an offer to finance a grocery store.

6.6.1 THE REPETITION COMPULSION

One of the goals of this work was to demonstrate how traumatic pasts beget painful futures. The first way that re-injury occurs is through how the world is framed and how that impacts worldviews. Lakota suffering creates value orientations, sensitivities, and perceptions that negate efforts to escape the dynamics that produce the suffering. The Lakotas adopt values that reflect what they could have, namely honor but not wealth, and contrast those with whites' behavior. The Lakotas see betrayal all around them as an omnipresent element of social relations.

In conjunction with the first dynamic of hypervigilance comes an important second set of psychoanalytic concepts based in the repetition compulsion. Why the Lakotas re-create social traumas—whether these injuries be the status of the Black Hills, negotiations over grocery stores and economic inclusion, or social violence from sexual abuse and alcohol—might be best understood as coming from the "conservative nature of living substance" (Freud [1920] 1961). This proposition holds that humanity might prefer the intensity of pain over the banality of pleasure, or, as Freud puts it, "Unpleasure corresponds to an increase in the quantity of excitation and pleasure to a diminution" ([1920] 1961, 30).

From the psychoanalytic perspective, the answer to this question lies in the in the interplay between the unconscious and the conscious. Early in *The Ego and the Id*, Freud states, "The division of mental life into what is conscious and what is unconscious is the fundamental premise on which psycho-analysis is based; and this division alone makes it possible for it to understand pathological mental processes, which are as common as they are important" (1923, 2). The answer to why people undermine themselves, according to Freud, is found in "pathological mental processes" rooted in the interplay between the unconscious and the conscious realms of human cognition (1923, 9).

The question of why some groups seem to enact environments to hurt themselves, which is fundamental to this project, is not new but has been excluded from the social sciences' more central discussions. Satisfying and unsatisfying behavior—as well as the peculiar way that some labor toward unsatisfying outcomes more than they should—are captured only by the gravitational metaphor of rationality, not the magnetized metaphor of rationality. In *Beyond the Pleasure Principle*, Freud proposes a similar question regarding the strange charisma undesirable outcomes have: "The most that can be said, therefore, is that there exists in the mind a strong *tendency* towards the pleasure principle but that tendency is opposed by certain other forces or circumstances, so that the final outcome cannot always be in harmony with the *tendency* towards pleasure" ([1920] 1961, 9).

As in this project, Freud willingly recognizes that most human behavior is pleasure-seeking and supports positive, self-preserving (often material) outcomes and that only a few of our many painful experiences are results of the reality principle. Freud states, "There can be no doubt, however, that the replacement of the pleasure principle by the reality principle can only be made responsible for a small number, and by no means the most intense, of unpleasureable experiences" ([1920] 1961, 4).

Why is the pleasure principle subverted by the reality principle? Why do people find themselves repeating painful experiences? To Freud, the answer was found in the unconscious. This realm of the unconsciousness where these experiences are held goads and guides our behavior to re-create situations similar to previous traumatic ones. The "psychology of consciousness is incapable," Freud says, "of solving the problems of dreams and hypnosis" (1923, 19). What Freud is saying, among other things, is that our minds do not fully process traumatizing events like other memories, and they become latent, not conscious but "capable of becoming conscious at any time" (1923, 13). Freud describes the logic of the repetition complex:

> As a consequence of the old conflict which ended in repression, a new breach has occurred in the pleasure principle at the very time when certain instincts were endeavouring, in according with the principle, to obtain fresh pleasure. The details of the process by which repression turns a possibility of pleasure into a source of unpleasure are not yet clearly understood or cannot be clearly represented; but there is no doubt that all neurotic unpleasure is of that kind—pleasure that cannot be felt as such. ([1920] 1961, 4)

This repression is not applicable to Lakotas regarding the Black Hills issue, which vividly recalls their community's trauma, but I do believe that the essence of this dynamic can occur without full repression to the point of amnesia. Though a segment of psychoanalytic scholars would suggest that one "is obliged to repeat the repressed material as a contemporary experience instead of . . . remembering it as something belonging to the past" (Freud [1920] 1961, 5), the Lakotas who talked about pain seemed to use it as a transcendental medium to reach communion with the pain of their ancestors. It is entirely possible that the compulsion to repeat one's own pain is a moment of return to the sacred from the profane, a socially constructed ritual or contemporary form of the "myth of the eternal return" as theorized by Mircea Eliade (1959). Precisely in the moments of hope and progress when the Rosebud Lakotas have an opportunity to satisfy material needs such as the grocery story offer and to live more fully, they find themselves re-injured and among new forms of an old pain, a fort/da, a peekaboo game of life and death, the future and the past that ends in tears not joy.[4]

6.6.2 LOSS, MELANCHOLY, AND POSSESSION

In Freudian analysis, powerful experiences of pain, such as massacres, recounting of massacres, removal, child abuse, and violent episodes involving drugs, are not entirely latent but often repressed memories. That traumatic memories are repressed is an insight from Freudian analysis that is unhelpful for the Lakotas who are aware of their history and what was taken. Of more help is the concept of repetition. A critical contribution of the psychoanalytical approach and Freud's work is the recognition that new situations are never really new. Individuals might have new opportunities, but these are tied to the past through the unconscious, memory residues, and memory traces (Freud 1923). The future is not itself but is often seen by the unconscious as a time in which to mitigate the inefficacy of the past to quell the agony of the unconscious. Using the future to deal with past pain is rarely a successful strategy and generally reinforces pain.

This reliving of past pain, along with the act of possession, is at the heart of the melancholic perspective. "In differentiating normal from pathological grief, Abraham and Freud characterized normal grief as feelings of painful dejection, with loss of interest in life functions and inhibition of activities," says Horowitz (1986, 243). In comparison, pathological grief is "marked by additional features such as panic, hostility toward the self, regression to narcissistic forms of self-preoccupation, and other signs of deflated self-esteem" (Horowitz 1986, 243). Accompanying the loss and anger are melancholy and an obsession that undermines healing. As Žižek describes the psychoanalytic perspective on loss and melancholy, "Therein resides the melancholic's stratagem: the only way to possess an object that we never had, that was from the very outset lost, is to treat an object that we still fully possess as if this object is already lost" (2000, 661). This melancholy not only harms retrospective attachments but also damages future and contemporary healthy relationships. Thus, Žižek states, "The melancholic's refusal to accomplish the work of mourning thus takes the form of its very opposite, a fake spectacle of the excessive, superfluous mourning for an object even before this object is lost" (2000, 661). It is this obsession, mixed with the characteristics of PTSD, that makes a future life beyond this loss difficult. "Mourning [successful healing] is a kind of betrayal, the second killing of the (lost) object, while the melancholic subject remains faithful to the lost object, refusing to renounce his or her attachment to it," as Žižek (2000, 661) describes the motivation to remember painfully. The melancholic, from the perspective of therapy, needs to remember how to forget.

6.7 THE VALUE OF PAIN AND TORTURED IDENTITIES: NIETZSCHE AND THE AMERICAN INDIAN

Few philosophers have confronted the relationship between context and value as directly as Friedrich Nietzsche in *On the Genealogy of Morals* and *Beyond Good and Evil*. These works followed Hegelian dialectical analysis in the thesis, antithesis, and synthesis (Hegel [1812] 2010) examination of the origins and variation in worldviews, values, and moral outlooks. As Nietzsche himself recognizes, "Would anyone like to take a look into the secret of how ideals are made of earth?" ([1887] 2000, 482). Despite Nietzsche's sometimes vitriolic and condescending framing of human context and value, a discussion of moral outlooks after crises would be only half complete without his perspectives.

Nietzsche was interested in the morality of the weak, or slave morality. In his opinion, the history of western civilization has been that of the weak subduing the strong through the creation of a moral system that lessens the efficacy of the strong and powerful by constructing them as evil and the weak as good. Nietzsche describes the weak conquering the strong as a slave revolt:

> The slave revolt in morality begins when *ressentiment* itself becomes creative and gives birth to values: the *ressentiment* of natures that are denied the true reaction, that of deeds, and compensate themselves with an imaginary revenge. While every noble morality develops from a triumphant affirmation of itself, slave morality from the outset says No to what is "outside," what is "different," what is "not itself"; and *this* No is its creative deed. This inversion of the value-positing eye—this *need* to direct one's view outward instead of back to oneself—is of the essence of *ressentiment*: in order to exist, slave morality always first needs a hostile external world; it needs, physiologically speaking external stimuli in order to act at all—its action is fundamentally reaction. . . .
>
> . . . The man of *ressentiment* is neither upright nor naïve nor honest and straightforward with himself. His soul squints; his spirit loves hiding places, secret paths and back doors. . . . He understands . . . how not to forget, how to wait, how to be provisionally self-deprecating and humble. ([1887] 2000, 472–73, 474)

In Nietzsche's assessment, what he calls ressentiment "gives birth" ([1887] 2000, 472) to the slave morality of the weak, which is designed to undermine the strong by changing societal values. I never gained the sense that the Lakotas were such a sinister priestly class. They possessed no identifiable desire to undermine non-Lakota civilization through a slow substitution of values of the ressentiment. This aggressive aspect of what Nietzsche describes does not hold true when applied to the Lakotas.

Nietzsche's charges that in slave morality and ressentiment, "weakness is being lied into something *meritorious*" (Nietzsche 1989, 47). Lakota identity has traces of being reactive but is not a "triumphant affirmation of itself," as Nietzsche claims that desirable or courageous forms of identity are ([1887] 2000, 472). Nietzsche's slave morality and ressentiment attempt to both undermine the strong and elevate the values of the weak. Yet there is a cost to the worldview and value system adopted by the weak in ressentiment. This subterfuge is psychologically subtle. This weak person with a worldview motivated by ressentiment, who inverts "the value-positing eye" (Nietzsche [1887] 2000, 472), might give some insight into the origin of Lakota deontological moral outlooks that prohibit accepting funds at such a heavy cost. As Nietzsche claims, "This *need* [to invert values] to direct one's view outward instead of back to oneself—is of the essence of *ressentiment*: in order to exist, slave morality always first needs a hostile external world" ([1887] 2000, 472–73). Indeed, the Lakotas do live in a hostile world that has betrayed them and conceivably bred in them a need to sustain themselves with absolutist perceptions that justify and find sustenance in the painful past.

A third point Nietzsche makes about the origin of values, though put too strongly for contemporary sensitivities, is the need to value one's pain and the ramifications when pain defines one's own values. Contemporary humanity's desire to examine, dissect, and embrace injury for emotional, identity, or political reasons has serious consequences for their freedom and psyche (see Nietzsche 1989, 46). As some authors working on intergenerational trauma point out, there is a flaw in the talking cure. As Nietzsche put it, "When he [the wounded] then stills the pain of the wound he at the same time infects the wound—for that is what he knows to do best of all" (1989, 36–38). The rejection of white values that lies at the center of much of the contemporary American Indian world's conception of power and authenticity, to a certain degree, could easily be turned on its head by applying a Nietzschean analysis, as Brown suggests doing for all social movements that arise out of injury (1995).

Nietzsche and Freud share a similar perspective on the internalization versus the externalization of violence resulting from trauma or weakness. Neither Freud's pathological nor Nietzsche's weak commit acts of violence against outsiders as much as they do against themselves. The *repetition compulsion* Freud describes does not function as a mechanism for self-hatred via self-punishment in the way contemporaries see it, although that is often the outcome. Nietzsche provides a greater understanding of blame than Freud. Philosopher Brian Leiter suggests that, to Nietzsche, "sufferers *instinctively* look for someone to blame because, more fundamentally (and more obviously), they instinctively want to relieve their suffering . . . but *ressentiment* can only be discharged when it has an object" (2004, 258). The embrace of this denial—our own role in our suffering—is discussed in the coming section.

In contrast to Nietzsche's ugly but aggressive investigation of the origin of values and Freud's honest recognition of our self-undermining dynamics (the repetition compulsion), investigations by scholars of indigenous communities seek flattery or even fail to ask difficult questions. Despite centuries of pain and loss at the center of many indigenous communities' experiences, scholarship is perhaps most comfortable discussing pain and loss via the creation of coping mechanisms or sorrow but not as central to the creation of moral outlooks, political culture, worldviews, or identity. Though pain, loss, and trauma are pronounced features of many tribal experiences and American Indian lives, these features are treated as frustrations to sooth, grievances to settle and wounds to heal rather than central features of why people and tribes make the decisions they do.

Scholars and communities themselves, American Indian or not, should not marginalize the role of loss and pain in shaping politics. One consequence is that questions go unasked. For instance, to my knowledge, no scholar has scrutinized the decisions about the Black Hills or probed beyond the surface-level politics or law into the worldviews or logics that support those decisions. This is a disappointment to the pursuit of knowledge and a glaring oversight.

6.8 GEOGRAPHIES OF EXPLOITATION: A CONCLUSION

Exploitation is used comfortably as a paradigm for relationships between heterogeneous groups (see the analysis in chapter 2 of the misconstrued discussion of sexual violence in American Indian communities, or consider the disinterest in the selling of cheap tobacco products to a population to whom it is a major health threat). For instance, it is relatively easy to use exploitation or a synonym when describing the abusive relationships between different civilizations. Yet exploitation as the conclusion is less comfortable when the exploitation is between American Indians. This moves the paradigm from what we wish to be true—that ethnicity is a protective factor against exploitation—to a way of thinking about things that is uncomfortable. This is an important point (and another common secret), so let it be restated: as the difference between exploited and exploiter is narrowed from heterogeneous to homogeneous; whether that difference is racial, geographic, civilizational, cultural, or economic, there exists more discomfort and liability when using exploitation as an analytical framework. For example, intertribal exploitation (between two tribes) is less comfortably analyzed than the conflict between American Indians and Europeans; and writing about intratribal exploitation (among members of the same tribe) is even more controversial than intertribal exploitation. This study goes so far as to suggest that the most unsettling form of exploitation can be found on the Rosebud Reservation: the potential for one to exploit oneself.

Much violence in Rosebud is self-harm. Regardless of whether the Rosebud Lakotas' actions are the result of melancholic logics merged with a communal Nietzschean value creation, they hurt each other and themselves often and severely. Analyses of self-exploitation, conflicts against oneself, and self-undermining processes have a contentious history in scholarship (see the term *false consciousness* in Marxist scholarship as an example). Rationality and irrationality, as non-exploited and self-exploited, occasionally are found in the nomenclature of these debates around exploitation (see Scott 1976; Popkin 1979). Considering the abundance of interethnic or civilizational conflict, one can assume that relationships between ethnic groups would be important locations for scholarship on conflict and exploitation. Massacres, removal, and genocide make exploitation an apt term for the interaction between non–American Indians and American Indians.

Community violence has been the subject of a growing body of literature in American Indian and Indigenous studies. Public health research has maintained a long-held interest in intratribal abuse and violence. This interest includes work on general vulnerability (Abril 2008a) or specific vulnerability, such as the high prevalence of elder abuse (Carson 1995) or traditional values (Abril 2008b). There are journals, such as *Native Social Work Journal*, which are now dedicated to exploring violence and its aftermath in American Indian communities. While these studies of violence indicate that violence is likely intra-ethnic and critical to how lives are shaped on some reservations, another direction in American Indian studies has heralded work claiming the opposite—or at least that the source of this violence is found outside, not within. Andrea Smith's *Conquest: Sexual Violence and American Indian Genocide* is a venerated example of such perspectives on communal violence (2005). Smith's work, which is followed widely, explains the high rates of violence against American Indian women as a product of non–American Indian perceptions of American Indian women as essentially "rape-able" (2003, 2005). This thesis fits neatly into the current normative paradigm, which posits that exploitation occurs mostly between American Indians and outsiders. When such exploitation is intra-ethnic, there is a strong tendency to externalize the causal factors. Studies that explore violence on the self and by the self fall even farther outside the normative scholarly paradigm.

Research on sexual violence that examines the link between exposure on reservations to childhood sexual abuse and the likelihood of sexual violence later in life receives less attention or praise than research that sees reservation sexual violence as interethnic. These two community problems—the sexual exploitation of children on American Indian reservations and the later sexual abuse of American Indian women—no doubt are linked as childhood sexual abuse drastically increases the risk of future sexual victimization in adulthood, whether as perpetrator or victim (Kellogg, Hoffman, and Taylor 1999; Noll, Trickett, and Putnam 2003; Peterson et al. 2003; Stock et al. 1997). This omission results from the discomfort in scholarship that increases the liability for reporting on intra-ethnic violence and exploitation. These liabilities may account for the substantial attention given to sexual abuse in Catholic boarding schools compared with what little attention the sexual abuse in American Indian communities, perpetrated by American Indians, has received. The inter-civilizational nature of boarding schools, for instance, has generated much scholarship, but the intratribal sexual abuse of children within American Indian families and communities has produced comparatively less work, and certainly this work has not captured the attention of the field as abuse in boarding schools has. One scholar, teaching an undergraduate lecture in which I sat, claimed that rape itself did not exist in American Indian communities before European contact.

For those willing to cast the geography of exploitation as occurring between civilizations, not community members, we overlook, whether intentionally or not, much of the world we purport to explain. By acknowledging exploitation as only between those who are different (in class, ethnicity, or civilization) and never as within oneself, we capture many of this world's processes but miss how many times life is against itself. To achieve the freedom Nietzsche proposed is impossible. Such freedom would require, as he proclaims in "On the Utility and Liability of History for Life," "[strength] to be able to live and forget how far life and injustice are one" (1995, 107). No community or individual might fully achieve an amnesia over past injustice, nor perhaps would they wish for such a state. To many American Indians, the request to forget resembles other non-indigenous suggestions that are considered insulting: "Why don't you get over it already?" "Isn't it time you move on?" As objectionable as these suggestions are, the other extreme of continual memory, captured in the statement "We will never forget," is not ideal either and has social ramifications. To remember, to hold dear to the point of sacrificing oneself and hindering the lives of future generations, is perhaps not strength, either. Understanding the world only as either just or unjust is a problematic way to live—though only if one wishes to avoid injury. If the social sciences continue to treat the phenomena of loss and pain as marginal players in human affairs and in cognitive architecture, we will, to paraphrase Nietzsche one last time, remain strangers to ourselves.

CHAPTER 7

Conclusion

7.1 CONCLUSIONS: BANAL AND PROVOCATIVE

It is time to draw a few conclusions from our examination of the conflicting worldviews presented in the preceding chapters. It should be obvious now that American Indians have meaningful, and contested, political relationships between each other. Reservations are not sanitary political spaces, and the evidence in this book of the veracity of intratribal politics demonstrates this. Co-membership in a tribe or ethnicity does not result in immunity from adversarial political or social relationships. Another conclusion, that is less provocative than that of the importance of intratribal relationships and that should emerge clearly is that lived experience is used to both gain meaning and inform a sense of appropriate action and perception. The intratribal emphasis this book argues for requires a continued willingness to study sensitive topics in American Indian politics. That an intratribal approach to politics is uncomfortable or to be avoided is perhaps itself a common secret and worthy of further discussion and debate. The two basic premises of this book—that tribal politics are central to the lives of Indians and that experiences are formative—are less debatable and should not be striking or novel.

Three more provocative conclusions stand out from this book. The first is that worldviews might be categorized into three logics with origins in the individual past (lived experiences) and collective past (ethnohistory). This is a highly simplistic way to organize the complexity of belief that includes one's sense of moral outlook, identity, values, perspectives, ontology, ethics, reflection of community, ethnicity, and so on. The parsimony necessary to nominate just three worldviews and logics—communal affect, self-interest, and melancholia—will miss much of this complexity. Let me offer two points to mitigate how relying on such a set of worldviews is limiting, imperfect, and reductionist. The first is that they are intended to be meaningful caricatures and exaggerate differences by taking what might be subtlety, concealed and complicated, and making it simple, even foolishly or impossibly so. Without these caricatures, these differences are lost in a Geertzian "thick web." Understandably, scholarship might say that a "thick web," as Geertz did, is the honest approach, and that is a fair criticism.

A second defense for simplicity is that all theories or perspectives will overlook immense complexity. A powerful theory or perspective (or worldview for that matter), is one whose simplicity or parsimony generates greater satisfaction than the dissatisfaction lost in what that simplicity overlooks or misses. By only using three worldviews, I constrain the complexities of American Indian political behavior to a narrow set of terms. Though these terms are broad enough to accommodate many commitments and motivations, they ultimately fail in capturing it all—and especially so considering the more than 566 tribes in the United States. These are meant to be poles, or representations upon which we can describe forms of belief and their provenance, rather than exact portrayals of complex beliefs.

The second provocative conclusion in this book is the causal claim found in the rise of self-interest and melancholia. Certain readers will reject the proposition that societies differ along such worldviews. For those who hold that view with firm commitment, there is little evidence that might sway them to the belief that peoples differ or that we might find adequate terms for such difference. Others might reject what seems a self-assured and simplistic relationship between lived experience, ethnohistory, and contemporary worldview. This book intends to be a starting point for a discussion about the effects of the past on contemporary politics that is explicit in its assumptions.

A third provocative part of this book is the existence of melancholic worldview or logic. This book does not present an optimistic view of those who experience—individually or collectively—searing trauma. What is absent in the account are resiliency and agency. It takes the possibility that our beliefs and behaviors (worldview, preference, frame) might be shaped by the past, outside of our control or in ways that we dislike. Melancholia, and seeing the world as formed in part by it, hints at unraveling the generous protections we afford our psyche and thereby allows the understanding of our worldviews and motivations as cussed. I could understand if few would want to go down this analytical path.

These conclusions have importance for how we understand American Indian politics, historical legacies, and political behavior. For American Indian politics, it is insufficient to ignore the political decisions and discussions of the polity. The relation between American Indians and other governments is important and its study should be continued, but dynamics *within* American Indian tribes is essential terrain for the field of American Indian studies and politics to engage. Such engagement might not examine divisions as this book has, by speculating on and explaining divergent worldviews, but might explore other areas such as risk tolerance, economic equality, allocation of budgeted resources, perceived obstacles to development, or other areas far afield from lived experiences and ethnohistories.

Certain historical legacies such as trauma and melancholia might be unflattering and uncomfortable. As is described in the Lakota and Citizen Potawatomi chapters, individual and collective trauma may alter how we understand political action and decisions. Such an interpretation of trauma and loss in American Indian communities requires a suspicious hermeneutics that is more generally focused on outsiders or non-Indians. A case in point is the Lakotas' refusal to accept the Black Hills settlement beyond the descriptions at the surface level that they are simply and only honoring the past or respecting the space. Such a decision may not be a function of historical trauma, or informed by it as this book claims, and perhaps the way to know such a belief's provenance is impossible, but the curiosity about the relationship between these past traumas and contemporary politics should not be left untouched.

7.2 CONCLUSIONS ABOUT
RESERVATION POLITICAL LIFE

If the theoretical points made in this work about worldview, ethnohistory, and lived experience are skeptically received by the reader, that intratribal political life is factious and important should not be. The variation of reservation and intratribal politics is stunning. The common secret that reservation and tribal politics are dynamic, contested, and widely varied should come through in this book. The Isletas chased witches inside an eight-hundred-year old village, the Citizen Potawatomis fought mercilessly even about the sexual motivations of each other's forbearers and their similarity or dissimilarity from other Indians, and the Rosebud Lakotas held a suspicious perspective of the outside world to protect themselves while potentially initiating further steps toward their own frustration. In total, these stories show only part of the remarkable diversity of politics within tribes.

What might come from such an exposé and analysis of sensitive subjects? This book is not an intervention into tribal political life nor is this look at reservation life designed to emancipate hidden oppression. The topic, however, is one about which there is little known in political and race scholarship, and is one concealed from open discussion. What we see is that the politics inside reservations and tribes are not markedly different from that of other polities, communities, political parties, organizations, or nations. An unintended externality is that we might examine the provenance and impact of our own worldviews. For the developmentalist or self-interested person in my tribe, the Citizen Potawatomis, it is now worth considering the loss that occurred in our own ethnohistory from the perspective of my Sacred Heart brothers and sisters. In this way, this book might have a normative result from it.

7.3 EMPIRICAL AND THEORETICAL ARCHIPELAGOS

Another way to consider this book's content is as arguing for comparisons to be made between American Indian polities, and for the value generated in such comparisons. In what ways do American Indians differ from each other (both within the same tribe and among different tribes)? How should we think about or consider these differences? If American Indians do differ along worldviews, and these worldviews can be or should be categorized—as this work advocates for—how does this complicate trends in studying or conceptualizing American Indians and indigenous peoples politically?

As much as this work is about division, it is also about integration. Ethnohistory and lived experience are infinitely complex—certainly more complicated than what has been presented in the previous pages. The Citizen Potawatomi, Isleta Pueblo, or Rosebud Sioux tribes are distinct cultural entities with dynamics beyond what can be described in such a limited work. It is my hope that this project has offered a picture that does not undermine the uniqueness of each community.

As complicated as the world might be, it is the social scientist's responsibility to provide some continuity to it—in a manner not dissimilar to how this study explains American Indians' own worldviews and logics as seeking order from complex experiences that betray even the best categories or terms. Even while providing perspectives that bring a sense of semi-uniformity to a rarefied reality, the framework provided has tried to respect variations in American Indian experience. This was an unusual challenge in a project as wide-ranging as this one: speculating simultaneously about the formation of a geographic continent and the formation of the human *psyche*, to use an inadequate term.

In a parallel with the studies of the American Indian communities themselves, theories borrowed from other students of society have provided complex supporting material that should have received greater rigor than what was afforded in this instance. This work has built upon the ideas from a range of social science theorists including Karl Polanyi, Albert Hirschman, James C. Scott, Sigmund Freud, Claude Lévi-Strauss, and Friedrich Nietzsche, among others. It is my hope that a subsequent work will return to these thinkers and how one might facilitate intellectual contact between their ideas and American Indian politics, as empirical political theory should.

Expecting a neat ordering of human experience, with few loose ends, would be foolish. Achieving a seamless continuity between all the actors involved in this work—American Indian communities and theorists, or between theories and communities—was not a goal; rather, creating fluidity among them was. To use a geographic metaphor, we might consider both the empirical (historical and geographic) and the theoretical part of this book as resembling archipelagoes somewhere between isolated atolls and existence on a contiguous landmass. As a framework, the theoretical parts of the book might be archipelagoes of experience and thought that respect similarities and differences. The peoples, theories, and experiences in this book are perhaps distinct islands, but these are still islands of the same chain. The logics of communal affect, melancholy, and self-interest, therefore, are my attempts to link these islands while recognizing both empirical and theoretical distinctiveness.

In order to make conceptual headway with other disciplines, American Indian scholarship must maintain a balance between similarity and difference. One means of achieving this is to consider the kinds of experiences that create commonality and divergence within and between tribes. If balance is not acheieved, Indian scholarship runs the risk of becoming more polarized in its levels of analysis. Consider, on the one end of the spectrum, the strong trend among some who analyze indigenous politics toward micro-level analysis that perceives tribes as incomparable to one another; while on the opposite pole there is scholarship that adopts a mega-level perspective, applying the term *indigenous* as a talisman to confirm an assumed similarity or universalization of experience. Such mega-level categorization puts indigenous peoples somewhere in the global nexus of indigenous identity, where the particulars of this web are scarce or deeply speculative.

The texture of American Indian (and indigenous) social and political life that is legible to others and important to political action may, in fact, reside in the *meso*-level; and it is only by exploring lived experiences that this level can be reached. This meso-level approach rejects the embedded or assumed ideological confraternity of the terms *tribe* (or community) or *indigenous*. In fact, using the terms *tribe, indigenous,* and *community* might imply or allow for an easy negation of important behavioral differences by assuming either overriding similarity (as *tribe* and *indigenous* both do) or distinctness (as *tribe* might do), and by failing to ask about beliefs that could supersede tribe (material self-interest over social harmony and communal affect, for instance). To put the point in different terms, American Indians might share greater commonality of political beliefs beyond the tribal level. Political scientists, for instance, divide survey responses by political party and belief, not only by race or geographic location. Thinking about American Indians not only in terms of tribe but also by looking at beliefs and worldviews (with more texture than the labels *progressive* and *traditional*) could allow for greater complexity and depth of analysis. In avoiding new terms, methods, spaces, and even common secrets, scholarship on American Indian politics may continue to distance itself from how political science approaches preferences and worldviews among other populations. As the study of American Indian politics is currently constituted, the most vivid politics and meaningful relationships can only be found in reality.

Notes

Chapter 2

1. Kuran's argument is shared with at least two other works. Lisa Wedeen's *Ambiguities of Domination: Politics, Rhetoric, and Symbols in Contemporary Syria* (1999) discusses a similar phenomenon in Syria. Wedeen's argument suggests that lies abound, but public ideologies are more committed to the power of the regime than truthfulness, and mainly ignore glaring discrepancies despite jokes outside the public sphere. James C. Scott's *Weapons of the Weak: Everyday Forms of Peasant Resistance* (1987) outlines a micro approach to studying power and resistance. Those who are subjects to domination, according to Scott, can pepper their deference to oppression and interaction with it in obsequious contempt.

2. During prior periods (pre-1980s), American Indian politics could be situated inside tribal communities. For instance, James Clifton's "Cultural Change, Structural Stability, and Factionalism in the Prairie Potawatomi Reservation Community," *Midcontinent American Studies Journal*, published in 1965, represents an example of intratribal politics. This work seems to have become unpopular among younger American Indian social scientists since the 1960s and 1970s, which coincides with the time of the Red Power movement, which sought to emphasize Pan-Indian identity and commonality. Another example might be Loretta Fowler's work, such as "Local-Level Politics and the Struggle for Self-Government," in *Struggle for Political Autonomy*, Occasional Papers in Curriculum, No. 11 (Chicago: D'Arcy McNickle Center for the History of the American Indian, 1989), 125–26; "Political Middlemen and the Headman Tradition among the Twentieth-Century Gros Ventres of Fort Belknap Reservation," *Journal of the West* 23 (July 1983): 54–63; or *Arapaho Politics, 1851–1978: Symbols in Crisis of Authority* (Lincoln: University of Nebraska Press, 1982).

3. The specific translation is closer to "hell is other people."

Chapter 3

1. For more description of a causal mechanism in the social sciences, see Emile Durkheim's (1912) *Les formes elementaries de la vie religieuse* (Paris: Aclan).

2. See the Native American Apology Resolution (2009) as a national example of redress through apology. H.R. 3326, Pub. L. No. 111–118.

3. Hume identifies these sentiments in terms of hostility and resentment more than self-destructiveness. Hume wrote centuries before Freud turned the project of the Enlightenment inward, toward the human mind. Hume's analysis of these dark passions recognized that they were what we might call *a-rational* and carried forth against one's own interest.

4. A necessary definitional point is required: the experience or event is *trauma*, with the outcome or condition from that traumatic event being *melancholia*, or in more clinical terms, post-traumatic stress disorder (PTSD).

5. Other regions are affected as well, such as the prefrontal cortex (see Nagel 1996, 239–41). The limbic system is the most significantly compromised.

6. Synapses are structures that transmit chemical signals in the nervous system.

7. It should be noted that historical mass trauma from political events results in trauma that might seem idiosyncratic. Wars displace families, create poverty, and strain family or social environments where less political forms of trauma might flourish. This is discussed in chapter 6, which examines political life on the Rosebud Lakota Reservation.

Chapter 4

1. A brief note might be necessary to explain the term "Citizen Potawatomi" or "Citizen Potawatomi Nation" and why many tribes have two-part names. The "Potawatomi" component refers to the larger linguistic, cultural, or political group, though there are no formal or binding political relationships between the seven distinct Potawatomi tribes in the United States. The second term, "Citizen" in this case, is the subgroup or what used to be referred to as the "band," though the term "nation" is now more common, and tribes have switched from using the term "band" as the Citizen Potawatomis did in the late 1990s. Motivating the switch was the idea that "nation" had greater claims to authority and sovereignty than "band."

2. Curiously, no scholarly study on American Indians has explored the presence of nostalgia explicitly. Such an absence indicates either that the

emotion is not found among American Indians, which is unlikely, or that the sentiments about the past we imagine American Indians as having do not conform with the triviality of the term.

Chapter 5

1. Isleta bricks were and still are made with mud from the Rio Grande. Adobe is made with straw and terron without straw.
2. Isleta Pueblos rarely sell homes in the village. Death rites are geographically bound, and the recently deceased are brought to the village center within a short time after dying. To secure this requirement for a proper afterlife, families need access to homes in the village for days at a time and therefore are reluctant to sell their ancestors' village homes and relinquish easy access to this space.
3. The Isleta Pueblos told me that these irrigation ditches have remained the same for centuries. The primary irrigation canals were only made concrete in the 1960s.
4. The Pueblo Revolt was 350 years ago and did not result in the slaughter of Isleta Pueblos by the Spanish even upon their return eight years later.
5. I regularly asked Isletas to clarify what they thought "rich" was. They generally said if someone had over $500,000 the person was rich.
6. A cattle squeeze is a piece of ranching equipment placed at the end of a cattle chute. Cattle are separated using a corral. Often referred to as a "squeeze," it traps and immobilizes the animal as it runs for what it perceives to be an exit. Once in the squeeze, the animal can be branded, immunized, castrated, etc.
7. Stories about non-Indians are often about ethnic differences and larger historical processes, but not in stories whose participants are uniquely Isleta.
8. The individual is referring to a lake that is near the recreational vehicle park and golf course. The casino stocked it with fish that have tags. The fish, if caught, can be exchanged for prize money. The ten-thousand-dollar fish was a special promotion for the summer.
9. Indians often call members of Oklahoma tribes "Oklahoma Indians." It is a slightly derogatory term that implies light skin and diluted blood quantum and culture. "Oklahoma Indians" also has the connotation of tribes that have benefited from professional success and the ability to use available resources for their advancement. The term is used in the context of Natives describing other Natives who make them uncomfortable. These include

Bureau of Indian Affairs employees, well-educated Natives who seem to create a certain anxiety among other Natives at conferences and professional events, and Natives who pretend to have solidarity with tribes not their own. Oklahoma Indians generally capture more prestigious positions in Indian country, and the term is used to subtly suggest that these Natives are lesser or inauthentic. "Oklahoma Indians" captures both the politics of muted class rage and cultural retaliation. (For the record, the author is an Oklahoma Indian.)

10. "Gut-eater" refers to the notion that the Navajo were scavengers who would eat the bowels of an animal that no others would. "Gallup-ass-Indian" captures something similar to the Citizen Potawatomis' "blanket-ass-Indian." I was told that the term refers to the notoriously sad condition of Indians who live in Gallup, New Mexico. An informant told me that the drug and alcohol abuse in Gallup is so high that "the police handcuff drunk Indians to park benches so they don't hurt themselves" (Informant, 2008). In my presence, a Navajo acquaintance called a Pueblo a "Gallup-ass-Indian." The Pueblo suggested strongly that the Navajo had crossed a line and demanded an apology. Afterward when I asked the Pueblo why he was unusually offended by that remark, he said something to the effect that it was because "Gallup is for Navajo" (Informant, 2008).

Chapter 6

1. Standing Rock Reservation straddles the North and South Dakota state line.

2. The issue and prevalence of unresolved grief is discussed at length in American Indian mental health research (see Brave Heart and DeBruyn 1998 for examples of the importance of mourning in American Indian communities).

3. Counting coup was the practice of a warrior slipping behind enemy lines and touching an opposing warrior with a coup stick without him noticing. This was usually done when the enemy was asleep. A warrior could also plant a coup stick before battle, daring an enemy to cross it.

4. Freud described our self-initiative in participating in loss and return as a game of *fort* (gone) and *da* (there). This method enables feeling empowered by the lack of control over loss of that which we love or need. The ultimate objective generally is to maintain control and create a sense of efficacy at the end of the game (Freud 1920, 1959).

Works Cited

Abraham, Karl. 1927. "A Short History of the Development of the Libido." In *Selected Papers on Psycho-Analysis*. Translated by Douglas Bryan and Alix Strachey. London: Hogarth Press.

Abril, Julie C. 2008a. *Bad Spirits: A Cultural Explanation for Intimate Family Violence: Inside One American Indian Family*. Cambridge, UK: Cambridge Scholars Publishing.

———. 2008b. "Cultural Conflict and Crime: Violations of Native American Indian Cultural Values." *International Journal of Criminal Justice Sciences* 2 (1): 44–62.

Aleksandrowicz, Dov. 1973. "Children of Concentration Camp Survivors." In *The Impact of Disease and Death*. The Child in His Family, vol. 2, edited by James E. Anthony and Cyrille Koupernik, 385–92. New York: Wiley.

Alfred, Taiaiake. 1999. *Peace, Power, Righteousness: An Indigenous Manifesto*. Ontario: Oxford University Press.

American Psychiatric Association. 1994. "Posttraumatic Stress Disorder American Psychiatric Association." In *Diagnostic and Statistical Manual of Mental Disorders*, 424–29. Washington, D.C.: American Psychiatric Association.

Appell, George N. 1993. "Hardin's Myth of the Commons: The Tragedy of Conceptual Confusions." Working paper, Social Transformation and Adaptation Research Institute, Phillips, Maine.

Bachman, Jerald G., Jr., John M. Wallace, Patrick M. O'Malley, Lloyd Johnson, Candace Kolars, and Harold W. Neighbors. 1991. "Racial/Ethnic Differences in Smoking, Drinking, and Illicit Drug Use among American High School Seniors, 1976–89." *American Journal of Public Health* 81 (3): 372–77.

Bahrick, Lorraine, and Gordon Hollich. 2008. "Intermodal Perception." In *Encyclopedia of Infant and Early Childhood Development*, vol. 2, edited by Marshall M. Haith and Janette B. Benson. 164–76. San Diego: Academic Press.

Baldwin, Laura-Mae, David C. Grossman, Elise H. Murochick, Eric H. Larson, Walter B. Hollow, Jonathan R. Sugarman, William L. Freeman, and Lawrence Gary Hart. 2009. "Trends in Perinatal and Infant Health Disparities

between Rural American Indians and Alaska Natives and Rural Whites."
American Journal of Public Health 99 (4): 638–46.

Banfield, Edward. 1970. *The Unheavenly City: The Nature and Future of Our Urban Crisis*. Boston: Little, Brown.

Barrett, Carole A. 2007. "Sitting Bull (ca. 1831–1890)." In *Encyclopedia of the Great Plains Indians*, edited by David J. Wishart, 88–89. Lincoln: University of Nebraska Press.

Barrett, John. 2008. Interview by Raymond I. Orr. Shawnee, Oklahoma.

Bassett, Deborah, Dedra Buchwald, and Spero Manson. 2014. "Posttraumatic Stress Disorder and Symptoms among American Indians and Alaska Natives: A Review of the Literature." *Social Psychiatry and Psychiatric Epidemiology* 49 (3): 417–33. doi: 10.1007/s00127-013-0759-y.

Beals, Janette, Annjeanette Belcourt-Dittloff, Eva M. Garroutte, Calvin Croy, Lori L. Jervis, Nancy Rumbaugh Whitesell, Christina M. Mitchell, and Spero M. Manson. 2013. "Trauma and Conditional Risk of Posttraumatic Stress Disorder in Two American Indian Reservation Communities." *Social Psychiatry and Psychiatric Epidemiology* 48 (6): 895–905. doi: 10.1007/s00127-012-0615-5.

Bechara, Antoine, Daniel Tranel, and Hanna Damasio. 2000. "Deficit of Patients with Ventromedial Prefrontal Cortex Lesions." *Brain* 123 (11): 2189–202.

Beebe, Gilbert W. 1975. "Follow-Up Studies of World War II and Korean War Prisoners II: Morbidity, Disability and Maladjustments." *American Journal of Epidemiology* 101 (5): 400–22.

Belsky, Jay, and Kevin M. Beaver. 2011. "Cumulative-Genetic Plasticity, Parenting and Adolescent Self-Regulation." *Journal of Child Psychology and Psychiatry* 52 (5): 619–26. doi: 10.1111/j.1469-7610.2010.02327.

Benedict, Ruth. 1989. *Patterns of Culture*. Boston: Houghton Mifflin.

Bergmann, Martin S., and Milton E. Jucovy. 1982 *Generations of the Holocaust*. New York: Basic Books.

Berkhofer, Robert F., Jr. 1971. "The Political Context of a New Indian History." *Pacific Historical Review* 40 (357): 379–81.

Biolsi, Thomas. 1989. "The American Indian and the Problem of Culture." *American Indian Quarterly* 13 (3): 261–69.

———. 1992. *Organizing the Lakota: The Political Economy of the New Deal on the Pine Ridge and Rosebud Reservations*. Tucson: University of Arizona Press.

———. 2001. *Deadliest Enemies: Law and the Making of Race Relations on and off Rosebud Reservation* Berkeley: University of California Press.

Blackhawk, Ned. 2006. *Violence over the Land: Indians and Empires in the Early American West* Cambridge, Mass.: Harvard University Press.

Blair, Clancy. 2012. "Stress Relief Can Be the Key to Success in School." *Scientific American Mind* 23 (4): 64–67.

Booth, James. 1994. "On the Idea of the Moral Economy." *American Political Science Review* 88 (September): 653–67.

Borowsky, Iris, Michael Resnick, Marjorie Ireland, and Robert Blum. 1999. "Suicide Attempts among American Indian and Alaska Native Youth: Risk and Protective Factors." *ARCH Pediatrics Medicine* 153 (6): 573–80.

Bouton, Mark, and Jaylyn Waddell. 2007. "Some Biobehavioral Insights into Persistent Effects of Emotional Trauma." In *Understanding Trauma: Integrating Biological, Clinical, and Cultural Perspectives*, edited by Laurence J. Kirmayer, Robert Lemelson, and Mark Barad, 41–59. Cambridge: Cambridge University Press.

Boym, Svetlana. 2001. *The Future of Nostalgia*. New York: Basic Books.

Brand, M., F. Grabenhorst, K. Starcke, M. M. Vandekerckhove, and H. J. Markowitsch. 2007. "Role of the Amygdala in Decisions under Ambiguity and Decisions under Risk: Evidence from Patients with Urbach-Wiethe Disease." *Neuropsychologia* 45 (6): 1305–17.

Bratton, Mary. 1998. *From Surviving to Thriving: A Therapist's Guide to Stage II Recovery for Survivors of Childhood Abuse*. Binghamton, N.Y.: Haworth Press.

Braun, Sebastian Felix. 2013. *Buffalo Inc.: American Indians and Economic Development*. Norman: University of Oklahoma Press.

Brave Heart, M. Y. H. 2000. "Wakiksuyapi: Carrying the Historical Trauma of the Lakota." *Tulane Studies in Social Welfare* 21–22: 245–66.

———. 2003. "Historical Trauma Response among Natives and Its Relationship with Substance Abuse: A Lakota Illustration." *Journal of Psychoactive Drugs* 35 (1): 7–13.

———. 2007. "The Impact of Historical Trauma: The Example of Native Community." In *Trauma Transformed: Empowerment Responses*, edited by Marian Wise Bussy and Judith Bula Wise, 176–93. New York: Columbia University Press.

Brave Heart, M. Y., and L. M. DeBruyn. 1998. "The American Indian Holocaust: Healing Historical Unresolved Grief." *American Indian and Alska Native Mental Health Research* 8 (2): 56–78.

Bremner, James D., Penny Randall, Tammy M. Scott, Sandi Capelli, Richard Delaney, Gregory McCarthy, and Dennis S. Charney. 1995. "Deficits in Short-Term Memory in Adult Survivors of Childhood Abuse." *Psychiatry Research* 59 (1–2): 97–107.

Bremner, James D., Tammy M. Scott, Richard. C. Delaney, Steven M. Southwick, John Wayne Mason, David R. Johnson, Robert B. Innis, Gregory

McCarthy, and Dennis S. Charney. 1993. "Deficits in Short-Term Memory in Posttraumatic Stress Disorder." *American Journal of Psychiatry* 150 (7): 1015–19.

Breslau, Naomi, Howard D. Chilcoat, Ronald C. Kessler, and Glenn. C. Davis. 1999. "Previous Exposure to Trauma and PTSD Effects of Subsequent Trauma: Results from the Detroit Area Survey of Trauma." *American Journal of Psychiatry* 156 (6): 902–7.

Brown, Paul, Malcolm B. Macmillan, Russell Meares, and Onno Van der Hart. 1996. "Janet and Freud: Revealing the Roots of Dynamic Psychiatry." *Australian and New Zealand Journal of Psychiatry* 30 (4): 480–89.

Brown, Wendy. 1995. *States of Injury: Power and Freedom in Late Modernity.* Princeton, N.J.: Princeton University Press.

Bunzel, Ruth L. 1932. *Introduction to Zuni Ceremonialism.* Annual Report No. 47. Washington, D.C.: Smithsonian Institution, Bureau of American Ethnology.

Bureau of Indian Affairs. 1997. *Indian Service Population and Labor Force Estimates Report.* Washington, D.C.: Department of Interior.

Bygren, Lars O., Gunnar Kaati, and Soren Edvinsson. 2001. "Longevity Determined by Paternal Ancestors' Nutrition during Their Slow Growth Period." *Acta Biotheoretica* 49 (1): 53–59.

Capps, Linda. 2007. Interview by Raymond I. Orr. Shawnee, Oklahoma. October.

Carrion, Victor, and Shane S. Wong. 2012. "Can Traumatic Stress Alter the Brain? Understanding the Implications of Early Trauma on Brain Development and Learning." *Journal of Adolescent Health* 51 (2): S23–S28.

Carson, David K. 1995. "American Indian Elder Abuse: Risk and Protective Factors among the Oldest Americans." *Journal of Elder Abuse and Neglect* 7 (1): 17–39.

Cattelino, Jessica R. 2006. "Florida Seminole Housing and the Social Meanings of Interdependency." *Comparative Studies in Society and History* 48 (3): 699–726.

———. 2008. *High Stakes: Florida Seminole Gaming and Sovereignty.* Durham, N.C.: Duke University Press.

Centers for Disease Control and Prevention. 2000. "Cigarette Smoking among Adults—United States, 1998." *Morbidity and Mortalality Weekly Report* 49 (39): 881–84.

———. 2011. "Vital Signs: Current Cigarette Smoking among Adults Aged ≥18 Years—United States, 2005–2010." *Morbidity and Mortality Weekly Report* 60 (35): 1207–12.

Chaloupka, Frank J., Kurt Straif, and Maria E. Leon. 2011. "Effectiveness of Tax and Price Policies in Tobacco Control." *Tobacco Control* 20 (3): 235–28. doi: 10.1136/tc.2010.039982.

Champagne, Duane. 1983. "Social Structure, Revitalization Movements, and State Building: Social Change in Four Native American Societies." *American Sociological Review* 48 (6): 754–63.

———. 1985. *American Indian Societies: Some Strategies and Conditions of Political and Cultural Survial.* Cambridge, Mass.: Cultural Survival.

———. 1989. *American Indian Societies: Strategies and Conditions of Political and Cultural Survival.* Cambridge, Mass.: Cultural Survival.

———. 2007. *Social Change and Cultural Continuity among Native Nations.* Lanham, Md.: AltaMirea Press.

Choi, Won S., Babalola Faseru, Laura A. Beebe, Allen K. Greiner, Hung-Wen Yeh, Theresa I. Shireman, Myrietta Talawyma, Lance Cully, Baljit Kaur, and Christine M. Daley. 2011. "Culturally-Tailored Smoking Cessation for American Indians: Study Protocol for a Randomized Controlled Trial." *Trials* 12: 126. doi: 10.1186/1745-6215-12-126.

Chugani, Harry T., Michael E. Behen, Otto Muzik, Csaba Juhasz, Ferenc Nagy, and Diane C. Chugani. 2001. "Local Brain Functional Activity Following Early Deprivation: A Study of Postinstitutionalized Romanian Orphans." *Neuroimage* 14 (6): 1290–301. doi: 10.1006/nimg.2001.0917.

Clark, Peter, and James Q. Wilson. 1961. "Incentive System: a Theory of Organization." *Administrative Science Quarterly* 6 (2): 129–66.

Clifford, James. 1990. *The Invented Indian: Cultural Fictions and Government Policies.* New Brunswick, N.J.: Transaction.

Clifton, James A. (1977) 1998. *The Prairie People: Continuity and Change in Potawatomi Indian Culture, 1665–1965.* Iowa City: University of Iowa Press. Citations refer to 1998 edition.

———. 1987. *The Potawatomi.* New York: Chelsea Hour Publications.

Cohen, Cathy J. 1999. *The Boundries of Blackness: AIDS and the Breakdown of Black Politics.* Chicago: University of Chicago Press.

Cornell, Stephn. 1986. "The New Indian Politics." *Wilson Quarterly* 10 (1): 113–31.

———. 1988. *The Return of the Native: American Indian Political Resurgence.* New York: Oxford University Press.

Cornell, Stephen, and Marta Cecilia Gil-Swedberg. 1995. "Sociohistorical Factors in Institutional Efficacy: Economic Development in Three American Indian Cases." *Economic Development and Cultural Change* 43 (2): 239–68.

Cornell, Stephen, and Joseph P. Kalt. 2010. "American Indian Self-Determination: The Political Economy of a Policy that Works." Faculty Research Working Paper Series. Cambridge, Mass.: Kennedy School of Government, Harvard University.

Danieli, Yael. 1981a. "The Aging Survivor of the Holocaust: Discussion on the Achievement of Integration in Aging Survivors of the Nazi Holocaust." *Journal of Geriatric Psychiatry* 14 (2): 191–210.

———. 1981b. "Differing Adaptational Styles in Families of Survivors of the Nazi Holocaust." *Child Today* 10 (5): 6–10.

Dannlowski, Udo, Anja Stuhrmann, Victoria Beutelmann, Peter Zwanzger, Thomas Lenzen, Dominik Grotegerd, Katharina Domschke, Christa Hohoff, Patricia Antonia Ohrmann, Jochen Bauer, Christian Lindner, Christian Postert, Carsten Konrad, Volker Arolt, Walter Heindel, Thomas Suslow, and Harald Kugel. 2011. "Limbic Scars: Long-Term Consequences of Childhood Maltreatment Revealed by Functional and Structural Magnetic Resonance Imaging." *Biological Psychiatry* 74 (4): 286–93.

D'Antonio, William V., Steven A. Tuch, and Josiah R. Baker. 2013. *Religion, Politics, and Polarization: How Religiopolitical Conflict Is Changing Congress and American Democracy*. Westport, Conn.: Rowman and Littlefield.

Davis, Michael. 1997. "Neurobiology of Fear Responses: The Role of the Amygdala." *Journal of Neuropsychiatry and Clinical Neurosciences* 9 (3): 382–402.

Dawson, Michael C. 2001. *Black Visions: The Roots of Contemporary African-American Political Ideologies*. Chicago: University of Chicago Press.

De Koning, Colleen. 2009. "Un-Freedom of the Press Potawatomi-Style." *OpEdNews*.

Dennison, Jean. 2012. *Colonial Entanglement: Constituting a Twenty-First Century Osage Nation*. Chapel Hill: University of North Carolina Press.

deRoon-Cassini, Terri A., Anthony D. Mancini, Mark D. Rusch, and George A. Bonanno. 2010. "Psychopathology and Resilience Following Traumatic Injury: A Latent Growth Mixture Model Analysis." *Rehabilitation Psychology* 55 (1): 1–11. doi: 10.1037/a0018601.

Deschenie, Tina. 2006. "Historical Trauma: Holocaust Victims, American Indians Recovering from Abuses of the Past." *Tribal College Journal of American Indian Higher Education* 17 (3): 8–11.

Dimsdale, Joel. 1980. *Survivors, Victims, and Perpetrators: Essays on the Nazi Holocaust*. Carlsbad, Calif.: Hemisphere Publishing.

Dombrowski, Kirk. 2001. *Against Culture: Development, Politics, and Religion in Indian Alaska*. Lincoln: University of Nebraska Press.

Dowd, Gregory E. 1992. *A Spirited Resistance: The North American Indian Struggle for Unity, 1745–1815*. Baltimore: Johns Hopkins University Press.

Dozier, Edward P. 1983. *The Pueblo Indians of North America.* Prospect Heights, Ill.: Waveland Press.

Drury, Keith. 2007. *Walking the Trail of Death*. Marion, Ind. www.TrailOfDeath .org.

Duran, Eduardo, and Bonnie Duran. 1995. *Native American Postcolonial Pyschology*. Albany: State University of New York Press.

Durkheim, Emile. 1966. *Suicide*. New York: Free Press.

———. 1976. *The Elementary Forms of the Religious Life*. Translated by Joseph Swain. New York: Routledge.

———. 1997. *Division of Labor in Society*. Translated by W. D. Halls. New York: Free Press.

Duthu, Bruce. 2008. "Broken Justice in Indian Country." *New York Times*, August 10, 2008. http://www.nytimes.com/2008/08/11/opinion/11duthu.html.

Edmunds, R. David. 1987. *The Potawatomis: Keepers of the Fire*. Norman: University of Oklahoma.

Ehlers, Anke, David M. Clark, Emma Dunmore, Lisa Jaycox, Elizabeth Meadows, and Edna B. Foa. 1998. "Predicting Response to Exposure Treatment in PTSD: The Role of Mental Defeat and Alienation " *Journal of Traumatic Stress* 11 (3): 457–71.

Eliade, Mircea 1959. *The Myth of the Eternal Return: Or, Cosmos and History*. Translated by Willard R. Trask. Princeton, N.J.: Princeton University Press.

Elliott, Stacey. 2004. "Linda Capps: Experiences as the Vice-Chairman of the Pottawatomie Tribe." *15th Street News*, Rose State College, Oklahoma.

Fassin, Didier, and Richard Rechtman. 2009. *The Empire of Trauma: An Inquiry into the Condition of Victimhood*. Translated by Rachel Gomme. Princeton, N.J.: Princeton University Press.

Fenelon, James V. 2000. "Traditional and Modern Perspectives on Indian Gaming." In *Indian Gaming: Who Wins?*, edited by David Kamper and Angela Mullis, 108–28. Los Angeles: UCLA American Indian Studies.

———. 2006. "Indian Gaming: Traditional Perspectives and Cultural Sovereignty." *American Behavioral Scientist* 50 (3): 381–409. doi: 10.1177/0002764206292577.

Fiorina, Morris P., Samuel J. Abrams, and Jeremy C. Pope. 2010. *Culture War? The Myth of a Polarized America*. New York: Longman.

Foster, George M. 1965. "Peasant Society and the Image of the Limited Good." *American Anthropologist* 67 (2): 293–315.

Foster, Morris W. 1991. *Being Comanche: The Social History of an American Indian Community.* Tucson: University of Arizona Press.

Fowler, Loretta. 1982. *Arapaho Politics, 1851–1978: Symbols in Crisis of Authority.* Lincoln: University of Nebraska Press.

———. 1984. "Political Middlemen and the Headman Tradition among the Twentieth-Century Gros Ventres of Fort Belknap Reservation." *Journal of the West* 23 (July): 54–63.

———. 1989. "Local-Level Politics and the Struggle for Self-Government." In *Struggle for Political Autonomy,* 125–26. Occasional Papers in Curriculum No. 11. Chicago: D'Arcy McNickle Center for the History of the American Indian.

Frank, Robert H., Thomas Gilovich, and Dennis T. Regan. 1993. "Does Studying Economics Inhibit Cooperation?" *Journal of Economic Perspectives* 7 (2): 159–71.

Freud, Sigmund. (1896) 1962. "The Aetiology of Hysteria." In *Early Psycho-Analytic Publications.* Vol. 3 of *The Standard Edition of the Complete Psychological Works of Sigmund Freud,* translated and edited by James Strachey, Anna Freud, and Alix Strachey, 191–221. London: Hogarth Press. Citations refer to 1962 edition.

———. (1920) 1961. *Beyond the Pleasure Principle.* Translated by James Strachey. New York: Norton. Citations refer to 1961 edition.

———. 1923. *The Ego and the Id.* New York: Norton.

———. (1923) 1971. "Mourning and Melancholy." In *On the History of the Psychoanalytic Movement: Papers on Metapsychology and Other Works.* Vol. 14 of *The Standard Edition of the Complete Psychological Works of Sigmund Freud,* translated and edited by James Strachey, Anna Freud, and Alix Strachey, 243–58. London: Hogarth Press. Citations refer to 1971 edition.

Frodl, Thomas, Elena Reinhold, Nikolaos Koutsouleris, Maximilian Reiser, and Eva M. Meisenzahl. 2010. "Interaction of Childhood Stress with Hippocampus and Prefrontal Cortex Volume Reduction in Major Depression." *Journal of Psychiatric Research* 44 (13): 799–807.

Galinsky, Adam D., Joe C. Magee, Deborah H. Gruenfeld, Jennifer A. Whitson, and Katie A. Liljenquist. 2008. "Power Reduces the Press of the Situation: Implications for Creativity, Conformity, and Dissonance." *Journal of Personality and Social Psychology* 95 (6): 1450–66. doi.org/10.1037/a0012633.

Galperin, Bella L., Rebecca J. Bennett, and Karl Aquino. 2011. "Status Differentiation and the Protean Self: A Social-Cognitive Model of Unethical Behavior in Organizations." *Journal of Business Ethics* 98 (3): 407–24.

Garbarino, James. 2010. Review of *Adolescents and War: How Youth Deal with Political Violence*, by Brian K. Barber, ed. *Political Psychology* 31 (4): 650–53. doi: 10.1111/j.1467-9221.2010.00777.x.

Garroutte, Eva Marie. 2003. *Real Indians: Identity and the Survival of Native America*. Berkeley: University of California Press.

Geertz, Clifford. 1973. *The Interpretation of Cultures: Selected Essays*. New York: Basic Books.

Giago, Tim. 2010. "Black Hills Claims Settlement Funds Top $1 Billion." *Huffington Post*. http://www.huffingtonpost.com/tim-giago/black-hills-claims-settle_b_533267.html.

———. [2007] 2011a. "The Black Hills: A Case of Dishonest Dealings." *Huffington Post*. http://www.huffingtonpost.com/tim-giago/the-black-hills-a-case-o_b_50480.html.

———. [2007] 2011b. "The Lakota Will Never Forget Wounded Knee 1890." *Huffington Post*. http://www.huffingtonpost.com/tim-giago/the-lakota-will-never-for_1_b_78621.html.

Goffman, Erving. 1974. *Frame Analysis: An Essay on the Organization of Experience*. London: Harper and Row.

Goldfrank, Esther S., and Elsie Clews Parsons. 1962. *Isleta Paintings*. Washington D.C.: Smithsonian Institution.

Gonzales, Angela. 2003. "Gaming and Displacement: Winners and Losers in American Indian Casino Development." *International Social Sciences Journal* 175 (1): 123–33.

Grabenhorst, Fabian, Edmund T. Rolls, and Benjamin A. Parris. 2008. "From Affective Value to Decision-Making in the Prefrontal Cortex." *European Journal of Neuroscience* 28 (9): 1930–39.

Graeber, David. 2008. *Lost People: Magic and the Legacy of Slavery in Madagascar*. Bloomington: Indiana University Press.

Green, Michael, and Theda Perdue. 2008. *The Cherokee Nation and the Trail of Tears*. Penguin Library of American Indian History Series. New York: Penguin.

Greenfeld, Lawrence A., and Steven K. Smith. 1999. *American Indians and Crime*. Washington, D.C.: U.S. Department of Justice.

Greenfield, Patricia M. 2013. "The Changing Psychology of Culture From 1800 through ." *Psychological Science* 24 (9): 1722–31.

Griffin-Pierce, Trudy. 2000. *Native Peoples of the Southwest*. Albuquerque: University of New Mexico Press.

Guinote, Ana. 2007. "Power and Goal Pursuit." *Personality and Social Psychology Bulletin* 33 (8): 1076–87. doi: 10.1177/0146167207301011.

Gurvits, Tamara V., Martha E. Shenton, Hiroto Hokama, Hirokazu Ohta, Natasha B. Lasko, Mark W. Gilbertson, Scott P. Orr, Ron Kikinis, Ferenc A. Jolesz, Robert W. McCarley, and Roger K. Pitman. 1996. "Magnetic Resonance Imaging Study of Hippocampal Volume in Chronic, Combat-Related Posttraumatic Stress Disorder." *Biological Psychiatry* 40 (11): 1091–99. doi: 10.1016/s0006–3223(96)00229–6.

Habermas, Jurgen. 1984. *Reason and the Rationalization of Society.* Vol 1 of *The Theory of Communicative Action.* Translated by Thomas McCarthy. Boston: Beacon Press.

Hamalainen, Pekka. 2008. *The Comanche Empire.* New Haven, Conn.: Yale University Press.

Hamilton, Alexander, James Madison, and John Jay. (1787–88) 2003. *The Federalist Papers.* New York: Bantam Dell.

Hanson, Allan. 1989. "The Making of the Maori: Culture Invention and Its Logic." *American Anthropologist* 91 (4): 890–902.

Harch, Charles. 1979. *The First Seventeen Years: Virgina 1607–1624.* Charlottesville: University of Virigina Press.

Hardin, Garrett. 1968. "Tragedy of the Commons." *Science* 162 (3859): 1243–48.

Harel, Zev, Boaz Kahana, and Eva Kahana. 1988. "Psychological Well-Being among Holocaust Survivors and Immigrants in Israel." *Journal of Traumatic Stress* 1 (4): 413–29.

Harmon, Alexandra. 2010. *Rich Indians: Native People and the Problem of Wealth in American History.* Chapel Hill: University of North Carolina Press.

Hassrick, Royal B. 1964. *The Sioux: Life and Customs of a Warrior Society.* Norman: University of Oklahoma Press.

Hegel, Georg Wilhelm Friedrich. (1812) 2010. *The Science of Logic.* Translated and edited by George di Giovanni. Cambridge: Cambridge University Press.

Herman, Judith. 1997. *Trauma and Recovery: The Aftermath of Violence—from Domestic Abuse to Political Terror.* New York: Basic Books.

Hermann, Knud, and Paul Thygesen. 1954. "KZ-syndromet hungerdystrofiends folgetilstand 8 ar efter" [The concentration camp syndrome: The sequelae of hunger dystrophy eight years later]. *Ugeskrift for Laeger* 116: 825–36.

Hirschman, Albert O. 1997. *The Passions and the Interests: Political Arguments for Capitalism before Its Triumph.* Princeton: Princeton University Press.

Hobbes, Thomas. (1651) 1909. *Leviathan.* Oxford: Oxford Claredon Press. Citations refer to 1909 edition.

———. (1651) 1988. *Leviathan.* London: Penguin. Citations refer to 1988 edition.

Hodge, Felicia. 2006. "Persistent Smoking among Northern Plains Indians: Lenient Attitudes, Low Harm Value, and Partiality Toward Cigarette Smoking." *Journal of Cultural Diversity* 13 (4): 181–85.

Holmes, Stephen 1988. "Gag Rules, or the Politics of Omission." In *Constitutionalism and Democracy*, edited by Jon Elseter and Rune Slagstad, 202–35. New York: Cambridge University Press.

Homans, George C. 1974. *Elementary Forms of Social Behavior.* 2nd ed. New York: Hardcourt Brace Jovanovich.

Horowitz, Mardi J. 1986. "Stress-Response Syndromes: A Review of Posttraumatic and Adjustment Disorders." *Hospital and Community Psychiatry* 37 (3): 241–49.

Hoxie, Frederick E. 1997. *Parading through History: The Making of the Crow Nation in America 1805–1935.* Studies in North American Indian History. New York: Cambridge University Press.

Hume, David. (1777) 1966. *Enquiries Concerning the Human Understanding and Concerning the Principles of Morals.* Edited by L. A. Selby-Bigge. Oxford: Oxford University Press. Citations refer to 1966 edition.

Indian Health Service. 2011. *Indian Health Focus: Injuries, 2002–2003 Edition.* Washington D.C.: U.S. Department of Health and Human Services, Indian Health Service, Office of Public Health Support, Office of Environmental Health and Engineering. https://www.ihs.gov/dps/includes/themes/newihstheme/display_objects/documents/IHS-FOCUS_Injuries2002-2003a.pdf.

Informant. 2007. Interview with research participant by Raymond I. Orr.

Informant. 2008. Interview with research participant by Raymond I. Orr.

Jablonka, E., and G. Raz. 2009. "Transgenerational Epigenetic Inheritance: Prevalence, Mechanisms, and Implications for the Study of Heredity and Evolution." *Quarterly Review of Biology* 84 (2): 131–76.

Jefferson, Thomas. 1814. Letter to Horatio G. Spafford. Monticello, dated March 17, 1814. *Founders Online, National Archives*, http://founders.archives.gov/documents/Jefferson/03-07-02-0167 (last update: 2016-03-28). Source: *The Papers of Thomas Jefferson*, Retirement Series, vol. 7, *28 November 1813 to 30 September 1814*, edited by J. Jefferson Looney, 248–49. Princeton, N.J.: Princeton University Press, 2010.

Jensen, Richard. 1995. "The Culture Wars, 1965–1995: A Historian's Map." *Journal of Social History* 29 (October): 17–37.

Jones, Monica C., Paul Dauphinais, William H. Sack, and Philip D. Somervell. 1997. "Trauma-Related Symptomatology among American Indian Adolescents." *Journal of Trauma Stress* 10 (2): 163–73.

Kappler, Charles J., ed. 1904. "Treaty of Fort Laramie with Sioux, Etc., 1851."
In *Indian Affairs: Laws and Treaties*. Vol. 2. Washington, D.C.: Government
Printing Office.

Keehn, Robert. 1980. "Follow-Up Studies of World War II and Korean Conflict
Prisoners III: Mortality to January 1, 1976." *American Journal of Epidemiology* 111 (2): 194–211.

Kehoe, Alice B. 1989. *The Ghost Dance: Ethnohistory and Revitalization*. New
York : Holt, Rinehart, and Winston.

Kellermann, Nathan. 2009. *Holocaust Trauma: Psychological Effects and Treat-
ments*. New York: iUniverse, Inc.

Kellogg, Nancy D., Thomas J. Hoffman, and Elizabeth R. Taylor. 1999. "Early
Sexual Experience among Pregnant and Parenting Adolescents." *Adolescence* 34 (134): 293–303.

Kemnitzer, Luis S. 1972. "The Structure of Country Drinking Parties on Pine
Ridge Reservation, South Dakota." *Plains Anthropology* 17 (56): 134–42.

Kingsbury, George Washington. 1915. *History of Dakota Territory*. Chicago: S. J.
Clarke.

Kochanska, Grazyna, Robert A. Philibert, and Robin A. Barry. 2009. "Inter-
play of Genes and Early Mother-Child Relationship in the Development of
Self-Regulation from Toddler to Preschool Age." *Journal of Child Psychology
Psychiatry* 50 (11): 1331–38. doi: 10.1111/j.1469-7610.2008.02050.x.

Kraus, Michael W., Paul K. Piff, and Dacher Keltner. 2009. "Social Class, Sense
of Control, and Social Explanation." *Journal of Personality and Social Pyschology* 97 (6): 992–1004.

Kraus, Michael W., Paul K. Piff, Rodolfo Mendoza-Denton, Michelle L. Rhein-
schmidt, and Dacher Keltner. 2012. "Social Class, Solipsism, and Contextu-
alism: How the Rich Are Different from the Poor." *Psychological Review* 119
(3): 546–72.

Kuran, Timur. 1997. *Private Truths, Public Lies: The Social Consequences of Preference Falsification*. Cambridge, Mass.: Harvard University Press.

Lawrence, Paul R., and Jay W. Lorsche. 1967. "Differentiation and Integration
in Complex Organizations." *Administrative Science Quarterly* 12 (1): 1–47.

Lear, Jonathan. 2006. *Radical Hope: Ethics in the Face of Cultural Devastation*.
Cambridge, Mass.: Harvard University Press.

Leighton, D., and J. Adair. 1966. *People of the Middle Place, Series: Behavioral
Science Monographs*. New Haven, Conn.: Human Relations Area Press.

Leiter, Brian. 2004. "The Hermeneutics of Suspicion: Recovering Marx, Nietzsche, and Freud." In *The Future for Philosophy*, edited by Brian Leiter,
74–105. Oxford: Oxford University Press.

Leon, Gloria R., James N. Butcher, Max Kleinman, Alan Goldberg, and Moshe Almagor. 1981. "Survivors of the Holocaust and Their Children: Current Status and Adjustment." *Journal of Personality and Social Psychology* 41 (3): 503–16.

Lévi-Strauss, Claude. 1955. "The Structural Study of Myth." *Journal of American Folklore* 68 (270): 428–44.

Lewis, David Rich. 1991. "Reservation Leadership and the Progressive-Traditional Dichotomy: William Wash and the Northern Utes, 1865–1928." *Ethnohistory* 38 (2): 124–48.

Lickliter, Bobbi. 2007. Interview by Raymond I. Orr. Ponca City, Oklahoma. October.

Lindaman, Kara, and Donald P. Haider-Markel. 2002. "Issue Evolution, Political Parties, and the Culture Wars." *Politcal Research Quarterly* 55 (1): 91–110.

Lindauer, R. J., M. Olff, E. P. van Meijel, I. V. Carlier, and B. P. Gersons. 2006. "Cortisol, Learning, Memory, and Attention in Relation to Smaller Hippocampal Volume in Police Officers with Posttraumatic Stress Disorder." *Biological Psychiatry* 59 (2): 171–77. doi: 10.1016/j.biopsych.2005.06.033.

Long, Larry, Rich Braunstein, Brenda Manning, and William D. Anderson. 2008. "Understanding Contextual Differences in American Indian Criminal Justice." *American Indian Culture and Research Journal* 32 (4): 41–65.

Madison, James. (1787) 2003. "Federalist No. 10." In *The Federalist Papers*, Alexander Hamilton, James Madison, and John Jay, 50–58. New York: Bantam Dell.

Magarinos, A. M., B. S. McEwen, G. Flugge, and E. Fuchs. 1996. "Chronic Psychosocial Stress Causes Apical Dendritic Atrophy of Hippocampal CA3 Pyramidal Neurons in Subordinate Tree Shrews." *Journal of Neuroscience* 16 (10): 3534–40.

Manning, Anita. 2005. "Shaping Up to Fight Diabetes." *USA Today*, November 13, 2005.

Mansbridge, Jane J., ed. 1990. *Beyond Self-Interest*. Chicago: University of Chicago Press.

Manson, S. M. 1996. "The Wounded Spirit: A Cultural Formulation of Post-Traumatic Stress Disorder." *Culture, Medicine, and Psychiatry* 20 (4): 489–98.

Manson, S. M., J. Beals, S. A. Klein, and C. D. Croy. 2005. "Social Epidemiology of Trauma among 2 American Indian Reservation Populations." *American Journal of Public Health* 95 (5): 851–59. doi: 10.2105/ajph.2004.054171.

McEwen, B. S. 1992. "Re-examination of the Glucocorticoid Hypothesis of Stress and Aging." *Progress in Brain Research* 93: 365–81. doi:10.1016/S0079-6123(08)64585-9.

———. 1999. "Stress and Hippocampal Plasticity." *Annual Review of Neuroscience* 22: 105–22. doi: 10.1146/annurev.neuro.22.1.105.

———. 2001. "Plasticity of the Hippocampus: Adaptation to Chronic Stress and Allostatic Load." *Annals of the New York Academy of Sciences* 933 (March): 265–77. doi: 10.1111/j.1749-6632.2001.tb05830.x.

McGowan, P. O., A. Sasaki, A. C. D'Alessio, S. Dymov, B. Labonte, M. Szyf, G. Turecki, and M. J. Meaney. 2009. "Epigenetic Regulation of the Glucocorticoid Receptor in Human Brain Associates with Childhood Abuse." *Nature Neuroscience* 12 (3): 342–48.

McGowan, P. O., M. Suderman, A. Sasaki, T. C. Huang, M. Hallett, M. J. Meaney, and M. Szyf. 2011. "Broad Epigenetic Signature of Maternal Care in the Brain of Adult Rats." *PLoS One* 6 (2): e14739. doi: 10.1371/journal.pone.0014739.

McNaney, Bob, and Becky Nahm. 2010. "Shakopee Man Who Assaulted Dying Teen Reneges on Settlement." *5 Eyewitness News.* ABC. March 1, 2010. http://kstp.com/news/stories/s1420217.shtml.

Medicine, Beatrice. 2006. *Drinking and Sobriety among the Lakota Sioux.* Lanham, Md.: Rowman Altamire.

Michaels, Marguerite. 2004. "A Trust Betrayed?" *Time Magazine,* January 18. http://content.time.com/time/magazine/article/0,9171,578961-1,00.html.

Mill, John Stuart. 1836. "On the Definition of Political Economy, and on the Method of Investigation Proper to It." In *Essays on Some Unsettled Questions of Political Economy.* London: Longmans, Green, Reader and Dyer.

Million, Dian. 2013. *Therapeutic Nations: Healing in an Age of Indigenous Human Rights.* Tucson: University of Arizona Press.

Mitchell, Chris. 2011. "A Critic Untroubled by Facts Who Seeks to Silence Dissent." *Australian,* September 17.

Morrissette, P. 1994. "The Holocaust of First Nations People: Residual Effects of Parenting and Treatment Implications." *Contemporary Family Therapy* 16 (5): 381–92.

Moynihan, Daniel Patrick. 1965. "The Negro Family: The Case for National Action." Washington, D.C.: U.S. Department of Labor, Office of Planning and Research. http://www.dol.gov/oasam/programs/history/webid-meynihan.htm.

Mueller, S. C., F. S. Maheu, M. Dozier, E. Peloso, D. Mandell, E. Leibenluft, D. S. Pine, and M. Ernst. 2010. "Early-Life Stress Is Associated with Impairment in Cognitive Control in Adolescence: An fMRI Study." *Neuropsychologia* 48 (10): 3037–44. doi: 10.1016/j.neuropsychologia.2010.06.013.

Munck, A., P. M. Guyre, and N. J. Holbrook. 1984. "Physiological Functions of Glucocorticoids in Stress and Their Relation to Pharmacological Actions." *Endocrine Reviews* 5 (1): 25–44.

Myers, Elissa, Miles Hewstone, and Ed Cairns. 2009. "Impact of Conflict on Mental Health in Northern Ireland: The Mediating Role of Intergroup Forgiveness and Collective Guilt." *Political Psychology* 30 (2): 269–90. doi: 10.2307/25655389.

Nagel, Joane. 1995. "American Indian Ethnic Renewal: Politics and the Resurgence of Identity." *American Sociological Review* 60: 947–65.

———. 1996. *American Indian Ethnic Renewal: Red Power and the Resurgence of Identity and Culture.* New York: Oxford University Press.

Nefzger, M. Dean. 1970. "Follow-Up Studies of World War II and Korean War Prisoners I: Study Plan and Mortality Findings." *American Journal of Epidemiology* 91 (2): 123–38.

Nickerson, R. 1998. "Confirmation Bias: A Ubiquitous Phenomenon in Many Guises." *Review of General Psychology* 2 (2): 175–220.

Nietzsche, Friedrich. 1989. *On the Genealogy of Morals.* Translated and edited by Walter Kaufman. New York: Vintage Books.

———. 1995. "On the Utility and Liability of History for Life." In *Unfashionable Observations*, vol. 2, translated by Richard T. Gray, 83–187. Stanford, Calif.: Stanford University Press.

———. (1887) 2000. *On the Genealogy of Morals.* In *Basic Writings of Nietzsche*, edited by Walter Kaufmann, 437–600. New York: Modern Library.

———. 2007. *Untimely Meditations.* Translated by Reginald. J. Hollingdale. New York: Cambridge University Press.

Nieves, Evelyn. 2007. "Indian Reservation Reeling in Wave of Youth Suicides and Attempts " *New York Times*, June 9.

Nisbett, Richard E. 2003. *The Geography of Thought: How Asians and Westerners Think Differently . . . and Why.* New York: Free Press.

Noll, Jennie G., Penelope K. Trickett, and Frank W. Putnam. 2003. "A Prospective Investigation of the Impact of Childhood Sexual Abuse on the Development of Sexuality." *Journal of Consulting and Clinical Psychology* 71 (3): 575–86.

O'Brien, Robert M. 1987. "The Interracial Nature of Violent Crimes: A Reexamination." *American Journal of Sociology* 92 (4): 817–35.

Obeyesekere, Gananath. 1992. *The Apotheosis of Captain Cook: European Myth-making in the Pacific* Princeton, N.J.: Princeton University Press.

Orr, Raymond I., Carolyn Noonan, Ron Whitener, and Stephen M. Schwartz. 2015. "Up in Smoke: A Tradeoff Study between Tobacco as an Economic

Development Tool or Public Health Liability in an American Indian Tribe." *American Indian Culture and Research Journal* 39 (3): 25–40. doi: http://dx .doi.org/10.17953/aicrj.39.3.orr.

Pace, David. 1983. *Claude Lévi-Strauss, the Bearer of Ashes*. Boston: Routledge and Kegan Paul.

Parsons, Talcott. 1966. *Societies*. Englewood Cliffs, N.J.: Prentice-Hall.

Parsons, Talcott, and Neil Smelser. 1956. *Economy and Society*. Glencoe: Free Press.

Patcho, N. Santiago, J. Ursano Robert, L. Gray Christine, S. Pynoos Robert, Spiegel David, Lewis-Fernandez Roberto, J. Friedman Matthew, and S. Fullerton Carol. 2013. "A Systematic Review of PTSD Prevalence and Trajectories in DSM-5 Defined Trauma Exposed Populations: Intentional and Non-Intentional Traumatic Events." *PLoS ONE* 8 (4). doi: 10.1371/journal.pone.0059236.

Perdue, Theda, and Michael D. Green. 2007. *The Cherokee Nation and the Trail of Tears*. New York: Viking.

Perez-Rincon, Hector. 2011. "Pierre Janet, Sigmund Freud and Charcot's Psychological and Psychiatric Legacy." *Monographs in Neural Sciences* 29: 115–24. doi: 10.1159/000321781.

Perlstein, Rick. 1995. "Hawaii KO." May 26, 1995. *Times Higher Education*, https://www.timeshighereducation.com/news/hawaii-ko/98271.article.

Perry, Barbara. 2008. *Silent Victims: Hate Crimes Against Native Americans*. Tucson: University of Arizona Press.

Person, Noel. 2009. *Up from the Mission: Selected Writings*. Melbourne: Black Inc.

Peterson, Lizette, George Trembaly, Bernard Ewigman, and Lisa Saldana. 2003. "Multilevel Selected Primary Prevention of Child Maltreatment." *Journal of Consulting and Clinical Psychology* 71 (3): 601–12.

Pickering, Kathleen Ann. 2004. *Lakota Culture, World Economy*. Lincoln: University of Nebraska Press.

Pietrzak, Robert H., Rise B. Goldstein, Steven M. Southwick, and Bridget F. Grant. 2011. "Prevalence and Axis I Comorbidity of Full and Partial Posttraumatic Stress Disorder in the United States: Results from Wave 2 of the National Epidemiologic Survey on Alcohol and Related Conditions." *Journal of Anxiety Disord* 25 (3): 456–65. doi: 10.1016/j.janxdis.2010.11.010.

Piff, Paul K. 2013. "Wealth and the Inflated Self: Class, Entitlement, and Narcissism." *Personality and Social Psychology Bulletin* 40 (1): 34–43. doi: 10.1177/0146167213501699.

Piff, Paul K., Daniel M. Stancato, Stéphane Côté, Rodolfo Mendoza-Denton, and Dacher Keltner. 2012. "Higher Social Class Predicts Increased Unethical

Behavior." *Proceedings of the National Academy of Sciences* 109 (11): 4086–91. doi: 10.1073/pnas.1118373109.

Pinney, Christopher. 1995. "Divine Cook?" *Times Higher Education*, September 29.

Podietz, Lenore, Herman Belmont, Marion Shapiro, Israel Zwerling, Ilda Ficher, Talia Eisenstein, and Myra Levick. 1984. "Engagment in Families of Holocaust Survivors." *Journal of Marital and Family Therapy* 10 (1): 43–51.

Polanyi, Karl. 2001. *The Great Transformation: The Political and Economic Origins of Our Time*. 3rd ed. Boston: Beacon Press.

Popkin, Samuel L. 1979. *The Rational Peasant: The Political Economy of Rural Society in Vietnam*. Berkeley: University of California Press.

Porter, Robert B. 1997. "Strengthening Tribal Sovereignty through Government Reform: What Are the Issues?" *Kansas Journal of Law and Public Policy* 72 (Winter): 1043–62.

Poundstone, William. 1993. *Prisoner's Dilemma*. Garden City, N.Y.: Anchor.

Prager, Kenneth M. 1972. "Alcoholism and the American Indian." *Harvard Medical Alumni Bulletin* 46: 20–25.

Pritzker, Barry. 1999. *Native America Today: A Guide to Community Politics and Culture*. Santa Barbara, Calif.: ABC-CLIO.

Rakoff, Vivian G. 1966. "Long-term Effects of the Concentration Camp Experience." *View-Points: Labor Zionist Movements of Canada* 1: 17–22.

Rakoff, Vivian G., John J. Sigal, and Nathan V. Epstein. 1966. "Children and Families of Concentration Camp Survivors." *Canada's Mental Health* 14: 24–25.

Robin, Robert W., Barbara Chester, Jolene K. Rasmussen, James M. Jaranson, and David Goldman. 1997. "Prevalence, Characteristics, and Impact of Childhood Sexual Abuse in a Southwestern American Indian Tribe." *Child Abuse and Neglect* 21 (8): 769–87.

Rogan, Michael P. 1975. *Fathers and Children: Andrew Jackson and the Subjugation of the American Indian*. New York: Knopf.

Rosebud political debate. 2008. Held at Sinte Gleska University, Mission, S.Dak. October 22.

Rosier, Paul C. 2001. *Rebirth of the Blackfeet Nation, 1912–1954*. Lincoln: University of Nebraska Press.

Rubia, K., A. B. Smith, J. Woolley, C. Nosarti, I. Heyman, E. Taylor, and M. Brammer. 2006. "Progressive Increase of Frontostriatal Brain Activation from Childhood to Adulthood During Event-Related Tasks of Cognitive Control." *Human Brain Mapping*. 27 (12): 973–93.

Safranski, Rudiger. 2003. *Nietzsche: A Philosophical Biography*. Translated by Shelley Frisch. London: Granta Books.

Sahlins, Marshall. 1976. *Culture and Practical Reason*. Chicago: University of Chicago Press.

———. 1987. *Islands of History*. Chicago: University of Chicago Press.

———. 1995. *How "Natives" Think: About Captain Cook, for Example*. Chicago: University of Chicago Press.

Sandefur, Gary D., and Carolyn A. Liebler. 1996. "The Demography of American Indian Families." In National Research Council Committee on Population, *Changing Numbers, Changing Needs: American Indian Demography and Public Health*, edited by Gary D. Sandefur, Ronald R. Rindfuss, and Barney Cohen, 196–217. Washington, D.C.: National Academy Press.

Sando, Joe S. 1992. *Pueblo Nations: Eight Centuries of Pueblo Indian History* Santa Fe, N.Mex.: Clear Light Publishers.

Sapolsky, R. M. 1996. "Why Stress Is Bad for Your Brain." *Science* 273 (5276): 749–50.

———. 2000. "Glucocorticoids and Hippocampal Atrophy in Neuropsychiatric Disorders." *Archives of General Psychiatry* 57 (10): 925–35.

Sapolsky, Robert M., L. Michael Romero, and Allan U. Munck. 2000. "How Do Glucocorticoids Influence Stress Responses? Integrating Permissive, Suppressive, Stimulatory, and Preparative Actions." *Endocrine Reviews* 21 (1): 55–89.

Sartre, Jean Paul. 1944. *Huis Clos (No Exit)*. Paris: Gallimard.

———. (1957) 1991. *The Transcendence of the Ego*. Translated by Forrest Williams and Robert Kirkpatrick. New York: Hill and Wang. Citations refer to 1991 edition.

Schwartz, Stephanie M. 2006. "The Arrogance of Ignorance: Hidden Away, Out of Sight and Out of Mind." Special Resource Report: Regarding Life, Conditions, and Hope on the Pine Ridge Oglala Lakota (Sioux) Reservation of SD. *The Written Works of Stephanie M. Schwartz*, www.SilvrDrach.homestead .com/Schwartz_2006_Oct_15.html.

Scott, James C. 1976. *The Moral Economy of the Peasant: Rebellion and Subsistence in Southeast Asia*. 2nd ed. New Haven, Conn.: Yale University Press.

———. 1987. *Weapons of the Weak: Everyday Forms of Peasant Resistance*. New Haven, Conn.: Yale University Press.

Shapiro, Ian. 2007. *The Flight from Reality in the Human Sciences*. Princeton: Princeton University Press.

Shepherd, Jeffrey P. 2010. *We Are an Indian Nation: A History of the Hualapai People*. Tucson: University of Arizona Press.

Shimizu, Shinji, Katsuro Aso, Tetsuro Noda, Ryukei So, Yoshiro Kochi, and Noriya Yamamoto. "Natural Disasters and Alcohol Consumption in a

Cultural Context: The Great Hanshin Earthquake in Japan." *Addiction* 95 (4): 529–36.

Sigal, John J., and Morton Weinfeld. 1989. *Trauma and Rebirth : Intergenerational Effects of the Holocaust.* New York: Praeger.

Simpson, Audra. 2000. "Paths toward a Mohawk Nation: Narratives of Citizenship and Nationhood in Kahnawake." In *Political Theory and the Rights of Indigenous Peoples,* edited by Duncan Ivison, Paul Patton, and Will Sanders, 113–36. Cambridge: Cambridge University Press.

Small, Mario Luis, David J. Harding, and Michèle Lamont. 2010. "Reconsidering Culture and Poverty." *Annals of the American Academy of Political and Social Science* 629 (1): 6–27. doi: 10.1177/0002716210362077.

Smith, Adam. 1994. *The Wealth of Nations.* New York: Modern Library, Random House Press.

———. 2010. "The Theory of Moral Sentiments." *EarlyModernTexts.com,* http://www.earlymoderntexts.com/assets/pdfs/smith1759.pdf.

Smith, Andrea. 2003. "Not an Indian Tradition: The Sexual Colonization of Native Peoples." *Hypatia* 18 (2): 70–85.

———. 2005. *Conquest: Sexual Violence and American Indian Genocide.* Cambridge, Mass.: South End Press.

Snibbe, Alana, and Hazel Markus. 2005. "You Can't Always Get What You Want: Educational Attainment, Agency, and Choice." *Journal of Personality and Social Psychology* 88 (4): 703–20.

Snipp, Matthew C. 1989. *American Indians: The First of This Land.* New York: Russell Sage Foundation.

Snow, David A., E. Burke Rochford, Steven K. Worden, and Robert D. Benford. 1986. "Frame Alignment Processes, Micromobilization, and Movement Participation." *American Sociological Review* 51 (4): 464.

Sowell, Thomas. 2005. *Black Rednecks and White Liberals.* New York: Encounter Books.

Stack, Carol B. 1974. *All Our Kin: Strategies for Survival in a Black Community.* New York: Harper and Row.

Stephens, Kari A., Stanley Sue, Peter Roy-Byrne, Jurgen Unutzer, Jin Wang, Fred P. Rivara, Gregory J. Jurkovich, and Douglas F. Zatzick. 2010. "Ethnoracial Variations in Acute PTSD Symptoms among Hospitalized Survivors of Traumatic Injury." *Journal of Traumatic Stress* 23 (3): 384–92. doi: 10.1002/jts.20534.

Stewart, Kathleen. 1988. "Nostalgia—A Polemic." *Cultural Anthropology* 3 (3): 227–41.

Stock, Jacquie L., Michelle A. Bell, Debra K. Boyer, and Frederick Connell. 1997. "Adolescent Pregnancy and Sexual Risk-Taking among Sexually Abused Girls." *Family Planning Perspectives* 29 (5): 200–203.

Streeck-Fischer, Annette, and Bessel van der Kolk. 2000. "Down Will Come Baby, Cradle and All: Diagnostic and Therapeutic Implications of Chronic Trauma on Child Development." *Australian and New Zealand Journal of Psychiatry* 34 (6): 903–18.

Strum, Circe D. 2002. *Blood Politics: Race, Culture, and Identity in the Cherokee Nation of Oklahoma.* Berkeley: University of California Press.

Suina, Joseph H. 1998. "Pueblo Secrecy: Result of Intrusions." *Common Ground.*

Tilly, Charles. 1984. *Big Structures, Large Processes, Huge Comparisons.* New York: Russell Sage Foundation.

Tomsen, Stephen 1997. "A TOP NIGHT: Social Protest, Masculinity and the Culture of Drinking Violence." *British Journal of Criminology* 37 (1): 90–102.

Truman, Jennifer, Lynn Langton, and Michael Planty. 2013. *Criminal Victimization, 2012.* U.S. Department of Justice, Bureau of Justice Statistics (October): 1–17. http://www.bjs.gov/content/pub/pdf/cv12.pdf.

Tullock, Gordon. 1971. "The Paradox of Revolution." *Public Choice* 11 (1): 89–99.

Tversky, Amos, and Daniel Kahneman. 1991. "Loss Aversion in Riskless Choice: A Reference-Dependent Model." *Quarterly Journal of Economics* 106 (4): 1039–61.

Uno, H., R. Tarara, J. G. Else, M. A. Suleman, and R. M. Sapolsky. 1989. "Hippocampal Damage Associated with Prolonged and Fatal Stress in Primates." *Journal of Neuroscience* 9 (5): 1705–11.

U.S. Bureau of Justice Statistics. 2002. *A BJS Statistical Profile, 1992–2002: American Indians and Crime.* Washington, D.C.: U.S. Department of Justice.

U.S. Census Bureau. 2000. *Census of Population and Housing, Profiles of General Demographic Characteristics.* Washington, D.C.: U.S. Department of Commerce.

———. 2012. *2006–2010: Selected Economic Characteristics: Pine Ridge.* Washington, D.C.: U.S. Department of Commerce.

———. 2014. *American Indian and Alaska Native Heritage Month: November 2014.* Washington, D.C.: U.S. Department of Commerce.

Villarreal, Gerardo, Derek A. Hamilton, Helen Petropoulos, Ira Driscoll, Laura M. Rowland, Jaqueline A. Griego, Piyadasa W. Kodituwakku, Blaine L. Hart, Rodrigo Escalona, and William M. Brooks. 2002. "Reduced Hippocampal Volume and Total White Matter Volume in Posttraumatic Stress Disorder." *Biological Psychiatry* 52 (2): 119–25.

Vizenor, Gerald, Jill Doefler, and David E. Wilkins. 2012. *The White Earth Nation: Ratification of a Native Democratic Constitution*. Lincoln: University of Nebraska Press.

Volz, Kirsten G., Ricard Ines Schubotz, and Yves von Cramon. 2006. "Decision-Making and the Frontal Lobes." *Current Opinion in Neurology* 19 (4): 401–6.

Wang, Long, Deepak Malhotra, and J. Keith Murnighan. 2011. "Economics Education and Greed." *Academy of Management Learning and Education* 10 (4): 643–60.

Weber, Max. 1949. "Objectivity in Social Science and Social Policy " In *The Methodology of the Social Sciences*, edited by E. A. Shils and H. A. Finch, 49–112 Glencoe, Ill.: Free Press.

Wedeen, Lisa. 1999. *Ambiguities of Domination: Politics, Rhetoric, and Symbols in Contemporary Syria*. Chicago: University of Chicago Press.

West, Lois A. 2001. "Negotiating Masculinities in American Drinking Subcultures." *Journal of Men's Studies* 9 (3): 371–92.

Whitbeck, Les. B., Melissa L. Walls, Kurt D. Johnson, Allan D. Morrisseau, and Cindy M. McDougall. 2009. "Depressed Affect and Historical Loss among North American Indigenous Adolescents." *American Indian and Alaska Native Mentental Health Research* 16 (3): 16–41.

White, Tracie. 2013. "Almost without Hope: Seeking a Path to Health on the Rosebud Indian Reservation." *Stanford Medicine* 30 (3): 34–49.

Wilbanks, William. 1985. "Is Violent Crime Intraracial?" *Crime and Delinquency* 31 (1): 117–29.

Wilcox, Michael V. 2009. *The Pueblo Revolt and the Mythology of Conquest: An Indigenous Archaeology of Contact*. Berkeley: University of California Press.

Wilkins, David. 2013. *Hollow Justice: A History of Indigenous Claims in the United States*. New Haven, Conn.: Yale University Press.

Wilson, Terry P. 1985. *The Underground Reservation: Osage Oil*. Lincoln: University of Nebraska Press.

Wishart, David J. 2007. *Encyclopedia of the Great Plains Indians*. Lincoln: University of Nebraska Press.

Yehuda, Rachel, Guiqing Cai, Julia A. Golier, Casey Sarapas, Sandro Galea, Marcus Ising, Theo Rein, James Schmeidler, Bertram Muller-Myhsok, Florian Holsboer, and Joseph D. Buxbaum. 2009. "Gene Expression Patterns Associated with Posttraumatic Stress Disorder Following Exposure to the World Trade Center Attacks." *Biological Psychiatry* 66 (7): 708–11. doi: 10.1016/j.biopsych.2009.02.034.

Yehuda, Rachel, Stephanie M. Engel, Sarah R. Brand, Jonathan Seckl, Sue M. Marcus, and Gertrud S. Berkowitz. 2005. "Transgenerational Effects of Posttraumatic Stress Disorder in Babies of Mothers Exposed to the World Trade Center Attacks During Pregnancy." *Journal of Clinical Endocrinology and Metabolism* 90 (7): 4115–18. doi: 10.1210/jc.2005–0550.

Youth Suicide in Indian Country: Hearing Before the U.S. Senate Committee on Indian Affairs. 2009. 1st Sess., 111th Cong. 18 (February 26) (Testimony of Robert Moore). https://www.gpo.gov/fdsys/pkg/CHRG-111shrg47726/html/CHRG-111shrg47726.htm.

Young, Alford, Jr. 2004. *The Minds of Marginalized Black Men: Making Sense of Mobility, Opportunity, and Future Life Chances.* Princeton, N.J.: Princeton University Press.

Zhang, Bo, Joanna E. Cohen, Roberta Ferrence, and Jurgen Rehm. 2006. "The Impact of Tobacco Tax Cuts on Smoking Initiation among Canadian Young Adults." *American Journal of Preventive Medicine* 30 (6): 474–79.

Žižek, Slavoj. 2000. "Melancholy and the Act." *Critical Inquiry* 26 (4): 657–81.

Index

www.ingramcontent.com/pod-product-compliance
Lightning Source LLC
Chambersburg PA
CBHW020853270326
41928CB00006B/686